FOR THE WAR YET TO COME

HIBA BOU AKAR

FOR THE WAR YET TO COME

PLANNING BEIRUT'S FRONTIERS

STANFORD UNIVERSITY PRESS • STANFORD, CALIFORNIA

Stanford University Press
Stanford, California

Printed in the United States of America on acid-free, archival-quality paper

Library of Congress Cataloging-in-Publication Data

Names: Bou Akar, Hiba, author.
Title: For the war yet to come : planning Beirut's frontiers / Hiba Bou Akar.
Description: Stanford, California : Stanford University Press, 2018. |
   Includes bibliographical references and index.
Identifiers: LCCN 2017050467| ISBN 9781503601918 (cloth : alk. paper) |
   ISBN 9781503605602 (pbk : alk. paper) | ISBN 9781503605619 (electronic)
Subjects: LCSH: City planning—Lebanon—Beirut. | City planning—Political
   aspects—Lebanon—Beirut. | Communalism—Lebanon—Beirut. | Beirut
   (Lebanon)—Politics and government.
Classification: LCC HT169.L42 B68 2018 | DDC 307.1/2160956925--dc23
LC record available at https://lccn.loc.gov/2017050467

Typeset by Bruce Lundquist in 10/15 Adobe Garamond Pro

To my parents, Sanaa and Chaouki; my grandma, Jamal;
and all the feisty women in my life, for lighting the way.
And for all those who make the future a better place.

CONTENTS

FIGURES

ACKNOWLEDGMENTS

This book was woven over many years, across multiple cities, and made possible by numerous relationships of mentorship, friendship, and love. I am forever grateful for these relationships that have nourished and sustained me, and enriched my life and the pages that follow.

I am, foremost, beholden to my wonderful mentors at the University of California, Berkeley. Ananya Roy has been an inspiration and pushed this work to new fronts with her exceptional scholarship, teaching, and mentorship. With unsurpassed eloquence and guidance, she helped nurture my trajectory as a student of cities. Teresa Caldeira's superb and critical engagement, coupled with her dedication and kindness, encouraged me to explore new intellectual and professional turfs. Gillian Hart's passion shaped my program of research since that first day of my first year at Berkeley. Many aspects of my work were also galvanized by Cihan Tuğal and Aihwa Ong.

My friends and mentors from my years at the American University of Beirut have been instrumental in my journey to the present. Mona Fawaz was always there to engage with my work, and cheer me on with her continuous support, friendship, and ingenuity. I am forever grateful for Marwan Ghandour's precious presence in my life as a mentor, teacher, and friend. Mona Harb's kindness, astute feedback, and relentless encouragement were extremely valuable to the development of this work. And since my early days at MIT, Bish Sanyal and Diane Davis have likewise been wonderful mentors.

Friends and colleagues were pillars of strength on my voyage, and their presence in my life made the long hours of work endurable. This book would not have been possible without the unsurpassed intellect and friendship of Nada Moumtaz and Ghenwa Hayek, who have been with me throughout the daily grind and at every twist and turn along the way. Sylvia Nam was always there for me, sharing on a daily basis her brainpower, spark, and humor during our late-night chats. Kathryn Moeller and I walked together every step of the way, with its highs and its lows. Her companionship made the journey far more exciting and tolerable. Suha Ballout provided a warm home away from home, patiently listening, sharing her wisdom, and making everything much better. I am fortunate to have all of them in my life.

The work on this book has been enriched by my own trajectory across a number of institutions. I completed this book amid wonderful colleagues at the Graduate School of Architecture, Planning and Preservation at Columbia University. From my first days at the school, Dean Amale Andraos and Weiping Wu have cultivated a supportive environment in which I could complete this work. I embarked on this book during my tenure at Hampshire College, surrounded by generous, wonderful colleagues. I am particularly grateful to Carollee Bengelsdorf, Aaron Berman, Michelle Bigenho, Roosbelinda Cárdenas, Margaret Cerullo, Kimberly Chang, Omar Dahi, Marlene Fried, Jennifer Hamilton, Elizabeth Hartmann, Annie Rogers, Will Ryan, Helen Scharber, Uditi Sen, Falguni Sheth, Jutta Sperling, and Barbara Yngvesson. A postdoctoral fellowship from the Mahindra Humanities Center at Harvard University afforded me the unparalleled experience of joining that center's Andrew W. Mellon Foundation Seminar on Violence and Non-Violence. I am grateful to Homi Bhabha for his support, engagement, and feedback. I am also thankful to Mahindra Humanities Center Fellows Ram Natarajan, Thiemo Breyer, Alex Fattal, Joseph Fronczak, and Sam Anderson for their insights and good company. Steven Biel and Mary Helpenny-Killip provided a stellar working environment. The Department of Architecture and Design and the Graduate Program in Urban Planning and Policy at the American University of Beirut made sure to keep their doors open, and provided me with a research and institutional home in Beirut. Their generosity granted me opportunities for teaching and intellectual engagement that further contributed to the development of some of the arguments here. I am indebted to Howayda al-Harithy, Mona Fawaz, and Mona Harb for making this possible.

My intellectual path has also been grounded through the influence and insight of wonderful scholars. AbdouMaliq Simone's work has been an inspiration for a long time, and I am grateful for his guidance, encouragement, and friendship. Eric Verdeil has provided amazing support, feedback, and research material that helped me develop aspects of this work. Kevin O'Neill generously read and pushed some of my ideas for the better. Farha Ghannam was always supportive and insightful. Mona Atia, Erin Collins, Hun Kim, Marieke Krijnen, Cecilia Lucas, Mpho Matsipa, Ram Natarajan, Nazanin Shahrokni, and Delia Duong Ba Wendel have also generously provided feedback on presentations and drafts of chapters of this book.

Several fellowships and grants have made this book possible. I am thankful for the financial support of UC Berkeley's The Berkeley Fellowship. I am also grateful to UC Berkeley's Center for Middle Eastern Studies and the Department of

City and Regional Planning for providing continuous professional and financial support during my time at Berkeley. My fieldwork research was funded by the National Science Foundation Dissertation Improvement Grant, the Social Science Research Council International Dissertation Research Fellowship, the Wenner-Gren Foundation Dissertation Fieldwork Grant and Engaged Anthropology Grant, and the Middle East Research Competition Grant. And the postdoctoral fellowship from Harvard University's Mahindra Humanities Center mentioned earlier was crucial to making revisions to the text.

The publication of this book was shepherded by a wonderful team at Stanford University Press. I am grateful to Kate Wahl for her enthusiasm and superb engagement with the project, and for Micah Siegel and later on Leah Pennywark for their great support. David Moffat's amazing ability to make words flow made this book a better read. Elspeth MacHattie did a terrific job with copyediting. Marwan Kaabour lent his magic touch to some of the book's maps and images. Amer Mohtar, Bernadette Baird-Zars, and Stephanie Chan provided wonderful assistance during the last stretch of the writing and publishing process.

Many relationships that sustained me emotionally, intellectually, and physically through this work started in Beirut and have spread across space and time. From London, Mohamad Hafeda has been an amazing work partner and an inspiration. In Boston, Philippe Saad and Anil Nair always provided me with a warm home and a beautiful friendship. From Ann Arbor and Cambridge, Rania Ghosn listened and engaged at crucial times. From Barcelona, Alia Alame's friendship has been instrumental in getting the work done.

Since my early days at Berkeley, Cecilia Lucas, Kathryn Moeller, and Rebecca Alexander have been there for me, unremittingly. Their brilliance, dedication, and support carried me through the tough times and the fun ones, through both tears and laughter. Words are not enough to express my love and gratitude for them. Nazanin Shahrokni's friendship is heartwarming. Reem Alissa, Mona Damluji, Michael Gonzales, Joseph Godlewski, Elena Ion, Kah Wee Lee, Saima Akhtar, and Monica Guerra made Berkeley home. Austin Zeiderman, Malini Ranganathan, Mpho Matsipa, Renu Desai, Emilio Martínez De Velasco, and Tiago Castela provided many stimulating discussions and good times. Diana Bernal's warmth and dedication have always made things better.

Life in Amherst, Massachusetts, was made much better with the company and intellectual engagement of Elif Babül, Pinky Hota, Sahar Sadjadi, Robert Samet, Helen Scharber, Krupa Shandilya, and Uditi Sen, who provided me with food for thought and for the soul. In Cambridge, Kerry Chance, Laurie McIntosh, and Delia Duong Ba Wendel were amazing companions and friends who made writing much more pleasurable.

In Beirut, fieldwork would not have been as rewarding without the adventures and heated debates I shared with Rabih Shehayeb, Rami Wehbi, Laila Al-Shaar, Daniel Hamadeh, Dima Kaasamani, Rana Abu Dargham, Wissam Hamze, Mirna Chehayeb, and Firas Hamdan, and our reconnection over delicious meals. Ali Yatim was there for me with his humor and support. Ramzi Ballout was there when I needed him. Mahassen Sinno made it all much more enjoyable.

The love, warmth, and brilliance of my extended family—particularly Hind Abou Reslan, Majida Abo Hasan, and Ghina Abo Hasan—have added joy to my life. I am especially grateful to my grandmother, Jamal, for setting the standard for women's achievement in our family. By learning to read and write at the age of sixty-five, she inspired me to dedicate my life to knowledge.

There are not enough words of gratitude for my parents, Sanaa and Chaouki, and my brother Amin, who have been there for me at every step in this process with their unconditional love and support. They continue to enrich my every day with their magical combination of hard work, brilliance, dedication, humor, and family love.

Last but not least, many people dedicated their precious time and opened their doors to share with me their valued views, passions, experiences, hopes, and anxieties to help me better understand Beirut's contemporary geography and urban politics. I am particularly grateful to Mr. Omar Kadi, Mr. Mohamad Fawaz, Dr. Abdallah Said, the late Samih Dakdouk, and the late Wassim Ali-Hassan. Many others remain anonymous on these pages. I am humbled by their generosity and courage, and I hope this work speaks for them.

TRANSLITERATION, TRANSLATION, AND PSEUDONYMS

This book largely follows the system of the *International Journal of Middle Eastern Studies* for transliterating Arabic into the Latin alphabet. For Lebanese names and place names, however, the conventional, local Latin spelling is used.

Unless otherwise noted, all English translations of Arabic and French sources are by the author.

To protect people's identities, I have used pseudonyms throughout the text for the people I spoke with, with the exception of those experts who explicitly gave me their consent to use their names.

ACRONYMS

ACE: Associated Consulting Engineers

ACSP: Association of Collegiate Schools of Planning

AFESD: Arab Fund for Economic and Social Development

AUB: American University of Beirut

CCSD: Consultative Center for Studies and Documentation

CDR: Council for Development and Reconstruction

CIAM: Congrès Internationaux d'Architecture Moderne

CIL: Compagnie Immobilière Libanaise Sal

DGU: Directorate General of Urbanism

GDP: gross domestic product

IAURIF: Institut d'Aménagement et d'Urbanisme de la Région d'Île-de-France

IDF: Israel Defense Forces

IRFED: Institut de Recherche et de Formation en Développement

ISIS: Islamic State in Iraq and Syria

NGOs: non-governmental organizations

NPMP: National Physical Master Plan for the Lebanese Territory

PSP: Progressive Socialist Party (a Druze religious-political organization)

SAF: Syrian Armed Forces

SDRMB: Schéma Directeur de la Région Métropolitaine de Beyrouth

UNRWA: United Nations Relief and Works Agency for Palestine Refugees

USAID: United States Agency for International Development

USOM: United States Operations Mission

FOR THE WAR YET TO COME

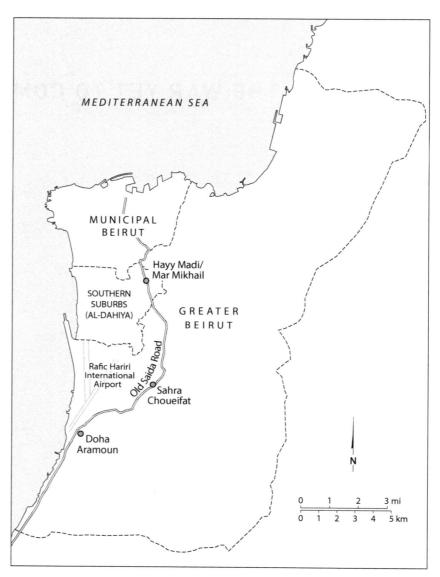

FIGURE 1. Beirut, the southern suburbs, and the three field sites: Hayy Madi/Mar Mikhail, Sahra Choueifat, and Doha Aramoun. Source: Adapted from Google Maps, 2017.

WAR IN TIMES OF PEACE

ON APRIL 26, 2011, I tuned in online from Berkeley, California, to a popular Lebanese radio show. It was the morning of the next day in Beirut, and the show's famous host, Rima, was asking her listeners to engage with her on what they thought were the most urgent problems facing Lebanon. People called in to express an array of concerns—among them health benefits, housing prices, and power outages. At one point, Rima paused and said, "I think we should all start thinking about urban planning. Look around you. I would say that in this city, urban planning lacks planning and order."

This was not the first time I had heard such a statement. While I was conducting fieldwork for this book in Beirut, people frequently asked me what I was studying. I often responded with what I thought was a simple answer: "I am studying urban planning in Beirut." But over and over, I would get the same reaction: "You came all the way back from the United States to study planning here?! Does planning even exist in this city?"

Once, three acquaintances and I were chatting on the balcony of a hillside apartment overlooking the city. "Look at how haphazard urbanization is in Beirut," one exclaimed. "Now, you tell me, is this planning?"

We had a view of Beirut and its southeastern periphery where Sahra Choueifat's remaining agricultural fields, striped with housing complexes and industries, merged with the international airport. On Beirut's southern fringe, buildings gradually blended into each other until they folded into a solid concrete mass with the city. The Mediterranean Sea framed the view (Figure 2). During the Lebanese civil war, our location had been a military site. Bullet holes from that long gone war still lined the balcony's walls. Pondering that, a second acquaintance asked: "See how buildings have different heights, different materials, and no street alignments? Where is planning?" His wife then added: "Tell me where are the sidewalks, the trees, the playgrounds? Many of these streets and highways remain unfinished."

My fieldwork notebooks hold dozens of such stories and encounters. And I realized that with each such encounter, I had become more curious about how

popular perceptions of planning are formed in a contested city like Beirut, mired in cycles of conflict. Why did people think there was "no planning" in Beirut? And how did urban planning become a subject of everyday discourse?

Beirut: A Contested City

For decades now, the name Beirut has been synonymous with war, chaos, and violence. Indeed, from 1975 to 1990, the city was the epicenter of the long Lebanese civil war. That conflict resulted in massive property destruction, while at least 120,000 people were killed and one million more were internally displaced.[1] During the war, Beirut was divided between a Christian east and a Muslim west along what became known as the Green Line. However, this represented only one facet of a new geography of violence that was partitioning a city that had, just a decade earlier, been celebrated for its vibrant, cultural, and intellectual society, prosperous and open economy, Mediterranean landscapes, and "Westernized" lifestyle.

Before the war, Lebanon had been internationally viewed as a young, decolonizing nation with a bright future. The country had recently gained its independence from France—the country that had been granted a mandate to rule it and its nearby areas in 1923 (following the partition of the Ottoman Empire). Soon after gaining independence in 1946, the country enjoyed an economic boom bolstered by local and regional investments.[2] Nonetheless, this narrative of economic development took little account of the socioeconomic disparities in Lebanon that resulted in the political upheavals and labor protests that were common throughout the 1950s and 1960s.[3] This same period witnessed the initiation of regional conflict attending the establishment of the state of Israel in 1948, the resultant mass displacement of Palestinians to Lebanon, and the subsequent onset of armed Palestinian resistance across Lebanon's southern border.

On the eve of the Lebanese civil war, tensions had escalated on a range of issues. These included Lebanese nationalism versus Pan-Arabism, the Palestinian armed presence, and uneven development and class inequality (as poverty in rural Lebanon forced many families to migrate to Beirut and its peripheral areas looking for jobs). There were thus many origin stories for the civil war; however, the nature of the war also changed over time to reflect the many regional and international interventions and shifting local alliances, eventually becoming, as it is most commonly understood today, a sectarian battle among Christian, Shiite, Sunni, and Druze militias.[4]

As is also well understood, the violence associated with the war at times took the form of sectarian cleansings that resulted in mass displacement, forcing people to flee their homes in "mixed" areas to seek refuge in areas under the control of militias corresponding to their sectarian affiliation. Thus, west Beirut became predominantly Muslim while east Beirut became predominantly Christian. Meanwhile, those Palestinians living in east Beirut who had survived the violence of Christian militias against their camps were forced to flee to west Beirut. Thousands of Shiite families, fleeing the violence on the Lebanese-Israeli border and the eventual Israeli occupation of southern Lebanon in 1982, also sought refuge there.

In 1989, the warring factions finally reached an agreement—the National Reconciliation Accord, also known as the Taif Agreement—to end the fighting. Signed in Saudi Arabia, the accord was brokered by Syria, other Arab countries, and the international community. Among other provisions, it ratified and institutionalized the sectarian-based power-sharing system originally set up informally in 1943 to create a system of national government.[5] But after the fighting came to a halt in 1990, this same governing framework allowed the militias that had fought the war to organize themselves as religious-political organizations overnight, and so continue to rule postwar Lebanon.

In the wake of the Taif Agreement, there followed a more or less peaceful period during the 1990s that allowed the reconstruction of downtown Beirut to begin, along with attempts to resolve the mass displacement caused by the civil war. However, in 2005, violence returned to the city in the form of a series of assassinations and bombings, only to be followed by a new Israeli war on Lebanon in July 2006.[6] Then, in May 2008, the ghost of the civil war returned, as what had appeared to be only sporadic episodes of sectarian violence unexpectedly erupted into full-scale battles in Beirut and its peripheries, as well as other areas of Lebanon. The violence lasted for five days and came to be known as the May 7 events.[7]

Ever since then, fear of sectarian tensions has risen, and the country has experienced one episode of political gridlock after another. Thus, in 2015, the Lebanese Parliament renewed itself without a vote, citing fear that elections would lead to sectarian violence. In addition, owing to gridlock, the country was without a president from May 2014 until October 2016. This tense political landscape was compounded by the ongoing war in Syria, which has seen the active participation of several Lebanese factions. By 2016, the Syrian war had also resulted in the flight of more than one million Syrian refugees to Lebanon.[8]

Planning without Progress

For many people, such as my acquaintances conversing on the balcony, who lived through the gruesome years of civil war and who continue to experience ongoing episodes of sectarian violence, a visualization of spatial order seems to hold great significance. Ordering the present with quality affordable housing, paved streets, playgrounds, and trees means improved living conditions. But it also signifies something more—the promise of a planned future that might finally dispel the specter of war that has loomed over the city and its peripheries for so long.

Although the task of organizing cities is an old one, it was the Western project of modernity that imbued it with a teleology of order and progress. Toward this end, the regulation of urbanization, redistribution of resources, and provision of public amenities are tasks that professional planners now pursue through tools like zoning ordinances, building and property laws, and investments in public infrastructure. Despite critiques, such as that by David Harvey, that the profession is a tool of the powerful (the state, capital, and dominant social groups)[9] to shape urban spaces in their image, hopes remain high among planners that their expertise can create better cities for the great majority of residents.[10] Among governments and the population at large, planning has likewise been celebrated as a way to mediate difference and provide a positive, coherent narrative of a shared urban future.

However, if the normative discourse within the planning profession is one of "progress," the reality in Beirut is quite different. In Beirut, planning has become a central domain of contest between religious-political organizations, governments, and profit-seeking developers. Several scholars, including Oren Yiftachel, Bent Flyvbjerg, and Ananya Roy, have described how planning outcomes are not always aimed at general improvement and betterment. My hope here is to contribute to understanding this darker reality of planning practice.[11] In Beirut, the ordinary tools of planners are commonly used by complex urban actors such as Lebanon's religious-political organizations in an overtly partisan manner. Such spatial practices challenge the common conception of planning as a tool through which to order the present in the interest of an improved future. They debunk modern narratives of peace, order, and progress; and they collapse distinctions between peace and war, order and chaos, construction and destruction, progress and stagnation. A practice of continuously planning for war in times of peace thus explains the underlying logic of Rima's assertion that "planning lacks planning" in Beirut.

With these conditions as a background, this book can be conceived as addressing a series of general questions. In cities in conflict, like Beirut—ones where the specter of war is always present; where state structures are not clear and public processes are frequently outsourced; and where fear, threats, rumors, and otherness provide as vital a ground for policy formation as statistics, censuses, and scientific findings—how are urban presents and futures configured and contested? What roles do spatial practitioners, including planners, engineers, and real estate brokers, occupy in such settings? And how are territories arranged, by whom, and for what purposes?

The specific territory in which I have chosen to investigate these issues is Beirut's southern and southeastern suburbs, particularly those peripheral areas known as Hayy Madi/Mar Mikhail, Sahra Choueifat, and Doha Aramoun (see Figure 1, preceding the Prologue). Beirut is a coastal city, bordered by the Mediterranean Sea to its west. Its downtown occupies a settlement site that is more than five thousand years old. But its contemporary development only began in the nineteenth century, when its port became a major transshipment point for regional produce. During the twentieth century, development began to sprawl both up and down the coastal plain from this downtown area and the rocky peninsula to its south that originally sheltered the port. Today this development has also spread part way up the hills that overlook the city, and that gradually morph into the Lebanese mountains.[12]

Originally, much of Beirut's population was concentrated near the city's historic core and its main roads.[13] However, the onset of civil war in 1975 caused a mass displacement from these central areas, resulting in the urbanization of outlying suburbs that grew exponentially after the end of the war.[14] While there are no authoritative numbers, a 2000 estimate put Lebanon's population at 3.2 million.[15] At the end of the 1990s, it was estimated that about 32 percent of these people lived in the greater Beirut area, and that Beirut's suburbs were home to 22 percent of Lebanon's entire population.[16] To further illustrate this urbanization pattern, another source estimated that in 1996 at least 80 percent of all buildings in Beirut's south and southeastern suburbs had been built since 1975.[17]

Since the end of the civil war, formal urban planning and development discussions in the city have been dominated by two topics: the progress of large-scale postwar reconstruction and redevelopment projects (such as Solidere, Elyssar, Linord, and more recently, Waad)[18] and the condition of Beirut's informal peripheries (such as Ouzaii and Hayy el-Selloum).[19] By contrast, the three neighborhoods I discuss here are peripheral yet formal, planned yet contested.[20] Located at the edge of the city, in 2008 these densely populated, understudied, overlooked areas suddenly found themselves at the frontier of renewed sectarian conflict.

Implicit in this analysis is a specific understanding of the notions of periphery and frontier. *Peripheries* are areas excluded by design, neglect, or circumstance from the formal ordering of a metropolitan center. For this reason, they are typically theorized as being governed by informal social, economic, and political arrangements. However, rather than understanding Beirut's peripheries as a geography of the unplanned, this book will attempt to show how they are in fact becoming ever more intricately planned within a logic of sectarian order. As such, they are increasingly taking on the spatial character of *frontiers*—areas often theorized as dystopic, where regimes of power and capital are actively involved in reconfiguring space in their own image. The principal agents in conflict in Beirut are religious-political organizations involved in post–civil war battles over land and access to housing. Among these, the four most prominent are Hezbollah (the main Shiite party in the region),[21] the Future Movement (the main Sunni party), the Progressive Socialist Party (PSP, the main Druze party), and the Maronite Christian Church[22] (as outlined in Figure 3).

Given these conditions, urban planning in Beirut must be viewed as embed-

Sectarian Affiliation	Religious-Political Organization
Druze	Progressive Socialist Party (PSP)
Shiite	Hezbollah Haraket Amal
Sunni	Future Movement
Maronite Christian (Catholic)	Maronite Church Free Patriotic Movement Phalange Party (Kata'ib) Lebanese Forces

FIGURE 3. The main religious-political organizations in Beirut's south and southeastern peripheries, and their sectarian affiliations. The Lebanese Constitution recognizes a total of 18 religious sects. Political offices are distributed among the largest of them. The National Pact of 1943 stipulates that the president, prime minister, and speaker of parliament must be Maronite Christian, Sunni, and Shiite, respectively. Distribution of political power among sects occurs at both national and local levels of government.

ded within a continuum of other social and spatial practices. This means it must frequently rely on innovative techniques to balance a spatiality of political differences to keep war at bay when possible, while simultaneously allowing for urban growth and development profit. Given such conditions, planning discourse and practice must continuously straddle tensions between the political, the technical, and the violent. However, by being simultaneously a tool of pacification, conflict, and development, it has actively transformed Beirut's peripheries into contested frontiers characterized by environmental degradation and ongoing cycles of violence. On the one hand, it has encouraged a patchwork of planned spaces that provide low-cost housing. On the other, it has created overlapping industrial and residential zones, towns where highways are never finished, and playgrounds and other amenities are planned but never built.

The Logic of Future War

The transformation of Beirut's peripheries into sectarian frontiers has been made possible through an overarching logic that I call *the war yet to come*. At its most basic, this logic does not treat war and peace as distinct categories. Aside from philosophical theorizations of war, the act of war is not considered the usual state of affairs; rather the war's absence, peace, is. However, as Hannah Arendt pointed out, "the Second World War was not followed by peace but by a cold war."[23] Similarly, in Lebanon, the end of civil war has not brought peace, only mutations in the logic of war. The war yet to come thus approaches war not as a temporal aberration in the flow of events, with a beginning and an end, but as a state of affairs expected to reoccur. The anticipation of future war has thus become a governing modality within Beirut's peripheries, with its imagined impetus drawn from a variety of possible sources, including local sectarian disputes, the Arab-Israeli conflict, the transnational geography of Islamic militarization, and the global "War on Terror."[24]

The politics of the war yet to come has both a temporal and a spatial dimension. Temporally, it involves a present moment from which the future can be imagined only as a time of further violent conflict. Spatially, it invokes a regulating logic according to which Beirut's peripheries are envisioned not only as spaces of urban growth and real estate profit but also as frontiers of future wars. These spaces are thus today continuously reconfigured through recursive cycles of violence, producing patchworks of destruction and construction, lavishness and poverty, otherness and marginality.

The arrangement of urban territories based on military logic is not new, nor is it unique to cities in conflict or geographies of the Global South.[25] It was equally constitutive of the project of modernization in the Global North. For example,

David Harvey, among others, has argued that Haussmann's nineteenth-century Parisian boulevards represented not only a modernization project but also a military strategy to counter frequent popular uprisings in the city.[26] However, the temporal logic of the spatial interventions of the war yet to come in Beirut sets the logic of planning in this city apart from Eurocentric approaches to urban development that characterized Haussmann's interventions and the post–World War II reconstruction of European cities. While these planning projects folded defense mechanisms into ideas of progress and modernization, planning for the war yet to come is shaped by expectations of future violence, terror, and economic ruin—devoid of the promise of a better future.

Two moments in recent Lebanese history are critical for understanding this framework: the end of the civil war in 1990 and the return of sectarian violence, peaking in the events of May 2008. During the Lebanese civil war, the three southeast peripheries that I discuss here were located in what was commonly known as Muslim west Beirut. However, this area was far from homogeneous, and changing global and regional geopolitics created powerful new schisms within it.[27] When these came to a head in May 2008, armed militias took to the streets, producing the worst sectarian fighting the city had witnessed since the end of the civil war.

This time around, however, the fighting was primarily between Muslim factions, and it represented a division of the country into two political coalitions, known as the March 14 and March 8 camps. The camps were named for the dates of two famous marches in 2005, which brought together hundreds of thousands of their respective supporters in response to the assassination of Prime Minister Rafic Hariri, the head of the Sunni Future Movement and at the time the nation's leading Sunni politician. Originally, the March 14 camp included the Druze PSP and the Sunni Future Movement (along with the majority Christian political parties), while the March 8 camp was led by the Shiite Hezbollah and Haraket Amal.[28] However, as is typical of Lebanese politics, certain aspects of these alliances have changed over time, as the country's various religious-political organizations have continued to reposition themselves.[29]

The actual spark that ignited the May 2008 fighting was a decision by a March 14–only government to condemn an independent telecommunications network constructed by Hezbollah as illegal.[30] Hezbollah responded by announcing that this was a "declaration of war" against it and its campaign of resistance against Israel's geopolitical project in the region. Thus, at dawn on May 7, 2008, one hundred or more armed Hezbollah fighters and their allies took over west Beirut. During the days that followed, Beirut's southern peripheries emerged as key battlegrounds—dozens were eventually killed and fighting spread to other parts of the country. At the time, Old Saida Road, which connects Hayy Madi/

Mar Mikhail, Sahra Choueifat, and Doha Aramoun—reemerged as a principal sectarian divide. This demarcation reinvoked the geography of the civil war, when Old Saida Road was part of the Green Line. But the city and its south and southeast peripheries had since been dissected even further, effectively transforming many neighborhoods into sectarian frontiers. Roadblocks, flags, posters, fortified positions, and informal neighborhood watches also came to line the city's streets, delineating zones, marking borders, and confining accessibility.[31]

Armed conflict, however, is not the only framework by which to understand how these peripheries were transformed into frontiers in post–civil war Beirut. When I began my research in earnest in 2004, fourteen years from the end of the civil war, (re)construction work was everywhere present in the city. But there was nonetheless a feeling of uneasiness. Residents and officials alike spoke to me of ongoing fear of the sectarian other, and these fears had already caused friction and led to episodes of youth violence. In my research at these peripheral sites, I not only sensed the ghosts of past wars but also the shadows of anticipated new ones.

Nevertheless, in 2004, there was no indication of the political upheaval the country would witness with the assassination of Prime Minister Hariri in 2005, or the extensive destruction that Israel's 2006 war on Lebanon would cause. But by 2008, that had all changed, as sectarian conflict, too, had come back. With a research perspective that spans times of "peace" and of "war," this book attempts to show how in the years since the civil war, religious-political organizations have sought to arrange Beirut's mundane peripheries into frontier geographies to reflect their imagined role in local and regional wars to come.

The resulting war in times of peace is not fought with tanks, artillery, and rifles, but through a geopolitical territorial contest, where the fear of domination of one group by another is played out over such issues as land and apartment sales, the occupation of ruins, access to housing, zoning and planning regulations, and infrastructure projects. The transnational circulations of real estate finance, militarization, and religious ideologies also play a role. Moreover, even though the pursuit of war during peacetime has not sought to define any particular future of war in Beirut, it has fundamentally redefined how the future is perceived and consequently how the present is arranged. Its logic lies in an evolving reconfiguration of "yet to." [32]

Even during the darkest days of the civil war in Lebanon, officials and spatial experts were still drawing and imagining a future of peace, order, and prosperity. However, gradually, in the years following the civil war, this expected future became less about peace and more about the inevitability of future conflict. This shift in perception has been informed by past experience, and by a sense that there can be no end to the many conflicts that now define the larger Middle East. Most critically, however, the war yet to come in Beirut forecloses the possibility of urban politics outside a sectarian order. And my analysis of these conditions aims to trace the twists and turns of engagement and estrangement through which such political difference is constructed, produced, managed, and contested. It illustrates the ways time and space may be curved into new complex configurations that construct safe and unsafe spaces—an accepted other versus an other to fear.

CHAPTER 1
CONSTRUCTING SECTARIAN GEOGRAPHIES

TALK OF SECTARIANISM is on the rise again in the Middle East in the wake of the Arab Spring, as wars continue to rage in Iraq and Syria and sectarian violence rocks cities like Cairo, Kuwait, and Manama. For a long time now, Lebanon has epitomized nations divided by sectarian conflict. And since the nineteenth century, much has been written on the issue of sectarianism in Lebanon. But what is interesting is that, despite its volume, much of this literature does not approach sectarianism ethnographically. In Lebanon, most studies of the topic are political theses or historiographies on the relationship between sectarianism and the formation of the nation state—debating, for example, whether sectarianism represents a traditional characteristic, a construct of colonial and/or modernization projects, or a project of class domination.[1] By contrast, this book focuses on understanding how sectarianism is constructed, lived, and practiced. Such questions have garnered more interest recently as scholars set out to examine "everyday sectarianism."[2] To that end, I have sought to unearth the spatial production of the sectarian order through ethnographic and archival investigation. My larger purpose, if such a thing can be presupposed, is to show how the production of sectarian difference is as unstable and contested as the spaces of conflict, domination, and profit that that difference produces. This, in turn, has involved investigating how the spatiality of the sectarian political order is constantly being negotiated, reconfigured, and reproduced, redefining what *sectarianism* may mean at each successive historical moment.

From the perspective of my two principal periods of fieldwork (in 2004 to 2005 and 2009 to 2010), for example, it was interesting to see how real estate deals that were once considered "normal" within Beirut's market-led economy were variously portrayed seven years later as a threat to the national coexistence of Lebanon's various religious groups, an "Islamization scheme of the Middle East," and a threat to all Christians and Druze in the region. It is in light of such fears that one must understand how the Lebanese Parliament came in 2011 to debate a proposed law that would have banned land sales between Christians and Muslims for a period of fifteen years. Passage of such a law, whose stated aim was to preserve "religious coexistence," would of course have represented the ultimate spatial manifestation of the war yet to come. Its effect would have been to lock the city into its present state because the future could not be conceived as anything less than bleak. Yet, as I will argue, territories of poverty and frontiers of sectarian violence in Beirut are constantly being negotiated and reconfigured. And it is within these unstable, continuously shifting spatial logics that one can also locate hope for urban politics in what are otherwise seen to be the dystopic planned geographies of the war yet to come.

Patching Stories and Maps

My methodology in this study can best be conceived as an *ethnography of spatial practices* that investigates how territories may be rearranged by practices and discourses of fear, rumors of conflict, and talk of war. It is based primarily on sixteen months of interviews and archival research I conducted in 2009 and 2010 in relation to three peripheral areas in Beirut—Hayy Madi/Mar Mikhail, Sahra Choueifat, and Doha Aramoun (see Figure 1). Yet my research engagement with Beirut's peripheries is actually much older. It dates to 1998 when I was an undergraduate studying architecture and urbanism at the American University of Beirut. My involvement with these areas then became more systematic following 2004, when I first began targeted research in Sahra Choueifat. I have also practiced urban planning and architecture in Beirut, which has allowed me to become professionally familiar with the spatial tools and products I analyze. In addition, I have a personal connection to one of the study sites: my family, members of the Druze minority who moved to Doha Aramoun in 1993, still live there. This is the location of my home in Lebanon.

At the time I performed the bulk of my research, I was living in Doha Aramoun and commuting to Hayy Madi/Mar Mikhail and Sahra Choueifat, my other two research sites. Among my informants were residents, government and municipal officials, developers, planners, landowners, real estate brokers, members of religious-political organizations, intellectuals, journalists, and former militiamen. I observed the work of planners and heads of planning units at public agencies and private consultancies. And I conducted extensive research in newspaper archives on the spatial quality of conflict in the city's peripheries since the beginning of the civil war. In addition, I reviewed master plans, planning proposals, and reports from public and private planning agencies, and examined reports and publications held in the archives of the American University of Beirut and the Council for Development and Reconstruction (CDR) that detailed expert discourse on planning and development in the city since the mid-1950s.[3]

Exploring the material and temporal "formations of violence"[4] in a deeply divided city like Beirut proved to be an extraordinarily complex exercise. The three areas my investigations targeted can be thought of as "zone[s] of awkward engagement," where a variety of entities think about, speak of, and approach the subject of urban growth and conflict quite differently.[5] These are not transparent, open sites of engagement; in these areas, what one group might consider natural, market-led urbanization might be deemed by others a hostile form of encroachment. And conducting research on a politically sensitive topic there, in a climate of violence, fear, and conflict, necessitated adopting a flexible methodology. Because of site conditions, I was frequently unable to take notes, record conversations, or take pictures—except when I could snap them discreetly. These limitations are not uncommon in spaces of conflict and volatility. But they meant I had to acknowledge that openings and closures of access in the field would shape the contours of knowledge production.

I came to call my methodology *patching stories and maps*, in reference to the particular way I juxtaposed information from interviews, observations, and popular discourse with archival fragments. My approach was first to collect what technical material I could, including maps, statistics, plans, urban regulations, building laws, private property documents, architectural drawings, and academic books on planning in Beirut. I then pieced these fragments together with public information available from news reports, visual surveys, and the virtual media posts of different political groups. Finally, I assembled these patchworks and matched them to the popular discourses,[6] stories, and rumors circulating in homes, public offices, streets, and social spaces like cafés, beauty salons, grocery stores, and gyms.

Such a "haphazard and patchwork"[7] approach to studying the construction of difference across space and time was necessary because it was difficult to talk to Beirut's residents deeply about such divisive topics as war, militarization, violence, and sectarianism. In this regard, I found conditions in Beirut's peripheries in 2009 and 2010 quite different from those I had encountered in 2004 and 2005. After the clashes in May 2008, talk of war and sectarian essentialism became so dominant and naturalized that it was often impossible to move any discussion beyond the rhetoric of conflict. This made it difficult to identify and understand the modalities of governance that had produced these discourses and spatialities in the first place.

Even though I had been engaged in field research for a long period and had an extensive network of contacts, the segmented political terrain in 2009 also meant that my access to information had always to be negotiated. Because I am Lebanese myself, my informants often tried to categorize me as "with" or "against" this or that group.[8] At times, residents in certain areas also felt uneasy discussing what they thought were sensitive topics, especially when they learned I was studying in the United States. Many of my informants were dependent on religious-political organizations for services, jobs, and (more importantly) security. In addition, during my research, politically motivated violence was taking place in and around my chosen areas of study on an almost weekly basis. Moreover, to understand diverse points of view, I had to cross emergent dividing lines again and again—both physical lines and social, political, and psychological ones. To overcome a number of these obstacles, I worked toward building trust among my informants by offering to be of help to them. For example, I sought out information for a number of families who wanted help with housing loans. And I offered advice to others who were unsure of the eviction and compensation processes being used to move displaced persons out of the buildings they had informally settled in two decades before (as discussed later). I also helped municipal officials by sharing data I had collected from other research venues. At times, these actions helped to bridge certain gaps. But at other times, I had to be satisfied with information provided in public forums.

A patchwork process was also necessary because Lebanon does not currently maintain a system of national archives. Neither do state agencies maintain formal systems of document storage and retrieval. Even when an agency has an archiving procedure, documents are quite often incomplete, randomly placed in drawers, or thrown in a corner. Tellingly, the most complete archives for public planning projects are locked up in the offices of a handful of prominent private planning firms that have received public commissions from the CDR or the Directorate General of Urbanism (DGU). As a result, my access to supposedly public discourse and data depended to a great extent on the benevolence of officials and other actors I interviewed. In this context, as in many others, "benevolence" and "at the mercy of" were two sides of the same coin, with conditions of access being defined along political lines. I also soon came to realize that the officials I interviewed were often only willing to disclose parts of a story.

Another challenge to archival work involved dependence on politically key people. Although such people could open doors, I had to find a way to connect to them. And in this search, my gender and class markers as well as the sectarian affiliation that people assumed about me frequently influenced what information key individuals would volunteer or withhold. As I discovered, the ability to do research on urban development in Beirut is determined by social and economic forms of capital as well as political connections. And the social capital that comes from class and sectarian affiliations is further crucial when attempting to access official sites. Lacking on both accounts, I was forced to rely on academic and personal connections to access high-profile decision-making networks. While I succeeded in many instances, at many other times I was simply denied access.

Moreover, gender played a further role in facilitating or impeding access, depending on how threatening a female researcher was perceived to be at different research sites. Gender was also relevant to how each office constructed the spaces in which I was allowed to examine documents. In particular, these arrangements often involved male supervision, and sometimes intimidation.

Yet another challenge was how to do fieldwork around what felt like a moving target. How could I research something that was simultaneously unfolding in multiple temporalities and spatialities? In Beirut in 2009, the very issues described in this book (such as the intervention of religious-political organizations in housing and land markets) had become central to local and national politics. These issues were taken up in multiple forums, including frequent media reports, legal proposals, planning schemes, and civil-society initiatives. They were also a frequent topic of conversation in cafés, gyms, and homes. In addition, political views around these issues were continuously in flux as new alliances formed and others dissolved. In ever-evolving real time, these shifts might facilitate data collection in one place while hindering it somewhere else. For example, in 2010 the Progressive Socialist Party (PSP) shifted its alliances away from the Sunni Future Movement, associated with the March 14 camp, to be closer to the Shiite Hezbollah, associated with March 8. This significantly weakened the March 14 forces, which (with the PSP support) had won the 2009 elections just a few months earlier. On the one hand, it was interesting to be doing fieldwork that seemed so inherent to the everyday lives of people. On the other, it was a challenge to have to continuously redefine the field of study. These conditions eventually meant that I had to integrate flows of information simultaneously unfolding in multiple spaces.

Ultimately, this "snowballing" method of data collection—as it unfolded in real time in a segmented political terrain, with only partial archival resources—resulted in certain limits to and fractures within the research. To address these problem areas, and to arrive at a more complete understanding of local conditions, I had to carefully seek out personal stories from informants in my research sites. This is where the archival aspect of my work interfaced most critically with ethnography to produce what I call an ethnography of spatial practices.

It is in this regard that this research work has also benefited most from being in part an auto-ethnography of my own engagements with a place I call home. I lived in Doha Aramoun for a large part of my adolescent life. My family still lives there, and it is where I stay when I visit Lebanon once or twice a year. It is also where I lived during my sixteen months of concentrated fieldwork. I have tried both to use and to lay bare the personal entanglements resulting from my being a Lebanese citizen and long-time resident of Doha Aramoun. This has at times meant collapsing the distinction between the expert and researcher on the one hand and the informant and resident on the other. Indeed, as a person who lived through the civil war in Lebanon, I have experienced firsthand the geographies of war, the itineraries of war displacement, and the ways in which the fear of future wars shapes everyday life.

In choosing the location of home as the site of investigation, my aim was to provide a lens that builds on the intertwined personal, professional, and political aspects of my life in order to understand the intricacies and intimacies of war and its geographies. To a certain extent, in the cases of Sahra Choueifat and Hayy Madi/Mar Mikhail, I was able to dissociate myself from my sites and subjects of study. But the intertwinement of my life history with that of Doha Aramoun since 1993 rendered it impossible to establish this same distance there. Over the course of my fieldwork, however, I found that it was not distance that I was striving for. On the contrary, I found myself excavating a sense of intimacy with a place where my family has long lived. Interestingly, this was also a place that had never felt completely like home to me. It was a place that always felt transient, in flux, floating, strange, uprooted, incomprehensible, and uncomfortable. I eventually realized that it was exactly these feelings of both entanglement and estrangement that I wished to interrogate—feelings that for many people made living in Beirut's peripheries an experience of "intimate estrangement."[9]

In excavating this sense of intimacy, I have also sought to elucidate the more general entanglements of the personal and the political that are constitutive of subjectivity in contested geographies. And I have sought to bear witness to the many ways—bold and subtle, fast and slow, formal and intimate—by which violent geographies are produced and reproduced through the intricacies of everyday life. This may become particularly significant as sites are reinscribed over time as nodes in the circulation of local and transnational real estate value, violence, ideology, and militarization. Ultimately, the violence and fear I bear witness to here is not that of emergency, terror, destruction, or death.[10] It is rather that caused by the gradual construction of buildings and infrastructure in ways designed to produce geographies of everyday life and militarization, of normalcy and exception, of peace and war—all at the same time. Eventually, therefore, what the yoking of multiple methodological approaches has allowed me to produce is a situated understanding of the changing geography of Beirut's peripheries as they have been shaped equally by master plans, territorial struggles, discourses, and everyday events.

Transforming Peripheries into Frontiers

As I mentioned in the Prologue, my three principal research sites are located in or adjacent to Beirut's southern suburbs. These southern suburbs are commonly and collectively known as al-Dahiya (the Suburb). In 2001, Mona Harb identified this area as comprising a geographic zone extending south from central Beirut to its airport, and east to the agricultural fields of al-Hadath and Choueifat. Considered to be Hezbollah's stronghold in Beirut, the area is densely inhabited and mostly by people who identify as Shiites. Even the name al-Dahiya today conveys an emotionally charged message that is often reinforced in the media and in conversation among Lebanese citizens. These discourses describe "the Suburb" as a belt of misery characterized by illegal urbanization, squatter settlement, and underdevelopment.[11]

Areas like al-Dahiya and its surroundings have been the subject of scrutiny by urban studies scholars for many years, largely through the conceptual distinction between the urban center and periphery. Within this framework, the periphery has been a powerful concept both in discussions of specific areas of cities in the Global South and with regard more generally to urban theory.[12] In the first instance, peripheries are usually seen as the spaces left out of the center, waiting for the center to engulf them. Commonly, such areas may form on the outskirts of a city.[13] In the second instance, peripheries have been seen as key sites for the discussion of urban informality.[14] As such, they are frequently theorized as receptors of "unwanted" populations, moved out of the way by the more profitable forces of "development."[15]

Whatever way they are viewed, peripheries are constituted and constructed according to social, economic, and political conditions quite different from those that govern the metropolitan center. Such an alternative logic both contributes to their exclusion from the center and asserts their potential for destabilizing it. Because of their exclusion, however, peripheries have also been theorized as spaces of hope. They thus accommodate "volatility that is permitted to go nowhere and a completion always yet to come."[16] And it is in such areas that "struggles . . . for the basic resources of daily life and shelter have also generated new movements of insurgent citizenship based on . . . claims to . . . a right to the city and a right to rights."[17]

However, in cities like Beirut, issues of sectarian identity and spatial competition have introduced a darker reality to such areas. In Beirut, this has largely resulted from the rapid expansion of al-Dahiya after the civil war into adjacent areas with land inhabited or owned by people of other sectarian affiliations—principally Christians in Hayy Madi/Mar Mikhail and Druze (and previously Christians) in Sahra Choueifat and Doha Aramoun. In conceptual terms, this expansion has created the social, political, and economic conditions by which al-Dahiya may now be viewed as a new center, defining the peripheral condition of adjacent areas. And in terms of lived reality, al-Dahiya's expansion is seen as "Shiite encroachment" on the territories of other sectarian groups and a challenge to their existence in the city. It was this sense of encroachment that ultimately produced interface zones characterized by friction, which were solidified as battle lines in May 2008.

Adding to the perception of al-Dahiya as a threatening new center is the fact that Hezbollah's headquarters, Haret Hreik, is located there, and that it emerged in the early 2000s as a node for the transnational circulation of religion, finance, militarization, and violence. Thus, during its war on Lebanon in July 2006, Israel bombed what it defined as areas of Beirut belonging to Hezbollah, and many of the buildings leveled were in Haret Hreik.[18] Surrounding areas, such as Hayy Madi/ Mar Mikhail and Sahra Choueifat, which were seen as extensions of these areas of Hezbollah control, were likewise targeted. Most recently, Haret Hreik and other supposed Shiite neighborhoods have also been the target of suicide bombings by Sunni extremists, with one such bomb being detonated on the road separating Shiite Sahra Choueifat from Druze Choueifat.

Such conditions are precisely what have led to the transformation of many of these peripheral areas into frontiers. Another powerful concept in urban theory, the frontier is often viewed as a dystopic space where regimes of power and capital are engaged in reconfiguring space in their own image. Within such a framework, frontiers are thought of as spaces of capital accumulation and/or racial or ethnic domination. Neil Smith thus examined how inner-city neighborhoods in American cities have become a new urban frontier, where poor people are displaced from old neighborhoods by the forces of gentrification.[19] And in another important study, Oren Yiftachel argued that the creation of frontier conditions in Israel has allowed control by a dominant group to expand into adjacent areas, assisting "both in the construction of national-Jewish identity, and in capturing physical space on which this identity could be territorially constructed."[20] The elasticity of such a frontier was shown by Eyal Weizman to allow it to "continually remold itself to absorb and accommodate opposition," diverting debate about its existence into issues of inclusion and exclusion.[21]

Frontiers have also shaped the geographies of the War on Terror. Derek Gregory and Steven Graham describe how spaces in Iraq and Afghanistan have been transformed to frontiers of war through their construction as "imaginative geographies," whose selective destruction is necessary to ensure the safety of "the West."[22] Frontiers are likewise spaces of uncertainty. Thus, in their account of borderlands, Akhil Gupta and James Ferguson described a frontier as a "place of incommensurable contradictions," and "an interstitial zone of displacement and de-territorialization that shapes the identity of the hybridized subject."[23] However, according to Helga Leitner, Eric Sheppard, and Kristin Sziarto, frontiers may also be "liminal zones of struggle, between different groups for power and influence—each seeking to expand its influence by shaping these zones on their own terms . . . [T]he frontier is a fuzzy geographic space where outcomes are uncertain."[24]

Within this discourse of peripheries as left-out, hopeful spaces and frontiers as contested and impendingly dystopic, how can the transformation of Beirut's peripheries into frontiers (or more accurately, into an increasingly overlapped geography) be understood? According to AbdouMaliq Simone, "the periphery can exist as a frontier in that it has a border with another city, nation, rural area, or periphery."[25] In such an overlapped condition, the periphery may become a hybrid space, "where different ways of doing things, of thinking about and living urban life, can come together."[26] In such a view, the periphery as frontier may be imagined as a hopeful space because it is able to "absorb tensions inherent in the intersection of substantially different ways of doing things." But, as I will show in succeeding chapters, the situation in Beirut contradicts such a hopeful narrative. In Beirut the transformation of peripheries into frontiers, or their coexistence, is a product of ongoing cycles of conflict and a constant effort by competing religious-political organizations to gain spatial advantage in anticipation of wars yet to come.

Interestingly, while the two concepts overlap to some extent, the war yet to come is in many ways the antithesis of Simone's "city yet to come." For Simone, the "city is the conjunction of seemingly endless possibilities of remaking." In such a view, precarious physical structures, provisional settlement sites, and potholed roads, "[e]ven in their supposedly depleted conditions, all are openings onto somewhere."[27] However, in cities in conflict like Beirut, the mundane geographies of peripheries turned frontiers instead prefigure the transformation of hope into dystopia. Thus, while these areas may provide affordable housing for low- and middle-income populations who could not otherwise afford to reside in the city, they are constructed as zones of conflict and contestation, where fear of future local or regional violence actively shapes both the lived present and imagined future. And while, as peripheries, such geographies may provide the possibility of a "right to the city,"[28] as frontiers, they are simultaneously spaces where the contours of future violent engagements and displacements are being drawn and redrawn every day.[29]

As concurrently peripheries of urban growth and frontiers of sectarian conflict, areas in Beirut such as Sahra Choueifat, Doha Aramoun, and Hayy Madi/ Mar Mikhail also dispute the current logic of center and periphery. Indeed, what is at stake in these areas is the very definition of the center, or core, of the urban region that constitutes contemporary Beirut. Geographic paradigms that consider these areas to be peripheries define them in relation to the municipality of Beirut—a center of finance and business, the seat of national government, and a hub of employment and leisure. However, Beirut is not the only center in relation to which the peripheralization of these neighborhoods may be understood. The expansion of Shiite al-Dahiya as a center in its own right equally defines them.

It is precisely this condition of not only being peripheries but of being peripheries of a periphery turned competing center that has transformed Sahra Choueifat, Doha Aramoun, and Hayy Madi/Mar Mikhail into frontiers. And as peripheral articulations of both Beirut and al-Dahiya, they are actively being shaped by the conflicting local, regional, and international dialogues of capital, real estate value, diaspora, war, and militarization that this juxtaposition entails. Most commonly, this tension may be felt in terms of anxiety around the expansion of al-Dahiya and its presumed Shiite population. And this frequently surfaces in discriminatory media reports, like a recent newspaper piece whose author claimed that one of these peripheries was "drowning in al-Dahiya's tsunami that swallows everything."[30]

Naturalizing Sectarian Formations

One gloomy November day in 2009, while I was sorting through maps in the municipality of Choueifat, one of its Druze employees, Hatem, told me he was busy moving to Deir Qoubil, a nearby town. Hatem was born and raised in Choueifat. When I asked him why he was leaving his well-located house there along the Old Saida Road and moving farther from his family and work, he unhesitatingly answered, "It is much more comfortable for one to live in his *bī'a* [natural environment], especially now that I am planning on starting my own family." I was struck by his answer. It was not as though Hatem had been living abroad and was moving back to Beirut to raise his family. This was literally a two-mile move. However, the unspoken crucial circumstance was that Hatem's house was now located alongside the now-Shiite district of Sahra Choueifat.

It also surprised me that Hatem opted to describe his situation by using the word *bī'a*. Initially, I did not pay much attention to this, filing it away as a matter of Hatem's personal choice of words. However, that same afternoon, while visiting one of Choueifat's neighborhoods, I asked Najib, a Druze young man originally from Choueifat, about his opinion on the largely segregated condition of Druze Choueifat and newly Shiite Sahra Choueifat. "This is not a problem!" Najib stated. "Why would it be a problem? Everyone would like to live in his own *bī'a*. Don't you think so?" Three doors down, I then chatted with Rawiya about the current geopolitics of Choueifat. From her window, she pointed to Sahra Choueifat in the valley below. "We can never live in their *bī'a*," she said. "So we sold our land in Sahra Choueifat. A Shiite developer bought it, I think."

It was at this moment that I became aware that the term *bī'a* seemed to have taken on a shared meaning in the city. Indeed, I realized it was a prime example of the discursive process by which the spatialization of sectarian identity proceeds. When I later asked informants at my research sites what *bī'a* meant, none were able to provide a dictionary definition, but all were able to describe what they meant by it. While their *bī'a* was inhabited by people who were "educated, civilized, spacious, and value good life," the constructed *bī'a* of the sectarian other (in most cases, Shiites) was inhabited by people who were "illiterate, uncivilized, overpopulated, and value death and martyrdom." Thus, while *bī'a* translates generally as "natural environment," talk of it in Lebanon had become a way for people to rationalize in everyday discourse the increasingly segregated sectarian spaces they inhabited.[31]

I soon came to see that such discourses circulate the other way around as well. A brief scan for the word *bī'a* in the local Lebanese newspapers (*As-Safir*, *An-Nahar*, and *Al-Akhbar*) for two weeks in 2010 (November 22–December 2) proved quite revealing in this regard. The term appeared frequently in these papers in discussions of the postwar political geography of Beirut, spanning a breadth of value judgments. But two common uses stood out: *bī'at al-muqāwama* and *al-bī'a al-ḥāḍina*: "the resistance environment" and "the incubating environment," respectively.[32] The first phrase has been used by Hezbollah generally to refer to its support base as a "natural environment" for the production of people ready for resistance, sacrifice, and resilience. The second was a more directed phrase, used by Hezbollah and its allies in 2010 after they had uncovered networks of Lebanese working as Israeli spies. Hezbollah denounced these spies not as corrupt individuals but as the expected product of a "natural environment" that endorsed, nourished, and produced treason. Both uses thus referred to a sectarian other. In the first instance, it designated a lesser outside, populated by people who were not willing to defend their land. In the second, it labeled spaces associated with a sectarian other as spaces of treason. Both usages had critical geopolitical implications in local and regional wars: Hezbollah's strongholds had been leveled during Israel's war on Lebanon in July 2006; and in May 2008, the sites of the sectarian other had been the target of attacks.

The principle of residential segregation embodied within contemporary use of the term *bī'a* in Beirut is neither a new phenomenon nor a new concern. The issue of segregation has long occupied the work of social scientists in their attempts to understand cities and urban spaces. Well-known examples of attempts to understand the phenomenon include studies of Chicago's racialized geographies;[33] of Johannesburg's apartheid landscape;[34] and of Belfast's religiously segregated neighborhoods.[35] Likewise, in Beirut, neighborhoods arranged on sectarian lines have been promoted as ideal places to live since the civil war began in 1975.[36] Thus, many people I talked with in Choueifat, Sahra Choueifat, and surrounding areas expressed a preference to live in one's *bī'a*. And these preferences became only more acute after these areas witnessed gruesome battles in 2008, during which houses were burned, people were killed, and families were temporally displaced.

Given many people's avowed preference for such a pattern of living, why is it important, then, to question the spatiality of sectarian order? Is homogeneous living a problem? Or does it just unsettle those people (planners, architects, and social scientists) who believe residents of urban areas should mix and mingle irrespective of difference? Why can't people just live separately if they prefer to?

Clearly, the answer to this question is that people ought to be able to self-segregate if they choose to. However, the mechanisms involved in this choice are never so clear. For example, problems frequently emerge in terms of how preference and choice are constructed. The particular issue here involves the tendency to label as problematic the othered geographies that groups "opt not to live in." At times, these areas may even become targets of intervention by governments, religious-political organizations, or non-governmental organizations (NGOs). And during war, these attempts to rearrange territories may take the form of ethnic or sectarian cleansing. This is just the type of situation that Beirut and Lebanon as a whole have witnessed during many of the episodes of local and regional war over the last four decades. The prevailing use of a term like *bī'a* as an instrument of segregation and othering, then, must be regarded not as idle chitchat but as a dangerous element of a fundamentally political discourse with foundational sociospatial implications. As such, it both creates and assumes an external and undisputed natural ecology from the top down. Such discursive formations are an established element within urban theory. Generally, they have been understood to reflect an attitude of environmental determinism, in which the ordering of the physical world is thought to determine both individual human abilities and broader social development.[37] But in the context of Beirut, such discourses are also critical because they co-constitute everyday contested geographies, and construct choices and preferences for living conditions. Thus, Lina's assumed *bī'a* may prohibit her from buying an apartment in Ras al-Nab' unless she can prove she is a Sunni, while Louay may not be able to rent an apartment in al-Hadath because he is a Shiite. Dalia may choose to sell her land in al-Hadath and Choueifat because she thinks there is no room for her "lifestyle" there anymore.[38] And Ayman, a Druze, may prefer not to rent in Achrafieh because of his fear he may be stuck there "*idhā 'ilqit*" (if a war were to happen).

As these examples indicate, the implications of such discourse are not trivial. Words like *bī'a* move the discussion of segregation, discrimination, and fear from the realm of the political to that of the natural. And when these conditions are thus naturalized, they become top-down structures with inevitable outcomes. In his lectures on the "birth of biopolitics," Michel Foucault described how constructing issues and conditions as "natural spontaneous mechanisms" implies that any "attempts to modify them will only impair and distort them."[39] By thinking of living enclaves as natural habitats, a discourse of *bī'a* thus justifies thinking of them as innately personal and depoliticized, and they are nullified as spaces of potential outside intervention or negotiation.

Joined with the talk of *bī'a* in contemporary Beirut is the notion of *dīmūghrāfīya* (demography). It is safe to say that any news article that touches on political change in Beirut will at some point use the phrase "*al-taghāyur al-dīmūghrāfī*" (the demographic changes), without further elaboration. Thus in 2010, a reporter for the newspaper *Al-Akhbar* described the context for an interview with the mayor of Christian al-Hadath (adjacent to Hayy Madi/Mar Mikhail) as follows: "Putting a map of al-Hadath on the table, [the mayor] explains the current *demography* of the area, dividing it into two parts." The mayor then described negotiations the municipality was holding with Hezbollah, "to help stop the Shiites from expanding beyond the line drawn for them on the map."[40]

As the scientific study of vital statistics about a population—including size, composition, distribution, density, births, deaths, diseases, and fertility—demography has long been considered an exercise in number crunching, a way to arrive at an apolitical, truthful reflection of reality. Yet, like any biopolitical science (in the Foucauldian sense), demography also has political implications. And what makes it further contentious in Lebanon is that even the most basic statistical effort that ordinarily underlies it does not exist here. Thus, people continuously refer to demographic change in their everyday talk when there has been no full population census in the country since 1932. So what are people referring to when they invoke the term? Crudely put, most of what individuals and news reports are indirectly referencing when they talk demography is fear of the encroaching Shiite (or Sunni) other.

In Lebanon (as in many other places) demography has become a passe-partout to refer to and justify the practice of sectarian discrimination without having to name it. Thus, in many interviews I conducted, residents lamented the "demographic changes" that Choueifat, Hayy Madi/Mar Mikhail, or Doha Aramoun was undergoing—even though these residents were often serving as the very agents of this change themselves by selling their land to Shiite developers. In addition, the urban planning, zoning, and construction measures of the municipality in these peripheries turned frontiers (in licit and illicit ways) "have been aggressive attempts to curb the demographic changes," as one engineer told me. The authority conveyed by demography's abstract concern for statistics has thus been appropriated into discourses that construct an unwanted threatening other, using demography's scientific terminology to obscure a fundamentally discriminatory view. As in the case of *bi'a,* a discourse of demography thus allows the construction of a supposedly depoliticized spatial discourse, when the reality is quite the opposite.

To these discourses of *bi'a* and demography in contemporary Beirut, one might add that of *sukkān aṣliyyīn* (natives). This is a concept that has, interestingly, been adapted to Lebanese political rhetoric from the context of settler colonies in North America. For example, the phrase has been used by PSP leaders to describe how minorities like the Druze (and more recently, Christians) are being forced into a geography of "reservations" by a sectarian other.[41] In a country where all citizens are supposedly equal, such discourses are made possible by obsolete policies that specify that voters must cast their ballots in their ancestors' villages, not in their present places of residence.

What the depoliticized discourses of environment, demography, and natives ultimately do, then, is construct certain spaces of the city as "white"—that is, the norm—while constructing others as outcast and unwanted, shaped by the threat of a problematic sectarian other. They are called upon to describe and justify the discrimination, fear, and anxiety that shape an urban geography that is increasingly being formed by the expectation of wars yet to come. In short, these natural and scientific discourses are politically produced.[42]

The Specter of the Other

At this historical juncture in Lebanon, all these discourses fold within them the anxiety associated with the presence of the Shiite figure in the city. Thus, when a new Shiite tenant moved into my building, my neighbor wondered if their religious identity would "tip the sectarian equilibrium we have reached in the building."

Typical of the public expression of these views,[43] since 2009, most of the stories in major newspapers about now-Shiite Sahra Choueifat have depicted it as a haven for gangs and drug dealers and as the center of a prostitution business that is affecting adjacent areas.[44] In May 2010, during an interview about geographic changes in Choueifat and Sahra Choueifat, a well-known local journalist told me, "one should not be *'unṣurī* [discriminatory based on difference], but we simply cannot live with them because they are of a lower class. They are of a different *bi'a.*" Pointing to the mostly Shiite Sahra Choueifat, he continued: "They are mostly illiterate down there. They have too many children, like seven to eight kids, and do not mind living in one- or two-room apartments. Have you been to some of the housing in Sahra Choueifat? Did you see how the garbage is everywhere? Who would want to be their neighbor? The Sunnis are different; you can at least negotiate and discuss issues with them." These comments, from an educated public figure, are in fact emblematic of how class, religion, poverty, and dispossession can become conflated, naturalized, and depoliticized vis-à-vis a constructed other.[45] Equally racist discourses circulate the other way around—that is, from the southern suburbs outward. Such reciprocal discourse typically centers on the figure of an effeminate, passive Sunni; a stubborn, non-tolerant Christian; or an untrustworthy, mysterious Druze.[46]

These sectarian discourses become especially problematic when institutionalized and adopted into quasi-formal practice. For example, a *tadbīr idārī*, or municipal ordinance, has been adopted in al-Hadath, an area adjacent to Hayy Madi/Mar Mikhail, prohibiting Christians from selling land to Shiites. And to better demarcate territories, the same municipality lobbied to have a sculpture of Jesus returned to "its 'proper' place on the roundabout that separates al-Hadath from al-Dahiya."[47] Meanwhile, at the national level, as mentioned previously, a fifteen-year ban on land sales between religious groups was proposed in the Lebanese Parliament in 2011 by one of its members, Boutrous Harb.

Anxiety around the presence of the Shiite figure in the city is not new. Haraket Amal (the political organization out of which Hezbollah emerged) was initially called Ḥarakat al-Maḥrūmīn, the Movement of the Dispossessed People. The reference was largely to Shiites, who for many years in Lebanon constituted a class of dispossessed, rural, and uneducated poor or rural-to-urban migrants who worked menial jobs in Beirut and its surroundings and who lived mostly in its informal peripheries.[48] Before the civil war, literature on urban conditions in Beirut cited a similar anxiety about the rural migrant who "does not know how to live the urban modern life."[49] At the time, such commentary did not attach a sectarian label to this figure, but it is easy in hindsight to put the two together. Indeed, this anxiety over the presence of the Shiite figure was a key justification for urban interventions in the decades leading up to the war. Such a figure was seen as disruptive and unsuited to modern urban life, and his or her presence was cited as a reason why interventions were needed in the form of development and planning.[50]

This anxiety, of course, is not unique to Beirut. It coincided with a moment characterized by an anxiety on how to deal with the rural to urban poor migrants across the globe after decolonization and with the emergence of newly independent nation-states. Indeed, successions of conjured figures to fear have helped to determine the practices, discourses, and policies of urban life. In Europe and America, this was true in the early twentieth century with regard to the presence of women in public spaces.[51] The rise of the Nazi party in Germany in the decades between the two World Wars was linked to anxiety around the presence of Jews in European cities.[52] And during most of the twentieth century, the figure of the revolutionary Communist caused anxiety throughout the major centers of capitalism as well as their peripheries.[53]

With the fall of the Soviet Union in the early 1990s, anxiety across the globe, and in cities across the Middle East, shifted to the ultra-religious figure. In particular, since the attacks of September 2001 in the United States, the feared other, in reaction to whom the present and the future of cities are being shaped, has become the Muslim suicidal bomber or Muslim "terrorist" more broadly, a global discourse that does not distinguish between Sunni and Shiite. The anxieties over the ultra-religious other have continued globally with the emergence of the Islamic State in Iraq and Syria (ISIS) and the recent spread of terrorist attacks in cities around the world. This focus on the ultra-religious figure is pervasive even in Middle Eastern countries, with predominantly Muslim populations, as the discourse on the war on terror has been widely used locally to construct various groups as threats to governments.

In Lebanon, the recent rise of ISIS (a principally Sunni organization) has also brought attention to the threat of the ultra-religious Sunni figure. However, the Lebanese othering of the ultra-religious figure was for the longest time focused locally on the Shiite figure. The construction of the Shiite figure as the threat was based on local as much as on geopolitical considerations. The Shiite figure was (and still is) constructed as a frugal, death-loving martyr. In this regard, he differed fundamentally from religiously moderate middle-class Sunnis, particularly those aligned with the Future Movement.[54] According to this view, Sunnis thus came to be seen as advocates of economic prosperity and the good life, and were assumed to represent the "real" Lebanon, "the Switzerland of the Middle East." Such a portrayal perhaps owes much to the leadership of Rafic Hariri, the country's most prominent post–civil war Sunni prime minister and a businessman who implemented a wide range of neoliberal economic measures.

Sectarian anxieties and fears of religiosity intertwine in Lebanon with the structure of the postwar state—and also that of quasi-state actors, such as Hezbollah. As Hezbollah gained more political and military power during the 1990s and managed to accrue the support of most Shiites, the fear of Hezbollah and, by extension, the fear of the Shiites were equated. This anxiety towards the Shiite figure deepened with the withdrawal of Israel in 2000 from territories it had occupied in southern Lebanon in 1982. This was the moment when rival political organizations argued that Hezbollah should disarm, as these other groups had been forced to do before, after the civil war. But this argument went unheeded for a variety of reasons, including continuing Israeli violations of Lebanon's sovereignty, and Hezbollah went on to survive the Israeli war against it in Lebanon in 2006. Hezbollah's subsequent show of arms during the May 2008 events even increased the group's clout as it did the fear of other sectarian groups. Today, the organization is involved directly in the fighting in Syria, and its leaders claim its military wing is more powerful than ever.[55]

Arms, however, do not constitute the only threat posed by Hezbollah to its rivals. Hezbollah also maintains a vast apparatus of social services,[56] and in addition, it coordinates a network of affiliated or sympathetic property developers who are deeply involved in Beirut's real estate markets.[57] These developers have the financial capacity to buy and develop land (sometimes with subsidies from Hezbollah). This has led to the massive urbanization of peripheral areas adjacent to al-Dahiya, and to a corresponding skyrocketing of real estate values there that has created concern among members of the other sectarian groups. At the frontiers of Hezbollah's territorial expansion, these fears range from increasingly unaffordable housing, which is seen as pushing other groups out, to the ever-present possibility of renewed sectarian violence.

Sectarian cleansing and forced displacement were central strategies during the civil war.[58] In a city where memories of that conflict are still vivid and where the possibility of its return are real, people are afraid that in a future war, a militarily and demographically dominant sectarian other will force them out of areas they have long considered home.

The Everyday Geography of Militarization

The rising military power of religious-political organizations is key to understanding the fears and anxieties that surround the urbanization of Beirut's peripheries. In Lebanon, there is no state monopoly over arms or territorial control. Indeed, state institutions in Lebanon, such as the army, have become increasingly less central to decisions about peace and war. Even before the civil war began in 1975, these decisions were becoming largely the domain of sectarian political parties, who retain that power to this day.

With the exception of the Maronite Church, the religious-political organizations in Lebanon that this book discusses are outgrowths of the main militias formed during the civil war. At its conclusion, they simply transformed themselves into political actors. Of these groups, the Druze PSP is the oldest, having first established itself as a secular political party in 1949. During the war, the PSP received military support from a wide range of sources, including Iraq, Syria, Libya, and the Soviet Union. By comparison, the Sunni Future Movement was officially established only in 2007. However, as a looser entity, with extensive financial and political support from Saudi Arabia, it exerted considerable influence after the civil war under the auspices of the late Prime Minister Rafic Hariri. Thus, even though it did not take part in the war, it ended up attracting many former Sunni militia fighters.

The Shiite Hezbollah is a more complex entity. It was born in 1982, primarily as a resistance movement to the Israeli occupation of Lebanon, and it has strong religious, political, and financial ties to Iran. Since 2011, Hezbollah has also been involved in the war in Syria, fighting on the side of the Assad regime, with which it has maintained long-standing ties. As part of the agreement ending the Lebanese civil war, the weapons belonging to the country's various militias were for the most part confiscated. Only Hezbollah was allowed to keep them, because its existence as an armed force was deemed necessary to prevent further Israeli encroachments on national territory. Depending on one's point of view, Hezbollah can be considered a non-governmental organization, a Lebanese political party, a resistance movement, and/or a transnational armed force.[59] However, such categories are often blurred because Hezbollah's activities blend characteristics of all these types of organization.

Today the Lebanese Parliament and government ministries contain representatives from all four of the groups described above, in addition to multiple other actors. And the functioning of government is further complicated by the postwar Taif Agreement to share public service appointments equally between Muslims and Christians (with all of Lebanon's religious entities being guaranteed a share). Each sect also maintains vast networks of supporters in the private sector[60] across real estate, finance, and industry.[61] And, despite the fact that only Hezbollah is supposed to be armed, in reality the recent reemergence of violence in the country and region has touched off an underground arms race.

Rather than being located outside the state or in opposition to it, each of these religious-political organizations functions through a constellation of affiliates who span the public and private sector. Their networks of loyalists include cabinet ministers, heads of municipalities, street-level bureaucrats, bankers, housing developers, landowners, draftsmen in public and private planning agencies, police officers, militiamen, religious charity workers, and even asphalt company employees. As hybrid entities, therefore, they cannot be defined simply as non-state actors or NGOs. Neither are they just political parties, since their activities range from organizing militias to distributing religious charity, passing through all other forms of social and political engagement in between.

Lebanon's religious-political organizations thus challenge established divisions between state and market, private and public, government and insurgency.[62] Together, they provide soldiers for the Lebanese army and contribute to the government functions essential to the maintenance of state sovereignty. Yet individually, they operate separate NGOs and paramilitary groups that have played roles in local and transnational wars in ways that challenge national sovereignty to varying degrees.[63] The drivers for these engagements include the unfolding regional Sunni-Shiite conflict, the fear of widespread "Islamization" in the Middle East among Lebanese Christians, Hezbollah's active participation in the Arab-Israeli conflict and more recently in the war in Syria, and the West's ongoing War on Terror against Islamic militarized organizations in the region.

In a country where the specter of war is ever present, involvement in past and ongoing conflicts is an element used to order territory. In Beirut's peripheries, in expectation of future violence, land has a religion, and everyday spaces are evaluated as strategic assets. In addition to being able to dominate and profit from real estate and housing markets, what matters to religious-political organizations is their ability (in the event of war) to control strategic hilltops, secure access to supplies of weapons, and control urban routes of movement. This signals a shift in what is usually thought of as militarized space. When a window in an apartment building can be understood both as an everyday source of light and air and a future sniper location, the distinction between living spaces and militarized spaces collapses. In such a context, construction is as much a feature of war as is destruction,[64] and every built space is a potential future battle space.[65] This doubleness of everyday and military geography is reshaping strategies toward warfare globally. For example, since its involvement in Iraq, the United States Army has rethought its training to emphasize what it calls *urban warfare*. It has even built mock "Arab towns" in the Nevada and California deserts in which to train—and the Israeli Army has built similar facilities in the Negev Desert.[66]

The war yet to come has therefore created the need to reconceptualize the interrelation of space and violence. Literature on the role of space in conflict, war, and violence has so far emphasized how social movements or factions use space (bridges, tunnels, public squares, streets) as resources for their activities.[67] Alternatively, it has examined how the ordering of everyday space may be used to produce meaning and demands for social change.[68] However, other concepts, such as *urbicide* (the killing of cities), have recently focused attention on how the destruction of urban space may itself be a primary objective of war, rather than its by-product.[69] Under this conception, space may be the target, agent, and receptor of violence.

However, the space-making practices of Hezbollah or the PSP in Sahra Choueifat, for example, illustrate an even more complex relationship between space and violence. Beyond being resources or receptors for violence, the geographies of post–civil war Beirut show how space and violence have become mutually constitutive. Thus, on a local level, the territorial contestations caused by the religious-political organizations' role in spatial production construct new and continuously shifting dividing lines, which in turn create new daily forms of violence and contestation. Meanwhile, the intervention of religious-political organizations in producing urban space (as Hezbollah has done in Sahra Choueifat, and in the southern suburbs of Beirut in general) positions these mundane geographies as targets in larger regional conflicts. Thus, in his discussion of the logic of Israel's July 2006 war on Lebanon, which was primarily directed at diminishing the capabilities of Hezbollah, Derek Gregory argued that by abstracting the assaulted areas as "targets," the IDF (Israel Defense Forces) could claim it was attacking "only 'structures, headquarters and weapon facilities,' 'vehicles, bridges and routes.'" Through such an abstraction, he argued, "the combat zone [could be] magically emptied of all human beings"[70] and ruthlessly bombed. The possibility of mapping strategic concerns onto the mundane geography of a city like Beirut may be seen as a primary cause for the transformation of urban peripheries into frontiers of violence in both local and regional conflicts.

It is also within this context that the very concept of the state must be questioned in Lebanon. The invocation of the state in the Middle East is always a political act. Layers of colonialism, political upheaval, war, and international economic and military intervention combine with issues of feudalism, ethnicity, sectarianism, and religion to complicate the task of identifying the extent and nature of a state's authority. In this regard, contemporary ethnographic works on the region have discussed the state in many different ways—as monolithic, as a non-state, as weak or hybrid, as multiple semi-states, as elusive or spectral, as states within a state, or as a state with holes.[71]

Ultimately, no discussion of urban spaces can escape considering the role of the state, since state agencies remain the generators of laws and urban policies. The difficulty in Lebanon is that people's conceptualization of the state differs across space and time. For example, its importance often fades completely in discussions of al-Dahiya, where the state is seen as absent and indifferent to the struggles of the Shiite poor. Its role here is widely assumed to have been taken over by Hezbollah—which other discourses have described as operating a "state within a state." Yet, when discussing the reconstruction of downtown Beirut, the same state may be invoked as strong and capable. The Lebanese state is thus seen as mobilizing massive power in consolidating capital and privatizing the heart of the city, while provincializing its poor peripheries. To make matters even more confusing, by simultaneously taking positions both "inside" the state and "outside" it, Lebanon's various sectarian groups may interpolate the idea of the state into the strategic positions they take in their struggle to rearrange Beirut's peripheries to advance their positions in anticipation of future wars.

The rising power of such complex actors is also not unique to Beirut. Religious-political organizations have played critical roles recently in a number of other post-conflict and post-colonial cities and territories, including Ahmadabad, Abidjan, Cairo, Gaza, Istanbul, Peshawar, Sarajevo, and Belfast.[72] Indeed, the growing number of such hybrid actors may be indicative of the current neoliberal moment, which has been marked by a worldwide decline in state services. Yet, despite the growing scale and breadth of their interventions, there has been little theorization of the role of such organizations in shaping urban space. Instead, discussions continue to prioritize a binary of state and private capital, in which such complex actors tend to be seen by default as private. Such a view does not fully account for the considerable complexity that has replaced the divide between public acts (by state agencies and government bodies) and private ones (by developers, companies, individuals, NGOs, and charities). Actors like Hezbollah and the PSP defy simple categorizations when it comes to the privatization of space and services or the fragmentation of urban space under conditions of violence. The same applies to other dichotomies, such as that between the state and private markets (where economic resources are seen as either public goods or private property) and that between state order and insurgency (where armed force is assumed to be under the control of either a government or a rebel group bent on challenging it).

As a result, the roles of these religious-political organizations in social change do not fit the usual narratives. It is therefore important to move away from thinking of their role in city making as exceptional. This is not the spatial exception of the urban revolution.[73] It is not the temporal exception manifested in a coalescing moment soon to dissipate.[74] And it is not even merely the exception of insurgency and terror. It is a condition that raises new questions.

At the periphery of the divided city of Beirut—where Hezbollah may act as an urban planner,[75] where residential developers must choose to be affiliated with Hezbollah or the Future Movement, where a municipality may serve as an administrative annex to the PSP, and where the planning of public amenities that are never built may be outsourced to private companies—how is it possible to conceive of spatial production as a process of positive social change? Indeed, what sort of sociospatial change is currently under way when the Maronite Church and Hezbollah—based on a discourse that imagines the Islamization of the entire Middle East—are engaged in a race to purchase land with the primary aim of dominating the street politics of the future?

In fact, the active participation of such groups in organizing space may position them as actors who *cannot but be central* to the functioning of contemporary cities. Understanding this new reality of urban life, however, requires also grasping how their increasing role is derived neither from the fragmentation of late capitalism nor from ethnic, religious, or racial discrimination alone. Rather, it is produced by the continuities and discontinuities between concurrent neoliberal economic practices, religious ideologies, transnational militarization, and the rise of sectarianism, territoriality, and violence.

Locations and Temporalities

In exploring these issues in relation to the transformation of my three principal research sites—Hayy Madi/Mar Mikhail, Sahra Choueifat, and Doha Aramoun—I will employ three spatial and temporal lenses based on processes of urban growth that I call *doubleness*, *lacework*, and *ballooning*. In each of the three following chapters, I will pair an explanation of one of these processes with an exploration of one of the research sites. However, I must stress that these processes of urban growth are not mutually exclusive. One must take them together if one is to understand the way urbanization currently operates in Beirut's southern and southeastern peripheries.

Conceptually, these three processes reveal how planning and space making in post-conflict cities mold space and time in labyrinthine ways. They thus challenge the typical modernization logic of urban planning, which assumes a narrative of progress toward a more equitable and harmonious future. This teleology is typically mapped onto urban space by means of plans that embody a certain temporal logic (e.g., a concentric model of urban expansion, or clearly designated zones for housing versus industrial growth). Lebanon's geopolitical location, however, has placed it in the middle of armed conflicts. And considering this condition of ever-evolving conflict, temporalities of future, present, and past have been folded into each other, resulting in an anticipated future that is always shaped by a past of war. What matters here is not that one particular new war will come or not, but rather that a general expectation of war has legitimized the claims of certain powerful actors (in this case, religious-political organizations) to shape the present. An anticipated future of violence and contestation has thus come to shape present geographies according to a cyclical temporality (of sectarian strife) instead of a teleological one (with a Eurocentric linear notion of time and planning).

Beirut's emerging geography involves the transformation of old peripheries into new centers, and the transformation of new peripheries into frontiers of conflict. Crucially, the city's southern suburbs, al-Dahiya, must today be seen as a locus of urbanization, not only a result of it. Al-Dahiya is as much a "center," shaped by unavoidable international circulations of finance, religion, and militarization, as is Beirut's central business district. And this condition has only become more pronounced since I began this research, as local political conditions now reflect the regional Sunni-Shiite confrontation, the ongoing Arab-Israeli conflict, and the civil war in Syria. One result on the ground today is that the high density of inhabitation in al-Dahiya has combined with the overall great demand for new housing in the city to create a situation in which al-Dahiya's peripheral pressures compete with those of central Beirut. Awareness of these processes is critical to understanding the construction of new sectarian frontiers.

In the chapters to come, what I further hope to show is that the relevance of the three urbanization concepts—doubleness, lacework, and ballooning—varies in proportion to the distance of a particular site from the Hezbollah headquarters of Haret Hreik and also from Beirut. In addition, ongoing development may be conditioned by material opportunities and physical and political constraints that make it feasible to build in one area at one time while freezing that possibility in other areas. Overall, however, emerging development patterns delineate new contours of separation between sectarian groups.

Of the three areas I studied, Hayy Madi/Mar Mikhail is the closest to Haret Hreik. Indeed, it is situated on the edge of al-Dahiya—but in a direction where al-Dahiya previously could not grow because these areas were part of a historically Christian village, and because the civil war transformed the Old Saida Road into a hardened frontier. At one point, this road was regarded by combatants as a literal "retaining wall" against the eastward expansion of al-Dahiya. My analysis will therefore examine this area's transformation according to spatial practices of *doubleness*. In this view, bombed-out building sites, whether redeveloped or retained as ruins, are understood both as the products of past war and as assets against the eventuality of future conflict.

The ruination of a former built environment in Hayy Madi/Mar Mikhail differentiates that area from Sahra Choueifat and Doha Aramoun, where contemporary conditions are typified more by massive construction than destruction. Moving out from the center of al-Dahiya, the development of Sahra Choueifat has been driven, since the war, by the need to rehouse displaced families, many of whom had been forced to squat in ruined structures such as those in Hayy Madi/Mar Mikhail. As a result of these pressures, areas of previously agricultural and industrial land have gradually been transformed by the construction of new apartment buildings, which have largely been marketed to Shiites. Druze and Christian property owners in this area initially facilitated this change by selling their land for a profit. But more recently, inhabitants of the Druze-dominated Choueifat municipality have used zoning plans and building laws in an attempt to resist establishment of an expanded Shiite stronghold. These efforts have now created a *lacework* of urbanization that folds areas for housing into industrial and agricultural zones, mixes areas controlled by Shiites with ones controlled by Druze, and delineates new contours of violence and engagement.

Of the three research sites, Doha Aramoun is the farthest from the center of al-Dahiya. Here I show how access to development sites and individual project characteristics reflect the simultaneous (and competitive) *ballooning* of Shiite al-Dahiya and of the city core (primarily Sunni west Beirut). Ballooning may take place at a variety of scales. On the level of an individual building, it may involve constructing more floors than initially permitted or encroaching on a setback to maximize profit. On the level of a municipality, it may involve working behind the scenes with government agencies or religious-political organizations to bypass market mechanisms and extend areas of sectarian control. And on the metropolitan level, it may involve the use of international aid to build infrastructure and engage in planning efforts that enable the extension of sectarian patterns of urbanization. Thus, in Doha Aramoun, the combination of large-scale, nationally sanctioned building and planning projects with the building-by-building efforts of Hezbollah-affiliated developers has transformed a formerly marginal periphery into a prime new site for sectarian violence.

What I hope to show through these case studies is that the failure of Beirut's new peripheral development to provide residents with safe environments is not the result of a failure of planning, nor is it a demonstration of the ways such spaces may defy the logic of planning. In fact, these peripheries are intricately planned. Their dysfunctional qualities may rather be traced to the way planning has been used as a tool to create the geographies of wars yet to come. Spaces and temporalities have been carved up in ways that allow for urban growth and development profit, while foreclosing the possibility of an urban politics that might enable anything other than a sectarian future imagined as equally as violent as the past. These conditions could come about because planning has been stripped of its development agenda, and experts have been reduced to the role of technicians of the war yet to come.

This book traces the production of Beirut's geographies of war in times of peace. But it also suggests that the twists and turns in the temporalities and spatialities of conflicts yet to come may be as relevant to cities across the globe as they are to Beirut. While the logic of anticipated sectarian war may be particular to Beirut, cities of both the Global North and the Global South are currently being governed, regulated, and contested according to a logic of future violence, based on imaginings of the likelihood and effects of gang war, destructive climate change, and international terror.

CHAPTER 2
THE DOUBLENESS OF RUINS

A QUARTER CENTURY after the negotiated end of the Lebanese civil war, ruins remain a common sight in the landscape of metropolitan Beirut. The fifteen-year conflict left an expansive geography of such scars, including buildings shelled and hollowed-out, pockmarked by thousands of bullets, or standing half-destroyed but in some cases still inhabited (Figure 4). Hayy Madi/Mar Mikhail is one area within Beirut's southern peripheries that still bears such traces of the long, brutal conflict. But, as I came to see, the persistence of ruins here has a special story to tell—one that reveals how a process of doubleness underlies the urbanization of a city in conflict.

The end of Lebanon's civil war in 1990 provoked a familiar debate on war ruins. As the reconstruction of Beirut's city center began in the 1990s, and ruined structures began to be cleared to make way for new construction, some writers and urbanists argued for the importance of retaining some of the ruins to preserve the memory of the civil war. If the Lebanese population were to forget this part of their history, the argument went, they would repeat it.[1] This view was bolstered by studies and examples of using war memorials not only to "commemorate and attempt to resolve memories of the traumatic experience that is war,"[2] but also as a as a form of peace education.[3] However, this position was ultimately no match for the potential of new real estate development. And except in a few notable cases like the Barakat building, a bullet-holed building that has been transformed into a museum and cultural center that documents Beirut's history and its civil war, or the iconic Holiday Inn that still towers with its bulleted façades over the city, awaiting its owners' decision on its redevelopment, a logic of future profit has prevailed over one of preservation, memory, and the past.[4] And as bulldozers brought down the ruins, Beirut's skyline began to sprout a glittering crop of new concrete, stone, and glass towers. In the city center today, as if to emphasize the point, billboards hang on the remaining ruined structures, promoting all sorts of products for a Lebanon that wants to be far from war. Nevertheless, the prospect of new war is never far away.

FIGURE 4. Ruins in
Hayy Madi/Mar Mikhail.
Source: Author, 2005.

In contemporary Lebanon, many consider the question of civil war ruins to
have been settled. And by and large, Beirut's remaining ruins recede into the background, forgotten, waiting their turn to be demolished. Yet as new residential
development reshapes the city and its peripheries, some ruins seem to defy the
dominant logic of redevelopment. In the face of a relentless construction boom,
skyrocketing land prices, and a seemingly insatiable demand for new housing, they
raise important questions. What, for example, explains the continued presence of
ruins in areas such as Hayy Madi/Mar Mikhail? And why do they seem to possess
a special ability to stop time and resist the ongoing urban development machine?

During my research, people offered several common responses when I asked why certain ruined buildings remained in the city. Among them, for example, were that the owners had emigrated some forty years ago, never to return; that the owners were awaiting a higher price and were not yet ready to sell; and that the sales that would have freed the land beneath them were being impeded by complications of inheritance. However, in the vicinity of Hayy Madi/Mar Mikhail, I also kept hearing of the Maronite Church and its campaign of real estate purchases. Thus, while answers elsewhere imagined pragmatic causes and concerns, I came to see the city's contemporary geography of ruins as also determined by an overlapping geography of past and present conflict, shaped by possible wars yet to come.

Through my two periods of ethnographic research (in 2004 to 2005 and 2009 to 2010), I came to understand the doubleness of certain ruins in Hayy Madi/Mar Mikhail as the product of overlapping conflicts.[5] The one that is past was about civil war, destruction, and displacement. The one that is ongoing concerns territory, housing construction, and demographic change. This second conflict explains the shifting condition of these ruins—from being partially destroyed structures inhabited for decades by war-displaced families to being empty shells caught and standing still in an ongoing conflict over territory.

In addition, the doubleness of the ruins in Hayy Madi/Mar Mikhail refers to how periphery and frontier, peace and war, construction and destruction, displacement and homemaking, expansion and containment, and sectarianism and pluralism overlap, coexist, and collide in contemporary Beirut. I was once asked with regard to my research: "Are these processes you describe for the war yet to come or for the peace? Is it about sectarian segregation or coexistence?" It is exactly this inability to distinguish between such categories that characterizes the doubleness of Beirut's contested geography. War displacement, compensation policies, land markets, and shifting political alliances have all shaped the city's checkerboard geography.

War ruins have been a subject of study in many urban contexts. But my aim here is not to examine the question of their preservation, or "to turn to ruins as memorialized monumental 'leftovers' or relics." Rather, it is to see them, as Ann Laura Stoler does in her discussion of "imperial debris," as "what people are *left with*: . . . the social afterlife of structures, sensibilities, and things."[6] In this sense, Beirut's ruins can be viewed as lingering objects of past conflicts in the landscape of the present, creating, through their materiality, sociopolitical and economic relations characteristic of a new geography of conflict.

A Site of Demarcations

Hayy Madi and Mar Mikhail are adjacent neighborhoods within the jurisdiction of the Chiyah municipality, a southern periphery of Beirut.[7] Adjoining the present Hezbollah stronghold of Haret Hreik, the Hayy Madi/Mar Mikhail area was a principal battleground during the civil war. Before the war, these neighborhoods had been home to a bustling Christian community, anchored by the Mar Mikhail church. However, during the early months of the war, the area was bombed and then abandoned, and the two neighborhoods eventually fell on the Muslim side of the Green Line dividing Beirut into a Muslim west and a Christian east. Today, as evidence of the intensity of this conflict, hollowed-out shells of fancy villas and ruined apartment buildings still line some of the side streets, amid the construction of upscale, modern apartment buildings.

As the war progressed and fighting moved to new areas, the character of the two neighborhoods changed markedly. During these later years of the conflict, their shattered buildings became home to hundreds of families who had been displaced by the fighting in southern Lebanon after 1976. Unlike the original landowners in Hayy Madi and Mar Mikhail, who had mostly been Christian, these newcomers were largely Shiite. And many of them (and others who settled there after being forced out of other areas of the country) stayed until 2005. This was when, through a series of postwar laws and government policies, they were granted monetary compensation to evacuate the ruined buildings they had occupied as squatters. The government's stated purpose in offering monetary compensation was to support the displaced families' return to their home villages in south Lebanon. However, after living in the city for decades, many of these families preferred to stay in Beirut's vicinity. The combination of their eviction and the government's monetary settlements thus created an overwhelming demand for new housing for them in the city's southern peripheries.

The most prominent landmark in Hayy Madi/Mar Mikhail is the Mar Mikhail church. A long, white structure, today it anchors a surrounding landscape of ruins and tall new buildings (Figure 5). The church stands on the Mar Mikhail side of the major road that separates the two neighborhoods, at the edge of one of the busiest intersections in Beirut's southern peripheries. A renovated, stone-clad structure, with a prominent yet subdued appearance, its façade facing the road is ornamented with arches framing crosses. The church's doors are largely closed, except on special occasions, reflecting the fact that the community it once served has itself been displaced.

Michel Zakkour Road separates Mar Mikhail from Hayy Madi. In recent years, it has been transformed into a four-lane arterial incorporating a traffic tunnel next to the church. While the aim of the expansion was to relieve traffic con-

FIGURE 5. Mar
Mikhail Church. Seen
here from Michel
Zakkour Road, the
church sits between
ruins and new
concrete and glass
buildings. Source:
Author, 2010.

gestion and make the area more accessible from the city center, it also created a
massive piece of urban infrastructure, whose concrete traffic dividers make it difficult to walk between the two neighborhoods. Meanwhile, to the west and south
of Hayy Madi, a vast stretch of empty land separates the area from Haret Hreik.
Lining the Hayy Madi side of Zakkour Road are a few unremarkable structures
that residents now identify as Hezbollah buildings, after they were targeted during
Israel's July 2006 war on Lebanon. The Old Saida Road, part of the former Green
Line, provides the border of both neighborhoods to the east (Figure 6).

Delineated and divided by main vehicular arteries, the interiors of Hayy Madi
and Mar Mikhail are nonetheless lightly trafficked. This calm is disrupted daily,
however, by noise generated by a number of massive building projects, located
primarily on the Hayy Madi side. The start of this construction boom generally
corresponded with the onset of reconstruction in the southern suburbs of Beirut
after the 2006 war. Today, cranes, stacks of cement blocks, concrete mixers, and
piles of steel rods are constant features of the landscape. Along with dozens of new
residential towers, the work associated with these elements includes a large new
public school. But the workers bustling around these sites are mostly Syrian migrants, and the billboards describing the projects mention the names of developers
who are mostly Shiite. The incoming apartment dwellers, the future population of
the neighborhood, I was told, are also Shiite.

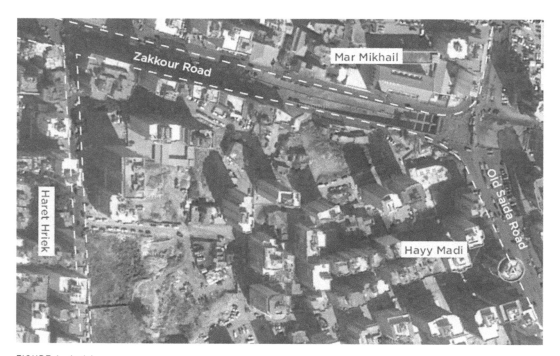

FIGURE 6. Aerial view of the Hayy Madi/Mar Mikhail area. Zakkour Road separates the two neighborhoods. Haret Hreik is to the west and south, and Old Saida Road to the east. Source: Adapted by the author from Google Maps, 2016.

Despite their veneer of affluence, these newly minted apartment buildings sit uncomfortably within an otherwise prominent geography of civil war ruins (Figure 7). The area also reemerged in 2008 as a site of sectarian violence.[8] These deadly episodes largely pitted Hezbollah and Haraket Amal against various groups—first, the Lebanese army, and then, during the May 7, 2008, events, against other sectarian armed factions.[9] These were among the battles that brought Beirut to the brink of a new civil war. Periodic episodes of violence since then have also marked this area as a frontier of al-Dahiya. Indeed, it is now seen as a site of strategic and symbolic demarcation—both for those attempting to delineate the borders of al-Dahiya (for either its expansion or its containment), and for those wishing to stage symbolic protests warning against the dangers of renewed civil war.[10]

The Making of a Periphery

Historically, the contest over the development of Hayy Madi/Mar Mikhail has resulted in the area being remade repeatedly as a periphery and a frontier. It was here, for example, that in 1975 Fuad Khuri conducted one of the first ethnographic studies of Beirut's peripheries. Titled *From Village to Suburb: Order and Change in Greater Beirut*, Khuri's ethnography traces the area's development from agricultural to residential use, and then to an industrial suburb. Khuri also shows how it had been transformed from a Christian village to a mixed Shiite and Chris-

FIGURE 7. Left: A Mar Mikhail building in ruins in 2004. These buildings were bought by the Maronite Church. Right: A typical high-rise building under construction in Hayy Madi in 2010. Source: Author, 2004 and 2010.

tian area through the migration, beginning in the 1930s, of job seekers from rural eastern and southern Lebanon.[11] Initially, the Christian village of Chiyah and neighboring Shiite settlement of Ghobeiri were part of the same municipality. However, as sectarian tensions mounted (for example, after the Shiite areas complained they were not receiving infrastructure services from the Christian municipality), the area was divided in two in 1956—with Ghobeiri becoming a separate municipality.

Bolstering Chiyah's status as a Christian-only town, however, did not end the conflict. In 1958, Beirut's suburbs, including this area, were the site of the first post-independence class and sectarian war in Lebanon. The fighting reflected an increase in class consciousness at a moment of heightened global communist and socialist influence. On the surface, the 1958 insurrection was directed at a perceived Christian monopoly over the country's resources, which reflected the fact that a majority of the country's poor and landless were Muslims. However, not all Christians were landowners either, and many poor Christians felt they were being squeezed out of Beirut's peripheries by both Christian landowners and Muslim migrants. Christian-Muslim antagonisms were based on fear of a Muslim rise to power, facilitated by Muslim spatial expansion in the peripheries through a combination of informal land subdivision and squatting.[12] But equally on the rise were Christian-Christian class antagonisms, spearheaded by right-wing parties like the Kata'ib, who championed the interests of low- and middle-income Christians against both Christian landowners and Muslims.

Although the armed uprising was put down after the appointment of a new president who promised a larger role for the state in balanced development, this class and sectarian conflict was soon apparent again in fighting over the arrangement of territories. In 1963, the French planner and architect Michel Ecochard was commissioned to produce a master plan for Beirut's suburbs, and his proposal contained controversial restrictions on development in Chiyah. The restrictions largely concerned calculations of minimum plot size and exploitation factors, which were seen as limiting who could afford to buy land or apartments there. Specifically, whereas landowners wanted to be able to build more densely on land in Chiyah, the Ecochard plan pushed for restricting the amount of building possible, which lowered the value of land.[13] At the time, many of Beirut's suburbs had already been informally subdivided and settled by Shiite migrants.[14] Thus, lower-income Christians and the Kata'ib supported building restrictions in Chiyah, hoping this would create opportunities for lower-income Christians, too, to obtain land at depreciated prices;[15] a plan landowners vehemently opposed. Ultimately, municipal elections in the area in 1964 were fought based on candidates' positions on the Ecochard plan.[16] And that contest prefigured how concern over planning and real estate would shape local politics in Beirut's peripheries in the run-up to full-scale civil war in 1975.[17]

Life in Displacement

As in much of the rest of Chiyah, the landowners and residents of Hayy Madi/ Mar Mikhail before the civil war were mostly Christians. The Maronite Church also owned large tracts of land as endowments in the area. However, early in the war, during the period known as the two-year war (1975–1976), buildings in Hayy Madi/Mar Mikhail—as elsewhere along the Green Line—were heavily shelled and eventually evacuated and abandoned by their original owners.[18]

Initially, the abandoned areas of Hayy Madi/Mar Mikhail were taken over by the Shiite Haraket Amal and a number of Palestinian fighters. However, around 1977 and 1978, life in Hayy Madi took a new turn. Fighting moved to other areas in the city, and the two neighborhoods became a primary destination for families fleeing the fighting in southern Lebanon between the Israel Defense Forces and Lebanese and Palestinian resistance factions. Typically, families arriving from the south would seek refuge in a neighborhood where there were abandoned apartments that had not yet been occupied. Information about such apartments was passed along to them either by the truck drivers who transported them to the city or by relatives who, evicted from the now Christian-dominated eastern suburbs, were in areas like Hayy Madi/Mar Mikhail themselves. Local militias settled the incoming population. As Imm Abbas, who was still living in Hayy Madi in 2004, explained to me:

The day that a bomb hit our neighbors' house, we escaped to our cousins' in Abbassieyeh. We spent three days in their house; fourteen people living in crowded conditions. We could not stay there longer. My sister, who was evicted from Nab'a, sent us a message saying that the militias were opening houses here in Chiyah. We hired a truck and came the next day.

Typically, such war-displaced people would simply set up makeshift houses inside hollowed-out buildings and call them home. But as more and more families moved in, the neighborhood began to flourish. And in the mid-1990s, a few new buildings were even built, with the spaces in them also being sold or rented mostly to nuclear or extended war-displaced families.

When I first visited the area in 2004, its shelled buildings, broken windows, and shattered structures brought back my own memories of living through the civil war. However, these feelings soon receded, and I realized that the area's new residents had brought new life to it over the last twenty-eight years. In between the buildings (which appeared to be ruins from the outside but in which improvised homes had been created) were streets filled with shops, toys, and food. Essentially, these outdoor areas were used as extensions of the private domain, providing space for children to play, elderly people to congregate, and families to gather. Such a rich social life reflected the fact that the inhabitants of entire villages had moved together to the area. People told me, for example, that the whole village of Bint Jbeil (a prominent town in southern Lebanon) had moved into Hayy Madi. Indeed, in 2004, one area resident, Ayad, described just such a move:

My parents hired a truck. The driver told them that he had heard of unoccupied evacuated apartments in Hayy Madi. We were the first family to squat in Hayy Madi, after which several families from Bint Jbeil followed us. After a few months, Hayy Madi was mostly inhabited by families from Bint Jbeil.

Among other things, the Bint Jbeil families brought with them a thriving shoemaking industry. Others started mechanic shops, some of which are still open today. Thus despite the area's physical condition, street-level space in the two neighborhoods gradually came alive and buzzed with the activity of light industry.

Toward the end of the civil war, the rise of Hezbollah divided the area politically. Generally, the displaced families in the vicinity of the Mar Mikhail church remained followers of Haraket Amal, while most of those in Hayy Madi, on the other side of Zakkour Road, became Hezbollah supporters. This situation became further polarized in 2004, after the government began to issue monetary compensation awards to displaced families. As mentioned, the awards were intended to allow families to leave the buildings they had been squatting in across the city and "return home" to villages from which they had been displaced. But Haraket Amal and Hezbollah were also able to benefit by putting themselves in charge of negotiating the compensation packages. Having established new lives in Beirut over the last thirty years, most families were not ready to go back to their former villages. And since families with strong relationships to one or the other of these religious-political organizations were more likely to secure higher compensation awards, the two organizations were able to solidify their grip on the local political terrain as soon-to-be-evicted families were forced to look for new apartments in areas close by.

The public relocation campaign of war-displaced families, which involved their eviction from their informal shelters across Beirut and its peripheries, ultimately created a huge new demand for low- and middle-income housing in the city. And since many of these displaced families were Shiites, it also fueled Hezbollah's intervention in housing and real estate markets in areas adjacent to al-Dahiya. Among these areas, some, like Sahra Choueifat, were deemed to be empty agricultural lands. However, the expansion also took aim at nearby built-up areas like Chiyah and al-Hadath, transforming them, too, into contested frontiers.[19] Because this massive new urbanization trend relied on available and affordable real estate and housing markets, pushback against it first came in the form of new municipal planning and zoning schemes that aimed to limit the possibilities of building housing in the area. Eventually, more politically controversial methods to counter "Shiite encroachment" soon emerged. It did not take long for violence to arrive. In May 2008, armed battles erupted across the area, and dozens were killed.

During the time I spent in the two neighborhoods in 2004, I had discussed the area's future with its remaining population of war-displaced families. Most were preparing to be evicted, and told me the government was going to hand the ruined villas and apartment buildings in which they had made their homes back to the original Christian owners. We then discussed the difficulty of finding alternative housing in light of the prohibitive price of apartments within Beirut and the limited supply of low-cost housing in its peripheries. At the time, the history of violence across the Green Line was still a vivid memory, and al-Dahiya could not expand beyond the Old Saida Road. As one resident told me, "This used to be a 'tough' war demarcation line. Think of these surrounding roads as barbed wires and retaining walls."

These conditions were similarly captured in an interview with Mr. E, a prominent Shiite housing developer in Haret Hreik and surrounding areas.[20] In it, he was frank about the politics that surrounded his earlier attempts to build housing on land across the divide between Haret Hreik and the adjacent "Christian" areas, mainly in Chiyah and neighboring al-Hadath in the 1990s:

They [the Christian parties and the Maronite Church] accused me of benefiting from Iranian funding to construct buildings that house Hezbollah supporters on the edges of Christian areas. Our goal, they said, was to overpower these areas. Even the Pope of Rome discussed my case. The Pope told Berri[21] that I needed to be stopped. . . . I bought the land . . . for $4.9 million by borrowing money from the bank. . . . They stopped us from building and zoned the area as "under study."[22] . . . No one supported my case. Even Hezbollah, of which I was a main financial supporter, was not able to help me.

As these comments indicate, in post–civil war Beirut, the perceived need to halt a particular land transaction or housing development could invoke local and transnational discourses of religion, finance, and militarization. In this case, it involved not only the Maronite Church and Hezbollah but also, allegedly, the Vatican and Iran. It is just such local and transnational spatial practices that underlie the doubleness of Beirut's peripheries as frontier geographies produced by territorial real estate wars in times of peace in anticipation of wars yet to come.

Despite such conditions, however, construction continued in the area throughout the early 2000s. And in July 2006, seen as part of al-Dahiya, Hayy Madi/Mar Mikhail became a target of Israel's new war against Lebanon. Residents I later interviewed said that only a few nonresidential structures in Hayy Madi had been damaged, and that the neighborhoods had otherwise been spared. However, many Shiite families, displaced from Haret Hreik by Israeli air attacks, subsequently relocated to Hayy Madi/Mar Mikhail. And many of them were still living there when I returned for my second round of fieldwork in 2009, either sharing apartments with other families or renting their own apartments while they waited for Hezbollah to rebuild their ruined homes in Haret Hreik.

Meanwhile, the targeted structures in Hayy Madi were clearly described to me by three of the people I interviewed as "Hezbollah buildings." One woman even pointed one of them out. It was a very small yellow building, basically a sealed concrete, four-by-four-meter structure at the edge of Zakkour Road, which had already been rebuilt. There was no indication of what it was used for. Nevertheless, the presence of such structures is what characterizes the mundane yet militarized geography of the peripheries turned frontiers on the edges of al-Dahiya.

From Vibrant Neighborhood to Emerging Frontier

Except for the noise from construction sites, the neighborhood I returned to in the 2009 to 2010 period seemed remarkably quiet—a stark contrast to the days of 2004 and 2005. What had then been a lively peripheral neighborhood in a war-scarred, dense, urban fabric was now dominated by a series of construction sites, which had replaced several of the ruined buildings that had formerly housed war-displaced families. These massive projects stood between other ruined structures that, contrary to the prevailing conditions in 2004, now stood empty. It was also clear from the moment I returned to the neighborhood in 2009 that it was no longer going to be easy to talk to people there. First, most of the families I had come to know in 2004 had moved away. And second, most residents and passersby also seemed suspicious of my presence because I was an unfamiliar face. Under such conditions, there was no easy way to take photos, and I found I could only snap shots discreetly.

Such conditions were not particular to Hayy Madi/Mar Mikhail. Indeed, they were typical of most areas of Beirut's southern suburbs where Hezbollah and Haraket Amal had a presence (and all other areas in the city that had been proclaimed "secure" by various political parties).[23] My own fieldwork presence became further questionable after local residents learned that the United Nation's Special Tribunal for Lebanon, which had been investigating Prime Minister Hariri's 2005 assassination, had offices in one of the new buildings in the neighborhood. The tribunal was then moving toward naming a number of Hezbollah officials as responsible for the assassination, and the UN's presence in the area was not welcomed.[24] As a result, seen as an outsider to the area, I had only limited opportunities to talk to people.[25]

In newly built-up sections of the neighborhood, the physical conditions and spatial experience had been radically transformed. Much of the area's former communal street life had been eliminated. Instead, its streets were mostly occupied by workers, such as day laborers, apartment building concierges, mechanics, and the like. In older areas that still reflected the area's prewar geography, I did find some remaining war-displaced families. But these areas had only a fraction of the vibrancy they had exhibited in 2004. And most of the ground-floor shoemaking workshops had gone out of business.

Although strategically located, the area felt like a ghost town.[26] In particular, on visit after visit to Hayy Madi, I had a recurring feeling of uneasiness. Its streets, once lively, were deserted and lined with piles of construction material, and areas that had once been filled with men, women, and children now seemed to have become an exclusively male domain. A few men who seemed always to be there watching were curious to know why I was there. I talked to a number of them, but this did not make any of us feel more at ease. And of the few women I encountered on the streets only a handful agreed to talk to me about the "face-lift" the neighborhood was undergoing. Children, meanwhile, were almost entirely absent, and most of the new apartments looked empty.

When I asked about the ghostliness of the place, some people said that all the apartments had been sold; they had just not been inhabited. Yet it was not clear why the new residents had not moved in—most of the buildings seemed fairly complete. One interviewee did suggest that the new buildings were not affordable for the local residents, so most buyers were "from outside the neighborhood." He added that people were buying the apartments for their strategic and accessible location within the city. Moreover, he said, apartments in the buildings had been sold mostly during the early stages of construction, based on the design plans, and with only the basic concrete skeleton in place. Ali, a concierge at one of the newly constructed projects, told me there was only one apartment left for sale in the three-building complex he managed. At the time, the sales price per square meter in the neighborhood had reached $1700.[27] This meant that 200-square-meter apartments were selling for $340,000.

This construction boom was clearly transforming an area that had provided a home for the poor and war-displaced for thirty years into a middle- and upper-middle-income neighborhood. The construction fever had even broken out in the older quarter, which, apart from a few bullet and bomb holes here and there, had remained mostly intact since the days before the civil war. Some of the new projects displayed descriptive billboards. A common practice in middle-income and upscale developments, such billboards typically advertise the name of the developer, the architect, and the size of the apartments for sale. They also provide information on how to contact the sales office. However, what was most striking in this case was that most of the billboards in the neighborhood (numbering about a dozen) mentioned the same architect and the same well-known developer, both known to be sympathetic to Hezbollah. The names of other, smaller developers showed up on only a couple of billboards. As these projects targeted middle- and upper-middle-income groups, Hayy Madi was thus in some ways returning to the socioeconomic condition it had been in before the war. But the new middle-class residents moving in were mostly Shiites, replacing the Christians who had mostly lived there before 1975.

As mentioned, the neighborhood did still contain a significant number of the ruined structures that had once housed war-displaced families. Starting from Zakkour Road and progressing inward, the scene in Hayy Madi in particular alternated between massive construction and brutal, yet aging and decaying destruction. Grass and garbage covered many of the spaces in between destroyed villas and new buildings (Figure 8). Some walls of the abandoned ruins displayed political graffiti, and plaques commemorating war martyrs who had lived in a particular building also sometimes appeared. It seems, from the few plaques I saw, that these martyrs were war-displaced individuals who had fought with

FIGURE 8. The outdoor area of a deserted villa in ruins, overlooked by residential buildings. Source: Author, 2010.

Hezbollah in south Lebanon. Overlooking these ruins today were mostly semi-luxurious buildings.

There was something uncanny about the presence of these new residential towers dotted within a landscape of bombed buildings, burned-out landscapes, and memorials to martyrs. During one of my visits, two fieldwork companions and I stopped to rest in front of a villa still in ruins, surrounded by burned trees. A plaque revealed that the villa had once been inhabited by Martyr Bazzi's family and that Bazzi had lost his life in 1989, fighting with Hezbollah (Figure 9). Sitting on a curb where weeds were growing out of the concrete, it was surreal to be able at the same time to see into the interiors of some of the surrounding buildings: beds with people sleeping, kitchens smelling of freshly made food, and laundry hanging out overlooking the destroyed villa. I had never before been in such an in between yet overlapping geography, where the spaces of the past—of standing still in time, of martyrdom, of civil war and its displaced families—and the spaces of the present—of the everyday with its beds, laundry, and pans—so starkly collided. These in between spaces projected a feeling of ghostliness that was not present when the ruins themselves were inhabited by these objects of everyday life.

FIGURE 9. A plaque mounted on the entrance to a ruined villa. It reads, "Martyr Farid Said Bazzi, martyred on January 23, 1989—Hezbollah." The villa has been purchased by the Maronite Church. Source: Author, 2010.

"It All Came to a Halt"

After several visits it occurred to me that there was clearly something strange about the pattern of redevelopment. As some new buildings reached for the sky, others were being prepared to be demolished. But there were signs that the condition of others was permanently frozen in time. When I asked why some buildings were still in ruins while many others had been demolished and replaced, a number of people gave me what seemed like a synchronized answer: "*khalaṣ waqqafūhun*"—"it all came to a halt," or "they stopped them." It was not obvious right away who had been able to stop what seemed to be a relentless tide of new construction, but I soon learned the Maronite Church was behind this effort.

Initially, none of the people I interviewed knew (or, perhaps, wanted to tell me) why the Church would take such a stand in a mundane peripheral neighborhood where real estate was booming—or how it had even been able to. But I then learned that almost all the people responsible for the Church's decisions lived and worked in places far away from Hayy Madi/Mar Mikhail. To talk to them, I had to visit prayer halls, Church offices, and Christian universities elsewhere in the city. It was only in these places that I was finally able to find people who could explain the role of the Mar Mikhail church, and the Maronite Church in general, in the pattern of urban development of the area.[28]

With its white walls and green foliage, the Mar Mikhail church has a powerful presence in the neighborhood. In 2004, its main building was renovated, and since then, its outdoor areas have also been upgraded and expanded to include an evergreen garden, ornamented with crosses and a new sculpture of Virgin Mary. But the Christians who formed its congregation now mostly live in Beirut's eastern suburbs, so that, for example, the school building on its grounds that used to be affiliated with the church is now rented out to a private school that serves students from the vicinity.

When I visited the church in 2010, only one couple lived on the premises. The husband told me he was the church's concierge. At first, he was reluctant to talk about my research in the neighborhood, and he only did so after asking about my place of birth and realizing I was not Shiite. The chat we eventually had inside the building was also very different from those I had been having outside. Like others in the neighborhood, this couple talked about the civil war, destruction, and displacement; but they talked about it as if it had happened yesterday. As tears rolled down their cheeks and their throats tightened, they showed me traces of the war they still bore on their bodies. Within the church compound, I felt that life had not moved much since 1975—or maybe that those feelings of loss had come back to haunt its residents. In particular, my hosts lamented the loss of "their community," people they now saw only at weddings and funerals. They also told me numerous stories about the pre–civil war neighborhood, its tight-knit quality, and the central role this church played in it. In particular, the concierge and his wife lamented the fact that the school, which had once been part of the church's outreach program, now taught only Shiite pupils. "All of this is gone. We [the Christians] are confined to the walls of the church," they told me.

FIGURE 10. Iconic ruins overlook the Mar Mikhail church's garden and a sculpture of Virgin Mary. Source: Author, 2010.

I also learned from them that it had been the Maronite Church that had bought the two adjacent buildings in ruins where I had conducted many of my interviews with war-displaced families in 2004. The two buildings were now fenced off, and part of the land they had occupied was used to expand the church garden (Figure 10). In the corner of one of these buildings was the local office of Haraket Amal. It remained because the Church did not have the political power to remove it. Thus, a number of armed men, some with amputated limbs and other traces of the civil war on their bodies, could always be found sitting in front, watching the roundabout. Sometimes they would question strangers to the neighborhood about their reasons for being there, and I had one such encounter. The entire area in front of the building was decorated with the green flags of Haraket Amal, along with pictures of Nabih Berri (its head) and Imam Musa al-Sadr (its religious leader and founder) (Figure 11). But these flags came to an abrupt end where the Mar Mikhail church's outdoor area began. From there on, the church's white walls, green shrubs, and crosses dominated the street.

Besides the two ruined buildings, the Church had also bought and cleared many of the ruins that were occupying the site across the street from the entrance of the Mar Mikhail church. It had then leveled these sites into several large park-

FIGURE 11. The office of Haraket Amal in Mar Mikhail, in one of the ruined buildings bought by the Maronite Church. Pictures of Nabih Berri and Imam Musa al-Sadr and flags of Haraket Amal delineate the area. Source: Author, 2010.

ing lots, awaiting development. One of these parking lots covered a site that had formerly been occupied by a building that had housed Huda, a woman who had become one of my fieldwork companions during my earlier research in the neighborhood. Huda, who had been displaced from southern Lebanon, had lived in Mar Mikhail informally for twenty-seven years. She was a secularist who never feared speaking her mind against all the religious-political organizations operating in the area.

Surprised by the scale of the Maronite Church's intervention in the surrounding geography of ruins (by fencing them off or demolishing them), and its general interest in acquiring such structures, I later asked a Church official, who served as director of one of the most prominent Christian universities in Lebanon, about plans for these sites. "They will remain as is for now until the Church decides what to do with them," he told me. In the near future, this meant "nothing." If one follows this logic, the Church's intervention in the real estate market was thus not related to the ruins themselves, but to the land they stand on. They were properties in a larger strategy of land acquisition aimed at curbing what the Church saw as Shiite expansion. According to Church logic, they would ultimately help Christians hold their ground against a larger scheme of "Islamization" and displacement. The goal, in other words, was to keep the land "Christian."

Holding Ground

One political event, in particular, that took place in Hayy Madi/Mar Mikhail may help to explain the Church's real estate strategy within the geographies of the war yet to come. On February 6, 2006, the Mar Mikhail church was the site of one of the most significant reshufflings of local and national alliances since the civil war. On that day, the Change and Reform Block,[29] led by the then Christian leader and member of parliament Michel Aoun,[30] signed a Memorandum of Understanding with Hezbollah, creating an alliance between the country's major Shiite and Christian religious-political organizations. That move has since had major political impacts and has led to power struggles across Lebanon.

The memorandum has often been described by the Change and Reform Block as a "gentlemen's agreement"—one that relies on the word of honor of the two parties for its fulfillment. It was further significant that it was signed in Mar Mikhail. The adjacent, mostly Shiite, area of Haret Hreik was Aoun's hometown, and it, too, had a preserved church. However, by holding the event in Mar Mikhail, both parties were recognizing how the area's surroundings have reemerged as a major contested frontier between Christians and Shiites. Land acquisition and housing development have been fundamental to this postwar struggle, and the two leaders seemed to be signaling their intent to (among other things) halt this particular territorial conflict. True to that expectation, the gentlemen's agreement has since been used to undo a number of large-scale land sales to Shiites in the area.

The struggle around land and housing sales is fueled in part by a discourse of fear among Lebanese Christians. As mentioned in the previous chapter, this conflict derives from an overarching anxiety over the Shiite figure in the city. Maronite Christians, who were one of the larger sects in Lebanon in 1932, have diminished in relative numbers since then. And this has coincided with a rise in the number of Shiites, who are now on the way to becoming a powerful new majority.[31] These conditions have resulted in a fear among Christians that they will in the future be excluded from the historic power-sharing formula in Lebanon, by which they were granted control over the presidency. And in general, Christians increasingly fear large-scale displacement from Lebanon (and indeed the entire Middle East) as the result of an "Islamization scheme" for the region. These views are often articulated in public discourses around the changing demography of Lebanon and the Middle East.

Many political analysts have also argued that the spatial mechanism for this systematic, gradual displacement is the real estate market.[32] This perceived threat provides the larger context for the Maronite Church's strategy of real estate acquisition to "reclaim the land as Christian." Thus as one Church official told me, "In order to stop the Shiite encroachment in Hayy Madi/Mar Mikhail, the Church has decided to buy land and buildings that the original Christian landowners want to sell." By buying land, the Mar Mikhail church, through the support of the Maronite Church, could avoid losing all its surrounding ground (and therefore, as he put it, its "raison d'être"). Thus, as soon as the Church learned of a Shiite developer bidding for a certain parcel in the area, it tried to contact the landowner to see if he or she would sell to the Church instead. The problem, according to the official, was that the Maronite Church did not have the resources needed to acquire all the land that was up for sale in what had become an inflated market. In many instances, therefore, the Maronite Church had not been able to match the offers of Shiite developers, and had lost properties to them. These were the sites being converted to new apartment buildings. In a number of instances, however, the Maronite Church had been able to convince landowners to sell to it, even at a lower price. These were the sites where buildings were either being demolished to leave the ground vacant, or where ruined structures were going to stay "as is."

Indeed, in the 2009 to 2010 period, on the sites the Maronite Church had bought so far, the ruins mostly remained as I had seen them in 2004 when they were still occupied by war-displaced families. As I came to understand, it was not that the Church had any sentimental connection to the structures as ruins or as evidence of how the former Christian neighborhood once looked. Rather, the

Church was primarily interested in the land and the possibility of its future development to benefit the Christian community. Thus, as Jihad Farah has pointed out, since 1998, the Mar Mikhail church and other Christian religious-political organizations have encouraged the Chiyah municipality to budget considerable resources to clear all traces of the civil war from the neighborhood.[33] They attempted this both by seeking help from government institutions to renovate the façades of structurally sound buildings and by destroying those buildings that cannot be repaired. However, this plan has not been highly successful. And the underlying reality is that Church-acquired ruins still exist because the Church doesn't have the funds to "do anything with them"—that is, develop them. As a result, the sites remain as they are—with their pitted and blasted walls, political graffiti, and overgrown shrubs—shaped concurrently by past and present conflict. For now, if the Church buys vacant land, it stays vacant; and if there is a war-scarred building on it, the ruins remain. This doubleness of construction and destruction, growth and arrested development, is a large contributor to the contrasting physical conditions that mark the area as a frontier.

The practice of holding ground through engaging in the real estate market is, however, currently proving unsustainable. As one Maronite official told me, the Church ran out of funds early in the game due to inflated land prices—which were themselves a consequence of battles over land. Its real estate activities thus seemed to be coming to a halt, and it was brainstorming new ways to keep its land acquisition project alive. Indeed, another official told me the Church was thinking of initiating its own development schemes to transform areas it had bought into income-generating properties. According to that official, however, the Church was not considering constructing apartment buildings, because "no Christian family would come live in the neighborhood anymore." Rather, it was looking for more "business-oriented types of projects—a mall, perhaps—that would actually serve this expanding Shiite area." Most importantly, such a development would bring in money to help fund a continuation of the holding-ground program.[34]

Before shifting to this commercial orientation, however, both the Chiyah municipality and the Mar Mikhail church had tried to invest in residential development along the demarcation line. Farah's interview with Chiyah's mayor illustrates how the municipality pushed for and "benefited from a presidential decree allowing it to build and sell housing to the people of Chiyah who are 'registered in the community.'"[35] The decree, the first of its kind, would, however, without mentioning them directly, have excluded Shiites from the housing effort. In the interest of not upsetting the sectarian balance in Lebanon, it is hard for residents to move their records from one place to another—even after they establish a new permanent residence.[36] Many Shiite inhabitants of Chiyah are thus not allowed to register as residents there, so they would have been excluded from participation. The housing scheme was thus clearly directed only toward people of Chiyah origin—in other words, the area's original Christian residents.

Land with a Religion

Reflecting the strategic nature of land acquisition and development efforts, the contest over Beirut's peripheries has now expanded into a transnational phenomenon. It today involves international activities revolving around philanthropic donations and real estate deals across the globe that are fueled by sectarian discourse over the religious identity of land. Behind this movement are local Lebanese actors such as the Maronite Church and Hezbollah-affiliated developers.[37] Among other things, these parties are racing each other to find civil war–displaced Lebanese landowners who had moved to cities like Sydney, São Paulo, and Washington, DC, and who may be willing to sell their land back in Beirut.

In 2010, I was able to conduct an interview via Skype with one such landowner, a woman who had migrated some thirty-five years ago to the United States and settled in Washington, DC. She told me that despite having held onto her land in Beirut's peripheries for decades, she had not been able to refuse a recent offer to sell.

It was 2008, the financial bubble had hit the housing market here in the United States. They sent me a messenger with an offer that was impossible to refuse. I sold my land, 5000 square meters in al-Hadath [right next to Hayy Madi], to a Shiite developer. With that money, I was able to invest in buying three houses here at the heart of Washington, DC.

In the context of this market frenzy, and with the Maronite Church's blessing, a constellation of Christian activists have launched a global campaign to raise funds to buy land in Beirut's peripheries that Christian landowners would like to sell. The international fundraising initiative is aimed at pushing back against what the activists see as encroachment on Christian territory by other religious groups (mainly Shiites).

Such anxiety, manifested here in a struggle over land and housing, is not new, yet it has never been discussed as publicly as it is nowadays. The issue was a particularly hot subject at the time I was conducting my second round of field research in Hayy Madi/Mar Mikhail. Indeed, it was being debated daily in news outlets, not only in Beirut but also in other areas of Lebanon. One reason was that the incoming administration of the municipality of al-Hadath—a predominantly Christian area governed by Aoun's Change and Reform Block (under the signed agreement with Hezbollah)—had issued an "informal" edict in June 2010 prohibiting Christians from selling land or housing to non-Christians. As the edict declared, "For al-Hadath to stay, don't sell your land, don't sell your house. The municipality will not sign your paperwork." This informal policy was then disseminated to the public by means of a large-scale campaign of billboard advertisements along the road separating al-Hadath from neighboring al-Dahiya. The municipality claimed that its initiative, described as a "reform" decision, represented an attempt to simultaneously preserve religious identity and promote religious coexistence. Its aim was to counter the anxieties generated by the expansion of "Shiite al-Dahiya" toward "Christian al-Hadath." According to the municipality, the decision was supported by and had been coordinated with Hezbollah within the framework of the gentlemen's agreement with the Change and Reform block.[38]

This advertising campaign in al-Hadath was the first major open public discourse on land sales along religious sectarian lines. However, since then, such discriminatory talk has become the norm when discussing urban issues and land politics, not only in Beirut but in many other areas in Lebanon. And the phenomenon now involves attempts by various entities to condition property sales between different groups. The best-known of these efforts, as mentioned in Chapter 1, is what has come to be known as the Harb land law. In December 2010, Boutros Harb, a Christian member of the Lebanese Parliament, submitted a controversial draft for a nationwide law prohibiting land sales between Christians and Muslims for a period of fifteen years. In a January 10, 2011 interview on MTV, a local Christian-leaning television station, he stated as a rationale that "it was time to bring out people's anxieties and fears expressed in chats behind closed doors by openly addressing and formalizing them in a law that would put people's minds at peace." Harb argued that by proposing to halt land sales and questioning the very foundation of Lebanese property rights, his law aimed to preserve "religious coexistence." In effect, however, it would have institutionalized the idea that every parcel of land had a religion.

Harb's proposal has remained only ink on paper.[39] But the Maronite Church continues to work with a number of legal experts to devise ways to change Lebanese real estate and building law to curb some of the freedoms it currently provides. The goal would be to maintain "Christian land in the hands of Christians," as one representative said in a TV interview. In particular, these Church-promoted legislative proposals imagine using, and expanding on, the right of preemption, known in Arabic as *haqq al-shuf'a*.[40] A common principle in Lebanese property law, the right of preemption requires a property owner to ask his or her neighbors if they are interested in buying a parcel or house before it can be sold to a stranger. The Church is looking into expanding the notion of *neighbor* to include the larger Christian community. Within this logic, any Christian individuals looking to sell their land would first be required to ask members of "their community"—defined as the Christian community and the Church at large—if they would be interested in buying the land, before it could be sold to someone "outside that community" (i.e., a religious other).

A Chess-and-Domino Logic of Urban Development

Many of the land sales that have spurred such responses may be seen to reflect what has been described as a chess-and-domino strategy of real estate investment. And such a logic is certainly central to understanding the doubleness of ruins in Hayy Madi/Mar Mikhail. In light of my interviews with developers, residents, and planners, it seems that this pattern of development involves two complementary processes that together can be used to break down barriers such as those Christian groups have tried to maintain around the municipalities of Chiyah and al-Hadath. The first process consists of finding the right market channels through which to buy land in areas tagged as belonging to a different religion. Political affiliations, brokers' networks, inflated prices, and access to information are all critical aspects of formulating such deals. But once these deals are sealed, they may be seen as representing strategic "chess moves" into the territory of the religious other. The second process begins when these initially isolated purchases lead to the perception that the demography of an area is shifting. After this, surrounding landowners may also start selling their land, producing what was described to me as a "domino effect."[41] The incentives for such a cascade of sales may include a surge in land prices and the inability of landowners to imagine living in an area that is increasingly identified with a religious other. In the case of Christians in Beirut, this other is typically Shiite, a group they have fought wars against and that they see as inhabiting a different *bī'a* (environment).[42] Such feelings were shared by a number of the landowners I interviewed.

Not all developers and landowners see these spatial processes as a deliberate assault on the domain of the religious other. Rather, they consider the underlying logic to be informed by what they see as the normal action of markets—real estate markets, in particular. As one developer said, he is always on the lookout for ways to open "new markets" in "cream-of-the-crop" areas—that is, sites with views that are accessible to infrastructure and services. As the first to open such a new market, a developer is typically able to secure lower land prices and better plots. This form of development typifies a political and economic logic in which, according to David Harvey, land has become, through real estate development, a commodity central to capital accumulation.[43] And in a theoretical sense, it may be no different than, say, the advancing frontiers of urban capital that Neil Smith describes in his analysis of gentrification.[44] However, on the peripheries of Beirut, there is more to this logic than just the workings of capital and profit. The chess-

and-domino logic here is one that combines real estate profit with planning for future conflict. It thus involves growth, fear, violence, and anticipation of local and regional wars to come.

Mr. E, the developer quoted earlier who had bought land on the "Christian side" of the former Green Line, saw himself as engaged in just such a normal market process. He described his purchase of land there in 1994 for $4.9 million as simply taking advantage of an opportunity to buy into in a lush, green area close to Beirut's city center. At the time, however, he was blocked from developing it by general fear it might spark a new civil war. In particular, he described a high-level meeting with influential representatives of Christian Maronite organizations to discuss his stalled investment. At that meeting, one Maronite representative told him: "In seventeen years of war you were not able to cross the Old Saida Road. Now with the advantage of this housing boom, you aim to occupy Baabda?!"[45] Mr. E replied:

Well, the war ended in our souls before it ended in our streets. Through our housing developments, we are in fact reaching out a hand to you to cooperate and work again together in a nation where Muslims, Christians, Druze live together. But apparently the war has not ended for you. . . . Our residential buildings in al-Hadath were going to be built with regular construction material—10 and 15 centimeters deep, regular hollow concrete blocks. But now we are going to build, on your side, buildings with walls made of reinforced concrete. . . .

After that exchange, said Mr. E,

I was determined to tell the story to Nabih Berri. I knew I could take him back to the [civil] war barricades against the Christians. I told Berri what the Maronite guy told me. He was angry and told me "Tell him, I want to build on the roof of the Baabda Palace."

Such aggressive comments illustrate the intertwined geographies of past wars, current territorial conflicts, and the spatial and temporal logic of the war yet to come. The Church representative was in effect accusing the Shiite developer of aiming to occupy, through the housing market, the seat of the Maronite president in Baabda (a material and symbolic reference to al-Dahiya's territorial expansion into "Christian land" and the project of "Islamizing" Lebanon). The developer, in return, was threatening to build residential structures that could double as military installations on the "Christian side." In Lebanese architecture-speak, walls made from hollow concrete blocks are thin, fragile, and cheap. They can thus be easily demolished, and bullets can go through them, as the expansive geography of civil war ruins illustrates. Reinforced concrete walls, conversely, are thick, made of a 100 percent concrete mix reinforced with steel bars. They are almost impossible to destroy or penetrate, and are used for foundations, bunkers, and shelters. For developer Mr. E, using reinforced concrete in construction signifies constructing apartment buildings that could double as bunkers in wars to come. In addition, reinforced concrete means a more durable inscription, one intended to forever alter the existing landscape. The developer was sure that such conversations about real estate construction could ignite another civil war between the Shiites and Christians.

Because housing projects are conceived and built largely through formal channels, both sides have been using planning and zoning tools to advance their own positions and impede others' positions. For example, Mr. E told the story of how his development was initially stopped when the al-Hadath municipality zoned the area as "under study." Resolution came only when the area was rezoned with the help of a Christian political leader who was a Hezbollah ally and when municipal officials who were against changes in the master plan were imprisoned. As Mr. E explained:

Suleiman Franjieh [a prominent Christian leader and a Hezbollah ally] was then the Minister of Interior and Municipal Affairs. Berri called him and told him, "If you want to become the Lebanese President, you would want the blessing of the Shiites. And to get this blessing, you have to solve this problem [the stalling of Mr. E's project]. Franjieh solved it. Franjieh told me, "the Pope sent his representative to me four times to stop you. . . . Everyone talked to me, all the Maronite leaders talked to me." But he took it upon himself to solve it. The local municipal board was against him. He put all the board members in prison, and he made a zoning settlement which stipulated decreasing the allowed height of buildings from nine to five floors in order to allow us to build . . . although we lost a sizeable investment.

Mr. E's case shows that as long as there is not much friction holding back land sales, the urban growth machine driving the development of Beirut's peripheries may run forward at full force. Yet the persistent geographies of the civil war have sometimes made this expansion impossible without one group making what is interpreted as a chess move into territory perceived as belonging to a religious other. This has clearly been the case with the expansion of al-Dahiya. The high population density of al-Dahiya has made its expansion into adjacent neighborhoods inevitable since the end of the civil war. And though this has occurred through largely formal market mechanisms, it has also resulted in considerable anxiety within and been met with significant resistance from the formerly Christian municipalities of al-Hadath and Chiyah.[46]

At the time I was engaged in fieldwork in the area, the Maronite Church and related Christian organizations were trying to halt this movement by undoing some of the moves that had already been made. On September 26, 2011, MTV aired a heated political talk show titled "Land Sales in al-Hadath."[47] The

show attempted to address ways to stop land sales and reacquire land that Shiite developers had already purchased in al-Hadath and its vicinity, including in
Hayy Madi/Mar Mikhail. A representative of the Shiite developers who participated in the debate, however, repeated over and over that the reason they had
bought land "on the Christian side" of Beirut's divided peripheries was for real
estate investment purposes. And when asked if the developers were willing to "return" the thousands of square meters they had bought there to Christian owners,
to honor "coexistence," he said that they would do so, but only if they were paid
current market value.

The debate focused on a few particularly large-scale deals involving property
on the hills surrounding and overlooking al-Hadath and Chiyah, and highlighted
one particular proposed deal to return one of these sites. However, the asking price
seemed to go well beyond the budget of the negotiating Christian entities. And
given the present real estate market, this price had already been bid much higher
than the original purchase price of the land four or five years earlier.

During the show, Christian members of parliament also accused each other
of selling land in Chiyah and al-Hadath to Shiites. One representative responded,
"What do you want me to do? I was the last one to sell in the area." His sale of his
land, in Hayy Madi, illustrated the way certain chess moves had already provoked
a domino effect, as more and more people had decided to sell their land.

The Spatial Logic of Ruins

As I mentioned in the introduction to this chapter, scholars from a number of
academic disciplines have debated the value of preserving ruins in Beirut.[48] Some
see them as holding aesthetic and historical value that should be preserved and
acknowledged, while others have called for them to be cleared to mark a new
beginning and leave the past behind.[49]

Beirut following the end of the civil war is only one place where such discus-
sion has taken place. For example, the value of war ruins to public culture and
political life was debated extensively in cities needing to be rebuilt after World
War II,[50] and a similar discussion surrounded reconstruction of the World Trade
Center in New York City following its destruction on September 11, 2001.[51]
Beirut, itself, witnessed a new round of debate after the end of Israel's war on
Lebanon in July 2006. At that time, a number of planners, mostly affiliated
with Hezbollah, wanted to reconstruct the destroyed neighborhoods as they had
been—only "better." Others, however, thought the destruction should be used as
an opportunity to rethink and improve the quality of urban space entirely.[52]

In general, as Simon Guy has pointed out, "[o]ur fascination with ruins of
war-torn cities might be viewed as being driven by our need to understand the

present in relation to our sense of both the past and imagined futures." [53] Within this framework, the presence of ruins is seen as a time capsule through which the past is carried into the present as a historical relic. War ruins may thus provide continuity with an unwanted past, while being imbued with hope for a different and better future. Preserved ruins are positioned within a teleology where the future is imagined to be different and better than the past, a past that people never want to go back to.

But urban ruins may also be interpreted in a darker light, devoid of such a teleology. Some scholars have even argued that physical destruction may be a fundamental aim of contemporary urban warfare, rather than a by-product. [54] In particular, they have theorized the destruction of built environments as a way to destroy social relationships—precisely to nullify heterogeneous coexistence in urban space in favor of homogeneity. [55] Deliberate physical destruction may also enable a "context-specific physical and epistemological rearrangement of contested urban territories." [56] The destruction of urban space in Beirut during the civil war attests to just such a logic of violence and forced population displacement.

The temporality of ruins may also be a central concern. Ruins may thus be thought of as evidence of a past that is still present—indeed, this is the most common debate around ruins, especially in Beirut. As I mentioned at the beginning of this chapter, such spaces may develop afterlives in contemporary geographies that attest to their violent past. [57] But they may also raise questions about the future. Interestingly, Walter Benjamin saw ruins as artifacts that might provide, through dialectical analysis, a closer understanding of modernity, its past and future, transience and decay. [58] Indeed, he thought such analysis had the capacity to reveal a path out of the illusion of capitalism. [59] Such geographies even, following Benjamin, might provide a moment of awakening—one of historical revelation, embodying the "possibility of a politics that emerges from the aesthetics of ruins, from the aesthetic experience of the debris of history." [60]

Yet as the case I have presented here shows, the persistence of ruins in the present may also indicate gridlock. In her discussion of the blockaded development of Kolkata as a world-class city, Ananya Roy thus describes how that city's eastern periphery of unfinished buildings marked the failure of middle-class dreams. [61] Indeed, she describes them as "spaces of 'standing still' . . . haunted by the sheer failure of planned development." Roy also explains that she has borrowed the term "standing still" from photographer Simryn Gill, who had used it in relation to an exhibition of her images showing urban development projects abandoned before their completion. The ruins, according to Gill, were "a place in time, where, one might say, the past lies in ruins, unkempt and untended, and the future also somehow has been abandoned and has started to crumble. No way forward, no way back." [62]

"No way forward, no way back" closely describes Hayy Madi/Mar Mikhail's landscapes of ruins and development, a gridlock that seems to foreclose political action outside the spatial-sectarian order. But these are also spaces that are not "standing still." While their materiality might indicate otherwise, the contest over the land they occupy is unfolding in multiple spatialities and temporalities, across the globe, shaped by local, national, and transnational conflicts. In fact, these ruins are currently being doubly produced through a territorial contest between religious-political organizations that is waged and configured through land and housing markets, property laws, and planning schemes.

It is within this context that this chapter has explored doubleness as a spatial process, practice, and outcome inherent to the geography of the war to come. Of the three peripheries discussed in this book, Hayy Madi/Mar Mikhail is the closest both to central Beirut and to the center of Hezbollah-dominated al-Dahiya at Haret Hreik. And unlike the other two, it was already urbanized before the war. Today, however, its remaining ruins do not simply represent the *ruins of* a contested past but are also *ruins in* a contested present and future. The two primary actors behind the checkered coexistence of its ruins and new construction are the Maronite Church and Shiite-affiliated property developers. In this contest, the ruins are largely Church owned, whereas Shiite developers are "filling in" the neighborhood with high-end residential towers. Indeed, mapping the continued existence of ruins might be one way of evaluating who is "winning" where in the battle over the area's future.

The doubleness of ruins—as products and leftovers of the civil war and as indicators of ongoing territorial conflict aimed at shaping the contours of the war to come—illustrates one of the ways that peripheries like Hayy Madi/Mar Mikhail have been transformed into contested frontiers. As part of their afterlife in renewed conflict, these geographies are today being shaped as much by construction, planning, and laws and regulations as they once were by destruction, militarization, and violence. Excavating the sociopolitical relations that have conditioned the continued presence of ruins in Beirut's emerging frontiers thus collapses the teleological order of time and space often assumed to underlie planning discourse. Standing next to glittering, new-minted buildings, the ruined spaces signify the transitory and continuously changing nature of progress, peace, and coexistence in contested cities. Rather than assuming that ruins are solely leftover objects of a past that is never to return, we can also seek to understand how their materiality likewise reveals the contradictions and crises hidden within constructed binaries of war and peace, future and past, progress and violence, construction and destruction, home and displacement, and segregation and coexistence.

CHAPTER 3
THE LACEWORK OF ZONING

SAHRA CHOUEIFAT is a peripheral area in the vicinity of Beirut's Rafic Hariri International Airport. One would pass through it only if one worked or lived there, and its roads are barely maintained. Nevertheless, it occupies a place of strategic and geopolitical importance among residential areas ascribed to different sectarian groups (Figure 12). Long before the 2008 violence brought sectarian conflict into the open, this area had emerged as a site of conflict. The battle over its future, however, was being fought not with guns but through housing development, real estate transactions, and the planning instruments of zoning. The key actors in this contest were the Shiite Hezbollah and the Druze Progressive Socialist Party (PSP), and for most of the period concerned, the PSP was in control of the local government (the Choueifat municipality), while Hezbollah-affiliated developers dominated Sahra Choueifat's real estate and housing markets.

I once asked Mr. I, a chief planner at a private planning company about his experience working on Sahra Choueifat. His company was hired by the Directorate General of Urbanism (DGU) in 1997 to prepare a master plan for Choueifat, which includes Sahra Choueifat. "Practicing planning here is like doing *takhrīm*," he said. *Takhrīm* is an Arabic word for creating a pattern with intervening spaces. It can be used in reference to a range of materials, such as metal, leather, or lace. Mr. I, however, gestured with his hands to simulate a needle working its way through lace to construct a fabric of openings and closures.

Because of his gesture, I have used the English word *lacework* to translate *takhrīm*. Specifically, Mr. I's use of *takhrīm* referred to the way zoning in Sahra Choueifat was done and undone, hewn and stitched, negotiated and fought over; and like lacework, the practice was fragile and delicate. Thus, when I looked at one of his zoning maps of the area, I saw zigzagged lines, residential zones in the middle of industrial ones, and lines that twisted and turned to enfold individual properties while excluding others. What the lines expressed, it turned out, was not the typical separation of industrial from residential zones or areas of agricultural

FIGURE 12. The
contentious
geopolitical location
of Sahra Choueifat.
By the end of the civil
war, the predominant
sectarian affiliations
of the surrounding
areas were clearly
established. Source:
Adapted from Google
Maps, 2010.

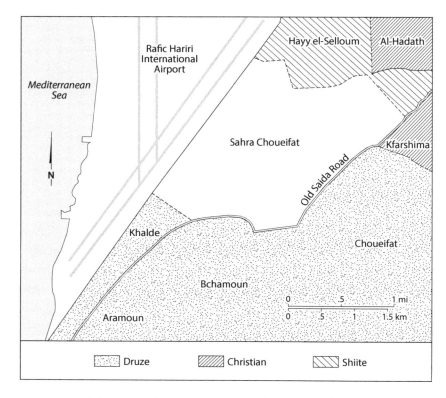

FIGURE 12. The contentious geopolitical location of Sahra Choueifat. By the end of the civil war, the predominant sectarian affiliations of the surrounding areas were clearly established. Source: Adapted from Google Maps, 2010.

land preserved from urbanization. Rather, these lines materialized the frontiers of segregation between sectarian groups.[1]

Takhrīm captures perfectly the urbanization of Beirut's second-tier southern peripheries within the logic of the war yet to come. In Sahra Choueifat, it encompasses how construction, zoning, and militarization are all implicated in transforming an area, first, into a poor periphery and, second, into a frontier of violence and environmental degradation. Lacework may be seen as a process, a logic, and an outcome. As a process of urbanization, it involves repeated layers of negotiation and conflict. It is shaped by channeled markets, zoning mutations, neoliberal government policies, outdated voting laws, and the activities of religious-political organizations both inside and outside the government. Through these mechanisms, much of the area's former agricultural land has been transformed into both industrial and residential zones, creating a patchwork of uses.

This process of lacework has stitched and woven the city and its southern peripheries to more distant areas, transforming the lands between into a second-tier periphery. To sort out these contested territories, the logic of lacework has called upon a variety of planning methods and expertise. That same expertise, however, may itself be called into question when instruments like zoning maps are compromised by pressure from sectarian groups. This has often been the case in Sahra Choueifat, where zoning maps are not simply the product of expert planning knowledge and a desire for profit from urban growth, but are inscribed within strategies and tactics of militarization and violence produced within a history, present, and future of local and regional wars. Given the stakes involved, planners have even at times been physically threatened in efforts to make changes to these maps.

A lacework planning process does not follow any zoning model. In Lebanon, the predominant model of planning once involved concentric circles of urban growth, from a dense center to a less dense periphery, within a progressive notion of time and space. But as a logic of territorial organization, lacework is a mutative process through which existing categories are split over and over, creating new subcategories whose aim is to facilitate urban growth while absorbing conflict, when possible. In Sahra Choueifat at times, entirely new zoning categories have been invented to address tactical considerations of paramilitary geographies.

Lacework planning, therefore, reflects a pattern of negotiation and contestation more than a coherent development vision. In times of peace, it points to a logic of negotiation, whose outcome is the coexistence of incongruent processes: profit and militarization, peace and war, the formal and the informal, green landscapes and environmental hazards. This is why it has produced conditions such as congested residential blocks next to greenhouses, unfinished buildings facing industries, and open spaces where children play when it is dry but where contaminated water pools when it rains. In times of war, the contours of this lacework are transformed into battle lines. Lacework also folds within it the possibilities of homemaking and displacement, as low-income populations arrive to inhabit the fringes of the city. Temporally, the logic, process, and outcome of lacework are all unpredictable, as its practices call into question what is past, present, and future; order and progress; peace and war.

A Marked Territory

Almost the same physical size as municipal Beirut, Choueifat, the municipality in which Sahra Choueifat is located, is situated 13 kilometers southeast of Beirut and contains most of Lebanon's only international airport within its boundaries.[2] In terms of geography, it is dominated by three hills that rise to a height of 150 meters and slope down toward the Mediterranean Sea.[3] Old Saida Road separates these hills from the plain that extends out toward the sea, and Sahra Choueifat refers to that portion of the plain between that road and the airport. To the north, Sahra Choueifat abuts the informal settlement of Hayy el-Selloum, which is mostly within Choueifat's jurisdiction but which also forms the south and east outskirts of the Hezbollah stronghold of al-Dahiya. Before the civil war, land in Sahra Choueifat was owned by Druze and Christian families. But the civil war displaced most of the Christians, and many Druze families also eventually sold their holdings.

For much of its history, low-lying Sahra Choueifat was an agricultural area. Longtime residents still remember when it contained groves that produced the highest-quality olive oil in the region. However, Michel Ecochard's 1964 master plan for Beirut's peripheries designated Sahra Choueifat as a future residential extension area, and in 1970, it was zoned for low-density residential development, with a small industrial strip alongside the airport. During the civil war, the Druze PSP militia protected the area against residential expansion southward from al-Dahiya. The olive groves, however, were burned down during the Israeli invasion of Beirut in 1982. After that, the area functioned mostly as a general agricultural and industrial center for west Beirut.

Choueifat's Druze residents have long been concerned about the urbanization of Sahra Choueifat. Thus, writing during the war on the problem of informal settlements, Shirine Hamadeh argued that while Sahra Choueifat might be an appropriate affordable housing site, this option was foreclosed by sectarian politics: "It is an important real estate reserve of 1.75 square miles, almost as large as the Airport. [Yet] it is . . . considered Druze territory. . . . It is [thus] for political and religious reasons that the extension of the Shiite illegal sector of Hay el-Selloum, north of it, was always impossible."[4] After the war, an expert report on housing in Beirut likewise noted that the government would face considerable opposition if it tried to enact a formal plan of residential expansion there:

If a new plan supplying 10,000 units in the Choueifat area, currently proposed by the government, is implemented it will occupy 15% of the generally available build out.

In this area, the majority of the population is Druze. This group has strongly opposed the new housing projects in that area, as they will bring other ethnic groups [a reference to the Shiites] into this Druze stronghold.[5]

Both these reports accurately summarized the logic of contestation that long hindered the urbanization of Sahra Choueifat. On the one hand, they described why the area had escaped informal development during the war as an extension of Hayy el-Selloum; on the other, they explained why the government was being blocked from pursuing various scenarios for a formal program of affordable housing there. What they did not imagine was how residential development would eventually transform the area through private real estate deals and channeled housing markets, and how such development would subsequently be twisted into strange new forms of urban development produced by battles over the area's zoning.

Sahra Choueifat's transformation became apparent soon after the end of the civil war. As early as 1993, large-scale housing complexes started mushrooming up, scattered between fields and greenhouses of tomatoes, strawberries, herbs, and other produce. Housing also appeared in industrial areas, in close proximity to pharmaceutical factories, concrete mixing stations, and packaging and bottling plants. The AA complex, with its 300 units, was the first and largest of these new developments (Figure 13). Located in Sahra Choueifat's northern sector, close to Hayy el-Selloum, it today consists of twelve buildings on 15,350 square meters of land, with a large (3000-square-meter) central open space that is used as a parking lot and playground. Its apartments are a mix of two-room and three-room units,

FIGURE 13. The AA complex and adjacent housing developments. Source: Author, 2017.

which were originally sold in the 1990s for the relatively low cost of $18,000 and $22,000, respectively.[6] The success of the AA complex at pushing the fringes of the city southward soon led other developers to copy that effort. Some of the new projects were successful, while others went bankrupt and were never finished. All seemed to exhibit a common appearance, however—perhaps reflecting an aesthetics of affordability. Built of hollow concrete blocks smoothed over with stucco, the exterior walls were painted with horizontal stripes: blue and white, brick and beige, or green and white (Figure 14). The outer walls of the AA complex were striped gray and white. Between the painted stripes, striped curtains enclosed the apartment balconies for privacy (Figure 15).

In the 1990s, many of these complexes stood empty. But the reason for their vacancy, I later learned, was that the buyers were largely war-displaced Shiite families living in areas like Hayy Madi/Mar Mikhail along Beirut's Green Line. For thirty years, these displaced families had inhabited makeshift homes in bullet-riddled buildings and ruins. They could not move to the new units because they were waiting for monetary compensation from the government to relocate, a sum that they could lose if they moved before being formally evicted. The scene began to change quickly after 2004, however, when, fourteen years after the end of the

FIGURE 14. A view from in between the housing complexes and Sahra Choueifat's agricultural area, looking toward Choueifat on the hill. Source: Author, 2010.

civil war, the Ministry of the Displaced decided to sort out all remaining displacement cases. As families received compensation packages, they were simultaneously handed notices of eviction from their existing squatter homes. Many subsequently began to move to areas like Sahra Choueifat; and thereafter, the area's few paved streets came alive with children, while adults could be seen sitting out in the open spaces of the housing complexes adjacent to the remaining agricultural fields.

The local Druze population was not happy with an incoming population of predominantly poor Shiite families. Just few years earlier, the two groups had been enemies in a brutal civil war, in which their militias had often battled each other. Thus, although the Druze PSP-led municipality had initially given permits for the construction of these projects, allowing the units there to be occupied through formal channels, it had never extended municipal water, sewage, or electricity service to the area. Instead, the developers and residents, supported by Hezbollah and Haraket Amal, had come together twice, in 1995 and 2004, to install this infrastructure on their own. In one complex, Naji, a resident who was a public utility electrician, told me he had volunteered to wire a number of buildings that had not been connected to the power grid. And his friend, Asem, who worked as a driver for an asphalt company, told me that on a daily basis he would leave a

FIGURE 15. An AA complex façade. Source: Author, 2010.

bit of asphalt in his truck and use it to pave open spaces and roads in the neighborhood. Meanwhile, between the housing complexes, there remained a long, winding space that had been set aside for a four-lane highway. This leftover space was frequently used by children to play soccer. It also served as an extension of the workshops of recycled car dealers and car mechanics, and local children found the junked steel frames, wheels, disks, and other parts perfect for play, too.

In 2004, when I began investigating conditions in this area, the lack of municipal concern for the area's residents was evident. Indeed, faced with the expansion southward of Shiite control, the PSP was busy trying to change the area's zoning from residential to industrial. The latent friction between the two sides had also now turned violent. Choueifat residents told me that just before the first confrontations, Hezbollah had erected arches throughout the area with pictures of martyrs and slogans of resistance. Druze residents of Choueifat took those public displays as an act of intimidation and an announcement that Sahra Choueifat had become a "Hezbollah area." As a result, small-scale rioting and youth violence broke out. These sectarian clashes were initially locally contained. However, during the upheavals of May 2008, sectarian violence took a dramatic turn between the Druze and Shiite religious-political organizations in the area. Dividing lines between Sahra Choueifat and the rest of Choueifat were transformed into battlegrounds, and the Old Saida Road was solidified as an armed demarcation line. Indeed, Choueifat witnessed the worst battles of May 2008, where dozens lost their lives. To this date, Lebanese army tanks are still positioned at key intersections between the two areas in hopes of deterring new outbreaks of violence.

As the situation stands today, Sahra Choueifat is considered a Shiite neighborhood, an extension of Hezbollah's al-Dahiya stronghold. More specifically, most Choueifat residents consider it a continuation of Hayy el-Selloum—although the latter is an informal settlement, while Sahra Choueifat was mostly developed legally. Choueifat residents' feelings, however, are based not on whether the area is legal or not but on who resides there. In this sense, their view of the incoming population has been constructed through discourses of *bi'a* (environment), demography, and nativeness.[7] The urbanization and transformation of Sahra Choueifat from Druze to Shiite territory has also inscribed it as a node in transnational conflicts, such as the current war in Syria and the Arab-Israeli conflict. Indeed, seen as extension of al-Dahiya, the area was bombed by Israeli warplanes during Israel's war on Lebanon in 2006. And on February 3, 2014, it witnessed a suicide bombing by a member of the Sunni extremist group, the Islamic State in Iraq and Syria (ISIS), as part of a campaign of violence against Hezbollah-affiliated territories in Lebanon. These transnational assaults have further alienated the area from its surroundings, and reinforced it as a sectarian frontier.

Residential Hopes and Perils

Among those I met when I began my research in Sahra Choueifat in 2004 were Zeina and Imm Yasmine. Like many others who had been evicted from makeshift housing in other areas of the city by the reconstruction of downtown Beirut and other major postwar infrastructure projects, they had been forced to look for alternative affordable housing on the fringes of the city. They eventually bought apartments in Sahra Choueifat. By the time they were looking for apartments, the AA complex was already sold out and the two families invested in adjacent housing developments.

Zeina was originally from southern Lebanon. In 1976, following the bombing of her village, she and her family had fled to a neighboring village, and then sought refuge in Beirut. For the next twenty-eight years, Zeina and her family had remained in an abandoned building in Hayy Madi/Mar Mikhail, along Beirut's former war demarcation line. However, in 2001, with news of their pending eviction, and with the help of her politically affiliated brother-in-law, she and her sons had bought apartments in a housing complex in Sahra Choueifat in the vicinity of the AA complex. Then, in August 2004, after receiving final eviction notices, they had finally moved to those Sahra Choueifat apartments. Two of Zeina's sisters had also moved to the same apartment complex. After living in overcrowded conditions in a bullet-riddled building, the families were finally enjoying life in new apartments surrounded by green areas, and breathing cleaner air.

Imm Yasmine had moved to Sahra Choueifat four years before Zeina, purchasing her apartment there in 1997. She had also originally been displaced from southern Lebanon, and had lived in downtown Beirut for twenty years. One day in 2004, while sipping coffee on her balcony overlooking a stretch of greenhouses, I asked Imm Yasmine what she liked most about her residence. Her building, striped in beige and maroon colors, was at the time at the edge of Sahra Choueifat's residential developments. She pointed to the fields and replied, "You know, people tell me that these empty lands are all zoned agriculture, so no new buildings will ever block our view. True, we are far from the city, but unlike al-Dahiya, it is quiet and green here." I pointed out to her that in reality the land she referred to was no longer zoned for agriculture. I tried to explain how the zoning of the area was in flux, and that the view she was pointing to could be blocked any day by more buildings like hers. She did not seem concerned. Instead, she took another sip from her cup and told me about her daughter's achievements in school. At the time, I decided not to pursue our discussion about zoning and her prized view. But in 2015, as I passed by Imm Yasmine's building again, I found that the view we had enjoyed in 2004 had indeed been blocked by a new row of buildings. Moreover, the small street I had used to take to her building was now a wide, four-lane road, and on that day it was clogged with cars, trucks, and vans pushing up toward al-Dahiya's southern entrance at Hayy el-Selloum. With no trace of Choueifat's municipal police or any form of traffic control, a few male drivers finally took charge and sorted the situation out. But it took forty minutes to make what used to be a five-minute trip.

Of course, not everything had been perfect in the area where Zeina and Imm Yasmine lived in 2004, either. During the course of my research, it soon became apparent that not all the new housing complexes there had been as successful as the AA complex (and a few adjacent projects) had been at providing displaced families with legal, affordable apartments with views (even if that latter condition was short-lived). Indeed, some of Sahra Choueifat's buildings had never even been finished. By most accounts, however, the AA complex was a success, and I was curious to know how it had accomplished advancing the urban edge into an agricultural area otherwise disconnected from the city. On separate occasions, I asked two of the AA developers, who were *hajjs*,[8] what had encouraged them to invest in low-cost housing—a rare phenomenon in Beirut. Both described their goal as being to provide shelter for the poor, without profit, and they also described other projects they had built. They attributed their success to minimizing management expenses, capitalizing on economies of scale, and selling units at cost.

But, I wondered, why would developers take on the risk of such a low-profit or no-profit investment? The answer I received from residents and officials alike was that the AA developers were affiliated with Hezbollah, and that they had received financial support and no-interest loans from related organizations in support of their project in Sahra Choueifat. When I tried to ask the two *hajjs* about their political connections, however, they would not answer the question directly. And when I asked about the three other business partners whom they referenced during our conversations, they told me they were unwilling to identify them. The affiliation of these people, nevertheless, seemed to be common knowledge. Scholars who have studied housing markets in the southern suburbs have identified the AA developer as either a Hezbollah NGO[9] or a politically affiliated, community-based organization that encourages housing development in Sahra Choueifat.[10] This did not concern the residents, however; aside from a few complaints about the low quality of the piping, paint, and tiling, those I interviewed all reported that their experience with the company had been positive.

As I later learned, Imm Yasmine's sister is one of the many people who had less success in her move to the area. She had bought an apartment—also with a view—from a different developer in a housing complex next to AA. However, this developer had never finished the building, and she had never received a title deed for her apartment. Despite paying most, or all, of the fees, therefore, the residents in this complex technically did not own their apartments, and they would never be able to legally sell or mortgage them. The situation was best explained by Rabah, a young man who lived in a first-floor unit. "After years of living in displacement, we decided to spend large sums of money to own a house and become legal residents. We ended up in Sahra Choueifat without a title deed, where we are still squatters in the eyes of the law."

As I soon discovered, there is a hidden logic to these circumstances. Originally, real estate developers in Sahra Choueifat had received the support of organizations like Hezbollah and Haraket Amal. And their seemingly lucrative projects had then provided incentives for nonaffiliated, independent developers to enter the housing market. But most of these other developers had failed to deliver on their promises. Thus, in 2004, many of these projects, like the one in which Imm Yasmine's sister lived, were being managed by banks, which had taken them over after the original developers had defaulted on their loans.

Two independent developers told me that the underlying reason for the problem was that they could not match the low prices of apartments in Hezbollah-supported developments. Indeed, in 1994, when units in Sahra Choueifat were first coming on the market, 64-square-meter apartments there were being sold for $18,000, compared to $30,000 for similar apartments elsewhere in the city's southern peripheries. Imm Yasmine's case thus illustrates how the development of Sahra Choueifat has indeed provided people like her with a chance to buy legal apartments at affordable prices close to Beirut. But her sister's case illustrates why some of these complexes have since failed, exposing their residents to new threats of displacement. In short, the difference has involved the role that religious-political organizations have played in shaping the real estate market in the area by directly subsidizing certain developments while leaving the others to market dynamics.

Thus, a number of families continue to live with the everyday threat of eviction. And this kind of informality has perpetuated the image of Sahra Choueifat as an informal area, despite the fact that many people have paid large sums for apartments there in hopes of gaining a formal foothold in the city. Indeed, when I visited Sahra Choueifat in 2017, these same unfinished housing complexes looked even more run-down. At that time, five women, who were picnicking in a green area next to their buildings, told me that thirteen years after moving into their units, they still did not hold title deeds for their apartments. Only the status of one building has been resolved.

Unfinished buildings, however, were only part of the peril faced by residents of the area. As I soon learned, another hazard was that every winter, the open spaces between Sahra Choueifat's housing complexes would flood with wastewater.

FIGURE 16. Wastewater flooding in Sahra Choueifat. Source: Al-Manar TV, 2004.
Reproduced with permission.

Before the area was developed, pipelines coming down from upland areas of the Choueifat municipality emptied their untreated effluent onto agricultural lands, where it would be absorbed into the ground. However, as residential complexes came to occupy much of this land, the wastewater instead pooled up in the remaining open spaces and on roads, especially during the winter.

Some of the most harmful conditions were created by the Ghandour factory, a sweets manufacturing plant located on a hill directly above the eastern part of Sahra Choueifat. Several times every winter, wastewater piped down the hill from the factory would fill up the lower open spaces to a depth of 35 to 50 centimeters, causing damage to both apartments and businesses, especially those on the ground floor. The wastewater created additional hazards to residents because it made surfaces slippery and led to injuries. It also smelled of sweets and grease, which caused lung problems. On severe flooding days, the wastewater even kept children from going to school. And it damaged the local economy, because ground-floor businesses had to close for days whenever the floods occurred. But the most affected people were those who lived in ground-floor apartments—in particular, in the AA complex. When the wastewater rose into their apartments, it ruined their furniture and other possessions. By August 2004, many of the families who had once lived in these apartments had already sold them for a loss and moved out. Others were in the process of searching for new apartments so they, too, could relocate.

In addition to the wastewater problem, several residents reported that floods were also being caused by overflowing water tanks for which the municipality of Choueifat was responsible. According to one storeowner, these tanks were located on the hill above the neighborhood, and there were claims that on several occasions they had been intentionally overfilled. The excess water had then run downhill, carrying soil from adjacent agricultural fields and transforming the lower neighborhood into a muddy pool. Neither the wastewater from the factory nor the overflowing tanks had created much concern among the municipal personnel, however. People had complained and sought help in addressing both situations, but their efforts had been in vain. On the municipality's end, officials told me that they had tried unsuccessfully to solve the wastewater problem. However, in 2004, al-Manar TV, a Hezbollah media outlet, presented a short report about the situation (Figure 16). One woman who was interviewed for the report commented: "If the people who were suffering from these horrible living conditions were Christians, the pipe would have been fixed tomorrow, not in six years. Just because we are Shiites, we have to take this dirt."

Her statement indicated how residents of Sahra Choueifat, and Shiites in general, saw themselves—treated as an unwanted other in their own country. In the worst cases, this inattention had led to the displacement from Sahra Choueifat of people who had already been twice displaced—first by the civil war and then by the reconstruction of the ruined areas of the central city. Reflecting the seriousness of this crisis, in 2005, the balconies of several apartments were hung with for sale signs. And when I returned a decade later, in 2015, the situation had barely improved. Residents of Sahra Choueifat still felt they were being ignored by the municipality and treated like second-class citizens.

Creating Channeled Markets

In part, the conflicts described here indicate the processes through which Sahra Choueifat gradually developed as a periphery following the civil war. Understanding the context of Sahra Choueifat's urbanization requires examining the socioeconomic context that has prevailed in Lebanon since the end of the civil war in 1990, and the opportunity this has afforded religious-political organizations to influence patterns of growth at the edges of the city.

Key to the new phase in the urbanization in Beirut after the war were the privatization policies of the government of Prime Minister Rafic Hariri. In particular, in 1992, the Hariri government made the controversial decision to award the reconstruction of downtown Beirut to the private real estate development company Solidere. This was accompanied in turn by a decision to evict war-displaced squatters from the city center.[11] Such policies were all part of the government's agenda of neoliberal economic restructuring, and reflected its desire to redevelop the central city as an area for business, tourism, and upscale housing.

As mentioned, an important aspect of the government initiative was the decision to award modest relocation funds to families displaced by the civil war who were still squatting in abandoned buildings in Beirut and beyond. Hayy Madi/Mar Mikhail, discussed in Chapter 2, was just one of the areas where these families were living. Thus, instead of devising a comprehensive relief and reconstruction plan—one that might have helped displaced, low-income residents find housing elsewhere in the city—the Hariri government opted for a hands-off, market-led approach. Typically, families were given short eviction notices and small compensation packages. Official packages were set at $5000 to $7000 per family, although some families were able to secure additional funds through their political affiliations.[12]

As described earlier, the alleged purpose of the government's compensation program was to support the war-displaced to "return home"—that is, to go back to villages they had left more than twenty years earlier. But for a large percentage of this war-displaced population, their preferred home was now Beirut. The government's policy thus forced most families to find alternative low-cost housing on their own, in an extremely tight market, and under the pressure of imminent eviction. Frequently, this meant families had no choice but to buy or rent apartments in al-Dahiya and surrounding peripheral areas.[13] Together, these factors also combined to transform second-tier peripheries, like the largely agricultural Sahra Choueifat, into potentially lucrative new real estate markets.

With the war over, in the early 1990s, Shiite religious-political organizations also began to explore the possibility of helping to provide affordable housing for their low-income supporters. Intent on keeping its population base centralized in the city, Hezbollah, in particular, became an important actor in this process. As explained to me by Hezbollah members, planners, and municipal officials, Sahra Choueifat's relatively flat, undeveloped lands presented the only possible "natural extension" to al-Dahiya. Yet, because Sahra Choueifat was a nonresidential area previously defended by Druze landowners, expanding into it required a campaign of intervention. Eventually, in addition to intervening in land and housing markets and installing infrastructure for new neighborhoods, Hezbollah and other organizations sponsored or encouraged the construction of communal spaces such as mosques, and also basketball courts for the young and coffee shops for the elderly.[14] But it was principally through affiliated housing developers that Hezbollah managed to steer the population it desired to new, low-cost apartments in the area. It is important to emphasize that Hezbollah did not directly house its supporters. Its approach was not top-down; rather, it worked by creating what I call *channeled markets* to ensure that many of Beirut's war-displaced families would settle there.[15]

As a market process, Hezbollah's strategy worked one housing complex a time. In the logic of lacework, each new apartment building represented a *stitch* that would expand the urban reach of al-Dahiya into the agricultural and industrial landscape of Sahra Choueifat. The first two such complexes (and the largest) were built by developers known to be affiliated with Hezbollah. But between 1993 and 1996, the area witnessed a construction boom, as these subsidized developments were followed by market-driven ones. Leading this effort, Hezbollah-affiliated developers were able to provide housing at extraordinarily low prices. Indeed, units in Sahra Choueifat were even cheaper than those being sold in the neighboring informal settlement of Hayy el-Selloum, where apartments—many without title deeds—were selling for $28,000.[16]

Such low prices, with good repayment schemes, attracted Shiite families, many of whom were on the verge of eviction and did not have stable jobs. In 2004, most such families I interviewed had originally been displaced from villages in southern Lebanon and had squatted for decades in abandoned buildings in the city before moving to these affordable apartments. Interestingly, however, the methods developers used to attract such buyers to the distant fringe of the city almost entirely avoided private advertising. Whereas the developers of complexes in nearby Hayy el-Selloum advertised their units on TV and radio, developers in Sahra Choueifat, such as those behind the AA complex, relied on social networks.

One of the first strategies used by the AA developers was political philanthropy. They made it known that they would donate two of their planned twelve buildings to the Martyrs Foundation and the Foundation for the Wounded. These two institutions supported families of Hezbollah members who had died or been injured during the civil war or in fighting against the Israeli occupation of southern Lebanon. This cast the work of AA in a positive light and resonated with Shiite families who supported Hezbollah.

A second strategy was to use Hezbollah party members and others as trusted intermediaries. When I asked residents of the Sahra Choueifat apartments how they had learned of the AA developers, about 80 percent said they had been recommended as loyal and truthful men who "fear God." Such social intermediaries— either kin, neighbors, friends, or shop owners—eventually played a large role within war-displaced communities in disseminating information about the AA project and boosting the reputation of its developers for trustworthiness. At the same time, such intermediaries were one way that Hajj L, one of the developers, said they could gain assurance that prospective buyers were well-respected and would honor their debts. Since most people living in the war-scarred neighborhoods were connected through kinship and other ties, it did not take long before many of the families there were seeking to buy apartments in the AA complex.

The AA developers' third social strategy relied on monetary incentives to attract people of like backgrounds. In particular, it involved a "ticketing system" to motivate people who had already bought apartments in Sahra Choueifat to convince relatives and friends to buy them too. The ticketing system reduced a resident's payment by $300 for every new person he or she could convince to buy an apartment from the AA developers. People thus sought to convince family members, neighbors in displacement, and friends to buy units in the AA complex. As a measure of how lucrative this could be, Hadia, who had convinced eight of her acquaintances to buy apartments from Hajj L, had had her first-year payments waived.

Ticketing was a very successful way to channel the Shiite population from areas like Hayy Madi/Mar Mikhail to Sahra Choueifat. But the AA developers also redefined the concept of a down payment by allowing people to pay it in installments. Instead of a prohibitive initial $6000 payment, therefore, a family might commit to paying monthly installments of $180 to $220, along with a year-end payment of $1200 for five years. In addition, all residents acquired a legal, "surveyed purchase contract," which gave them a ten-year grace period before they would have to pay government registration fees.[17]

In addition to these social strategies, the AA developers made the decision to locate sales offices in areas of the city that soon-to-be-displaced families visited when searching for cheap apartments. Hayy Madi/Mar Mikhail was one such area with an AA sales office. Such forms of recruitment decreased the likelihood that random people would seek to buy housing in the complexes. But in my fieldwork, I also found that they allowed related groups to move to the new area together. For example, I might find agglomerations of four or five nearby apartments owned by members of the same extended family. The creation of channeled markets thus might afford family members the opportunity to continue to live in proximity to one another, preserving some aspect of their community. Neighbors might likewise move together out of their previous makeshift living conditions. However, these markets also led to the formation of a Shiite enclave in Druze territory.

Inducing Land Sales

Two other important factors helped to break down attitudes that had initially marked the territory of Sahra Choueifat as Druze, and that had previously blocked its urbanization: the failed promise of Sahra Choueifat's industrial zone, and a consequent readiness among landowners to sell to whomever offered to buy their land. Thus, despite complaints by Choueifat's existing, largely Druze residents that Sahra Choueifat was becoming an extension of al-Dahiya, some of these same people benefited greatly from selling their land for this purpose. Such sales, however, were also the result of a campaign of inducements on the part of Hezbollah and affiliated entities. Indeed, Hezbollah may be seen as having set up the channeled market, by molding a supposedly free real estate market into an instrument for channeling a new population to the area.

In the postwar, high-growth days of the early 1990s, landowners in Sahra Choueifat had been promised that their property's proximity to the airport would result in its being transformed into a cutting-edge industrial zone. Residents, planners, and political officials all described how Prime Minister Hariri and his planning team had discussed a vision of Sahra Choueifat as a regional industrial, storage, and packaging center. According to one official, a Boston-based firm was even hired to design a plan for it. Initially, land prices boomed when these plans became known. However, the economic crisis that hit Lebanon in 1996 torpedoed this vision. And when land prices subsequently collapsed, many landowners in the area sought to unload their properties in exchange for a more secure source of income. That was when Hezbollah-affiliated housing developers stepped in, offering much more for the land than the owners imagined they would receive if they continued to hold it for industrial development. Indeed, many landowners sold their parcels as an "income-security strategy" (as one landowner described it to me), not caring much to whom they sold or for what purpose.

What this meant was that the failure to transform Sahra Choueifat into a cutting-edge industrial area coupled with the economic crisis compelled individual landowners to sell their land to ensure income. Many went into agreements with developers under which they provided land and received in exchange apartments that they sold on the market. At such a difficult economic time, landowners were not concerned with larger goals—specifically, with how individual sales or the resulting housing projects could restructure the area in geopolitical terms (which had been a concern during the civil war). Working through individual sales also meant that Hezbollah was able to use the real estate market and avoid going through formal planning channels. This allowed Hezbollah to prevent the political resistance that might have emerged among Choueifat's Druze residents had the development of Sahra Choueifat been discussed publicly. Neither did the subsequent development rely on municipal funding. As mentioned, Hezbollah-supported developers, without help from the PSP-dominated local government, eventually installed infrastructure to make the area livable. For example, they installed a sanitation infrastructure (with each new resident family contributing $100).

Initially, the transformation of the area went smoothly and was portrayed by all involved parties, the landowners, developers, and the municipality, as a function of normal real estate markets. However, fifteen years later, these same transactions were retrospectively being described by Choueifat residents (including those who had sold their land in Sahra Choueifat) as Hezbollah's attempt to "take over" a Druze minority territory and/or part of a scheme for the "Islamization" of Lebanon. What had started as a market phenomenon had been transformed into a new spatial practice. As in Hayy Madi/Mar Mikhail, this process is today described by many of the Druze residents of Choueifat as powered by a domino effect. As soon as one landowner learned that a neighbor's plot had been sold to a Shiite, she or he, too, became ready to sell.

During my fieldwork, this process was often described to me in charged, essentialist, sectarian terms directed toward the Shiite religious other. Older residents of Choueifat, especially ones who vividly remembered the civil war, were particularly uncomfortable with the construction of low-cost residential complexes nearby inhabited mostly by Shiites. Thus, during one conversation on a sidewalk in the old area of Choueifat, four elderly Druze residents told me that, initially, most of Sahra Choueifat's agricultural land had been sold to Shiite developers by displaced or émigré Christian landowners. The Druze landowners only followed suit, they claimed. As one of them, Rashid, explained: "Let's not hide from reality. As we recover from fifteen years of civil war, it has not been easy to accept the idea of coexistence with other sects, especially those that may cause a threat to our traditions and ways of life—to our *bī'a*."[18]

Residents of Choueifat also claimed that the real estate brokers operating in Sahra Choueifat were politically affiliated, and that their practices had contributed to the way the area was urbanizing. In particular, many people I interviewed believed that Hezbollah and its allies had intervened to fix land prices. One journalist was explicit in these allegations. Most of the real estate agents in Sahra Choueifat were affiliated with Hezbollah, he said, and "these brokers engage in what we call in the market 'price-fixing.'"[19] Specifically, he alleged, realtors would fix the price per square meter among themselves, eliminating competition and establishing a form of monopoly. He continued, "I know most of them. This technique allows Hezbollah to dominate the market. No one can sell or buy for a different price. They decide the direction of the urban development of Sahra Choueifat." He paused and then added, "I just heard a rumor—they recently decided to push the land prices down. Expect prices in Sahra Choueifat to start falling."[20]

The domination of Hezbollah-affiliated real estate brokers in Sahra Choueifat was eventually made plain to me by one of my own family members. Mr. A was once a landowner in Sahra Choueifat, but like many others, he had sold his land there. He had always avoided discussing my research because its subject was uncomfortable for him. He was also a member of a Druze religious-political organization affiliated with Hezbollah. Nevertheless, his membership in that organization did not translate into a different view about the urbanization of Sahra Choueifat or the essentialized view of its inhabitants. It had ultimately been his family's poor economic circumstances that had led him to follow the domino effect and sell a number of holdings in Sahra Choueifat. And our extended family celebrated the day he announced he had sold his land for a good sum of money: no one cared to whom it had been sold as long as his family would be better off.

One day, I asked Mr. A if he had sold his land for industrial or residential use. He instantly assumed I was asking about the sectarian affiliation of the buyer, and he replied, "I sold it to them" (meaning to Shiite developers and/or Hezbollah). He continued: "Who else would pay that sum of money for land in Sahra Choueifat? They also promised to consider buying this other land tract from me." I never received a direct answer to my question about whether the land had been sold for industrial or residential use. Instead, his answer confirmed for me how land-use questions automatically transformed into questions about the spatiality of the sectarian other. It also showed that there was one dominant entity buying land in Sahra Choueifat, and that it was setting the price. In a monopolized market, Mr. A had not been waiting for the best price on an open market; he had been waiting for the best offer he could secure from Hezbollah-affiliated real estate brokers and developers.

The Pre-2008 Zoning Mutations

The development of Sahra Choueifat initially took place through private land and housing markets, but the contest over its expansion unfolded through battles over zoning, planning, and building law. By tracking the changes to zoning plans over the years, it is possible to show how the lacework process has shaped Sahra Choueifat into a frontier. Many of these changes were initiated through the municipal government of Choueifat, which until May 2010 was controlled by the main Druze political party, the PSP.[21] Meanwhile, the Shiite families who have moved to Sahra Choueifat have not been able to translate their growing numbers into local political power or representation because Lebanese voting laws stipulate that people can register only in their areas of origin.

Zoning designations are not easy to change in Lebanon. Any proposed master plan must be endorsed by the DGU and studied both by the Prime Minister's advisory board on planning and development and by the national council of ministers. If the plan is approved, the changes it calls for, including zoning changes, are then issued as a government decree, which must be signed by the President of the Lebanese Republic, the Prime Minister of the Lebanese government, and concerned ministers, among whom is always the Minister of Public Works and Transport. When the decree is signed and is finally published in the official government gazette, it becomes law and is immediately applicable. Considering this cumbersome process, it is indicative of the high stakes involved in the contest over Sahra Choueifat that different parties managed to make eight large-scale legal changes to the zoning there in the twelve years between 1996 and 2008 (Figure 17). Other small changes have been made using a correction fluid commonly referred to in Lebanon by its brand name, Tipp-Ex. This white brush has been used to literally move zoning lines on official maps in order to repeatedly reclassify areas for either residential or industrial use.

These many changes ultimately reflect the ongoing dispute between Hezbollah, which has in general pushed for the entire area to be zoned for high-density residential development, and the PSP-dominated Choueifat municipal government, which has continued to advocate that Sahra Choueifat be zoned for industrial use. The result was a lacework process that created maps with areas of overlapping industrial, residential, and agricultural use. Sahra Choueifat now hosts a patchwork of apartment buildings in the vicinity of industries, next to one of the most active urban agricultural areas in the Beirut area. And a further consequence is the growing environmental crisis I outlined earlier, as every winter, wastewater mixes with rainwater coming down from Choueifat's hills, carrying with it industrial waste and soil.

The zoning battle over the area's future started after the first large-scale housing complexes began to appear there. At the end of the civil war, development in

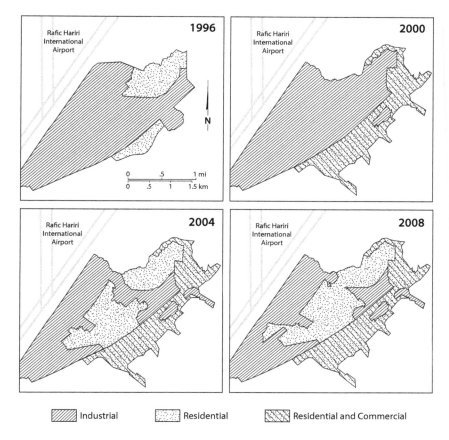

FIGURE 17. Zoning changes between industrial and residential in Sahra Choueifat, 1996–2008. Source: Adapted from DGU Zoning Maps, 1996, 2000, 2004, and 2008.

Sahra Choueifat was still governed by the 1970 zoning law, which designated it as a low-density, residential extension area where agricultural and industrial uses remained. However, in the early 1990s, as the first housing complexes started to appear, political pressure produced by the overlapping interests of the PSP and the Hariri government led to the entire area being rezoned for industrial use in association with the airport.

Attempts to transform Sahra Choueifat into an industrial area may seem like a normal outcome of a market rationale and a desire for profit maximization among landowners and industrial concerns. However, this designation was clearly informed by the past geographies of the civil war and paramilitarization. It carries out the logic of the 1986 master plan for the area, known as the Schéma Directeur de la Région Métropolitaine de Beyrouth (SDRMB). In "Methodological and Political Issues in the Lebanese Planning Experiences," Eric Verdeil describes how this zoning plan had been developed after the Israeli invasion in 1982 and finalized in 1986, but was never officially approved.[22] In analyzing the impact of the war on the SDRMB scheme, Verdeil observes that "the location of an industrial zone in Choueifat between the Shiite and Druze areas best illustrates the overlap of technical and political stakes. It served as a buffer to the Druze militias that have not accepted the growth of a Shiite neighborhood in proximity to their territory."[23]

Given such polarized conditions, it is hard to believe that just ten years later, the antagonistic sentiments between these two groups would have simply have disappeared and been replaced by pure concern among landowners for profit through industrial development. Indeed, a former high-ranking official of the municipality confirmed that older patterns of territorial conflict remained embedded in the rezoning process. As he explained it to me:

During my service at the municipality, I was against any residential permit in the Sahra Choueifat area, especially for people who are from a different religion [the Shiites]. Sahra Choueifat is not prepared to handle such a large-scale residential development. The buildings that were built there are not up to any building standards. . . . The previous municipality members say that they gave permits to ensure financial resources for the municipality after the end of war. However, I am not sure about the truthfulness of these claims. I tend to believe the permits that were approved ensured huge personal gains in side payments for the former cabinet.

When plans for an industrial area associated with the airport succumbed to the economic collapse of 1996, the existence of sentiments such as these refused to let the idea die. Thus, in 1998, a newly elected, PSP-affiliated municipal government made a second attempt to zone the entire area industrial—irrespective of the fact that people were already living there. The effort was headed by the mayor, a PSP member who had been the PSP's militia leader in Choueifat and surrounding areas during the civil war, and a logic of militarization was clearly central to his thinking. At that time, the mayor established a task force to lobby to rezone the area as industrial, an effort accompanied by an official campaign to stop new residential construction. These efforts ultimately failed. But in 2004, another municipal cabinet was elected that vowed, again unsuccessfully, to pursue a similar strategy.

Conflicting efforts to zone Sahra Choueifat for residential expansion and industrial use have since produced a number of mutations. In 1994, when the original plans for the industrial area were being drawn up by a constellation of planners, these alterations first appeared in attempts to address the problem of existing residential use. The solution at the time was to propose a new zoning category, Zone T (or "transition zone"). This category, which was created for the special case of Sahra Choueifat, was a light industrial zone where additional residential development was not allowed. When I asked Mr. Mohammad Fawaz, the former head of DGU, about the logic of Zone T, he replied: "Zone T is a *bid'a*. There is nothing like that in the Lebanese planning law." A *bid'a* is an "innovation," and it sometimes carries a connotation of disapproval or dissent, such as in this case.[24] In effect, Mr. Fawaz was indicating that Zone T did not correspond to the larger logic of planning practice in Lebanon.

According to Mr. B, one of the planners who worked on the area from 1994 to 1996, this zone was created to address the problem of the area's possible future urbanization. Specifically, use of Zone T was intended to postpone the decision on how to categorize certain areas. As Mr. B explained, "It is mainly a reserved zone where urbanization is to be delayed. It is a zone frozen in time, to be revisited later informed by the development of its surroundings." He then explained the dilemma faced by planners hired to create an industrial zone in an area that was already partially inhabited. In effect, the planners had to invent this zoning category because the activities already in place were frequently incompatible with each other. "Ethically, we could not zone the area industrial because residences were already built there. We also could not zone it residential because of health issues of locating residences in the vicinity of industries."

Mr. B then explained how landowners in Sahra Choueifat had opposed the new Zone T, which would have allowed only light industrial activities, such as carpentry and car repair, along with offices. At the time, "the landowners believed their land would be devalued and not utilized," he told me. He did not mention the spatiality of the sectarian order. Instead, he said that profit was the primary consideration at the time. Nevertheless, the profit concerns of landowners who had attempted to pressure the planning team to make "unethical zoning decisions," had ultimately led him to quit the project.

When the 1996 rezoning was rejected, the DGU placed Sahra Choueifat "under study."[25] According to Lebanese law, areas that need to be zoned or rezoned can be placed under study for one year, renewable for another year, after which time a final designation must be made.[26] During the time areas are thus classified, building permits cannot be issued and reconfigurations of land plots are not allowed. In Sahra Choueifat, the under study designation was renewed not just for one year but repeatedly, and remained in effect from 1996 until 2004. During this time no new building permits were, technically, allowed to be approved in Sahra Choueifat. Nevertheless, construction continued with previously acquired permits, many of which were likely processed fraudulently. Indeed, according to one official, developers were frequently able to change the dates of their building permits to before 1996 with the help of municipal employees.

The under study status is also not as technical a tool as it sounds. As was the case in al-Hadath, under study may indeed be understood as principally a mechanism of delay, to freeze the process of development.[27] Supposedly, while an area is under study, planners are evaluating larger forces that should inform its zoning. However, during my fieldwork it became clear that the final decision on how to zone a piece of land under study depended little on the actual need of a city for new affordable housing or industrial lands. What mattered were negotiations among religious-political organizations and affiliated developers, brokers, and landowners over territories, profits, military concerns, and expected strategies for wars yet to come. And when alliances changed and shifted over time, zoning plans would follow, resulting in a lacework of different zones that twisted and turned, zigzagging around individual properties, to delineate the territory of each sectarian group and its other.

In Sahra Choueifat the result of this process was that, between 1996 and 2004, the actual zoning and building laws were continuously in flux, with the underlying political struggle being manifest in multiple rezoning plans submitted back and forth between the DGU and the municipality. Sometimes these schemes would vary over a single year from an area entirely designated for owner-occupied heavy industries to one that was residential with light industries. For example, the maps from June 2000 show Sahra Choueifat as entirely industrial, while those of April 2004 and November 2008 show it as increasingly residential.

Throughout the zoning revisions, the existence of a transitional Zone T between the Shiite informal settlement of Hayy el-Selloum and the Druze town of Choueifat was always preserved. However, not only were the actual areas designated for residential or industrial use changed over time, but the definition of Zone T, too, developed a life of its own. Specifically, this unorthodox category evolved from an area frozen in time to, in 2002, a residential area where light industrial uses were also allowed. The new mutation was labeled "Zone T′." The 1996 approved scheme said that in Zone T, "all kinds of investments are allowed (industries, trade, offices, storage space, etc.) *except for* heavy industries . . . and *residences*" (emphasis added). Whereas, the 2002 zoning plan, which introduced Zone T′, stated that in Zone T′, "all kinds of investments *and residences* are allowed (industries, trade, offices, storage space, etc.) except for heavy industries" (emphasis added).

By 2008, Zone T′ had itself mutated, to become a completely residential and commercial zone without any permitted industrial uses. According to that approved scheme, in Zone T′, "only residences, offices, schools, exhibition rooms, commercial stores, hospitals, hotels, restaurants, and pharmacies are allowed." Figure 18 shows a sample of the zoning and building law changes that Zone T and T′ categories underwent. Above all, Figure 18 demonstrates that the variation between residential and industrial use did not depend merely on technical input but also on political intervention. As a top-level planning official told me in

	Zone	Type	Minimum Plot Area after Parcelization (m²)	% Surface Exploitation	Maximum Allowed Built-up Area	No. of Floors	Maximum Height (m)
1971	No Zone T	N/A	N/A	N/A	N/A	N/A	N/A
1996	Zone T	Industries	1000	40	1.2	N/A	12
2002 & 2004	Zone T′	Light Industries and Residential	500	30	1.5	N/A	15
2008	Zone T′	Residential	750	30	1.2	4	12

FIGURE 18. Sample of zoning laws for Zone T and Zone T′. Source: DGU, compiled by the author.

2010: "Do you really think the few remaining industries constitute an industrial zone? An industrial zone in Sahra Choueifat is a synonym for Druze territory, and a residential zone for Shiite territory." What he was outlining were the facts on the ground—that Hezbollah was pushing to zone the area residential to help house more of its supporters, and that by attempting to retain the area's industrial designation, the PSP was trying to avoid its further urbanization, which was synonymous with more Shiites living there.

The Post-2008 Militarization of Zoning

After the clashes of May 2008, the planning discourse shifted, exposing people's fears and anxieties. After this time, changes that planning officials had previously described as normal were now openly articulated as security measures that would "curb the threat" to Choueifat and protect it from another outbreak like that of the May 7 events. The same municipal office employees who told me in 2004 that their job was "simply technical, to make sure that construction follows the laws," thus informed me in 2009 that "we have been all along trying to stop this influx that attempts to take over 'our area.'"

As I started a second round of fieldwork in the municipal offices in June 2009, people were enthusiastically whispering about the new zoning law. At the same time, people were secretive about just what that planning and zoning law contained, even though it was supposed to be public knowledge. I asked Hatem, a municipal engineer whom I have known since I started research in the area in 2004, about what I had been hearing. He told me he hadn't seen the plan. When I asked him why, he said, "The mayor does not want anyone to see it. The zoning map was an *under the table* deal." I was surprised by this approach to what was supposedly a public plan, but since I was familiar with the politics of planning in Choueifat, I did not pressure him. Nor could I subsequently find any copies of the new master plan anywhere in the municipal offices.

A few weeks later, while I was visiting the American University of Beirut's Department of Architecture and Design, I did, however, spot a copy of the new zoning plans in a colleague's office. When I told Hatem that I was able to obtain a copy, he asked if I could show it to him, which I did. It was truly surprising that I (who had found it by chance) had been able to share the new master plan with the very municipal engineers who were supposed to be consulted about it, and who were in charge of implementing it.

This last iteration of the master plan for the area was approved on November 26, 2008. The action came just a few months after the May 2008 events, which had transformed the area into one of Beirut's most prominent post–civil war battlegrounds. Taking advantage of the twists and turns of political alliances at that time, the PSP-influenced municipal government of Choueifat had managed to snatch approval from its March 14 allies for the new zoning plan.[28] Therefore, the zoning changes this plan incorporated must be understood in relation to the battles that had just been fought in the area and the new demarcation lines, fears, and anxieties that had emerged.

Despite the fact that the 2008 iteration of the area's zoning law had expanded the residential area, Zone T′, to cover most of Sahra Choueifat, the PSP municipal government celebrated the new law as a triumph. The reason was that this new iteration decreased the height and density of future buildings there. The changes shown in Figure 18 illustrate the logic. From the 2002 to the 2008 iterations, the minimum land plot allowed after parcelization had been increased from 500 to 750 square meters. And while the percentage of surface exploitation stayed the same, the built-up (floor area) ratio had been decreased from 1.5 to 1.2, and the allowable height had been decreased from 15 to 12 meters. The 3-meter decrease in building height meant a reduction in maximum building height from five floors to four.[29]

In addition to these changes to exploitation factors and building heights, other regulations such as those on façade materials and the number of apartments per floor were also critical. These affected not only the quality of construction in Sahra Choueifat but also the area's density and the socioeconomic profile of its future residents. The regulations were thus not only about material requirements but also about how these requirements would collectively produce a shift in the mode and logic of urbanization. Figure 19 provides a brief comparison of the 2002 and 2008 façade regulations.

A major change between the 2002 and the 2008 zoning and building laws is their reduction of implicit densities. Under the 2002 laws, a 1000-square-meter piece of land could be developed with 1500 square meters of floor area (five floors of 300 square meters each). The law, however, did not limit the number of apart-

2002 Zoning Plan Regulations	2008 Zoning Plan Regulations
The façade can be built from hollow concrete, smoothed or painted. In the case that the façade is to be built from rough concrete (béton brut), prior approval from the General Director of DGU is necessary. In case of the use of corrugated or tin sheets, prior approval from the General Director of DGU is necessary.	The façades should be clad with 60% natural stone. 60% of the roof should be covered with red tiles. It is prohibited to have more than 2 apartments per floor per block. If the plot has several blocks, each block is to be treated independently (i.e., ensure double the setback distance between every two blocks). After providing adequate parking areas, remaining spaces should be tree-planted. The residency permit will be provided only after landscaping work is done.

FIGURE 19. Zoning plan building regulations: 2002 versus 2008. Source: DGU, compiled by the author.

ments per floor. In fact, a typical arrangement in the Sahra Choueifat buildings I visited during my fieldwork consisted of dividing each floor into three apartments of about 75 square meters each, resulting in a total of fifteen apartments per building. On the same plot, under the 2008 zoning law, a 1000-square-meter parcel may only be developed with 1200 square meters of floor area on four floors. Each floor would still be 300 square meters in size, but the 2008 zoning law also prohibited buildings from having more than two apartments per floor (see Figure 19). Therefore, the same plot could only be developed for eight apartments, and the size of each apartment would need to be larger—around 112 square meters.[30]

This hypothetical example shows the significant spatial implications of the new zoning laws. While a developer in 2004 would have been entitled to house fifteen families, in 75-square-meter apartments, the 2008 law allowed the developer to house only eight families, in 112-square-meter apartments. Not only were overall densities decreased, but the families who could afford 112-square-meter apartments would be of a higher socioeconomic background than those who would have typically been interested in the smaller units.

The decline in density, and thus profitability, was even more pronounced in the case of large tracts, which a developer might plan to subdivide and develop as two or more separate dwellings. Under the 2002 zoning law, a 4000-square-meter parcel of land could be subdivided into six building sites. Each plot would therefore be 500 square meters in size, after subtracting 25 percent of the total area for public use. Under the 2008 law, however, the same plot could be subdivided into only four plots of 750 square meters each. As a result, the same site could accommodate only four buildings, and thirty-two apartments instead of sixty. This would result in a significant (almost 50 percent) decrease in the number of families, and in density in general. Moreover, the fact that the new law required that such large-scale projects treat each building independently—doubling the effect of setbacks—meant that developers would lose significant portions of their land to open space. In particular, the new law specified that the distance between buildings needed to be 9 meters instead of the prior 4.5 meters.

Overall, such changes to the zoning law can be seen as being aimed at decreasing the profitability of development in Sahra Choueifat and shifting the kind of housing permitted. Alternatively, some claimed, it was intended to bringing development to a halt, since it would be more difficult, if not impossible, to sell more expensive units there, considering the environmental, political, and economic situation.

By increasing minimum plot size, reducing allowable floor areas, and decreasing the number of floors, the 2008 law fundamentally rewrote the rules of development in Sahra Choueifat. In addition, it required the use of more costly exterior finish materials (stone cladding, instead of paint). Its projected socioeconomic effect, therefore, would be to change the background of Sahra Choueifat's future residents by roughly doubling the cost of apartments there. According to one planner, the new law would result in fewer apartments per plot, a lower overall population density, and higher apartment prices. If it were to be impossible to curb the expansion of Sahra Choueifat as a "Shiite area," the plan would make it harder for developers to build affordable housing there for the poorer section of al-Dahiya's population. The 2008 plan, according to one advocate, meant "fewer Hezbollah followers will afford apartments under our new zoning laws." As he further boasted, "[T]hose who do will at least be of a higher class and less ideologically committed than what we have now."

The spatial implications of the "under the table" 2008 zoning plan may help to explain why rumor had it (according to both the journalist and the family member I mentioned earlier) that Hezbollah-affiliated real estate brokers were pushing land prices down. Such a step might have been their response to a decrease in demand for land in the Zone T′ now that zoning rules had redefined it as a higher-income area. Such action may even have reflected the sense that further urbanization of Sahra Choueifat had stalled for now. A second possibility, however, was that by depressing prices, Hezbollah was seeking to pressure landowners to lobby the municipality to undo the new zoning. This scenario would imply that Hezbollah was again seeking to use market forces, and their antitheses (such as price-fixing), to arm-twist the municipality into changing the law again to accommodate more affordable housing. It was further possible that by depressing land prices, developers were simply seeking to limit their losses as they continued to develop Sahra Choueifat. In this case, urbanization would continue under the new law, but using other innovative building and marketing techniques. Only time will tell. But as of

January 2017, all the new buildings I visited in Sahra Choueifat had red-tiled roofs and were partially clad in stone, in major contrast to older buildings, like those of the AA complex, which had only a basic painted stucco finish.

Zoning for the War Yet to Come

The 2008 zoning plan for Choueifat featured yet another *bid'a*: the invention of Zone V (where the letter V designated villas) (Figure 20).[31] One of the main achievements celebrated by the Choueifat municipal government following approval of the

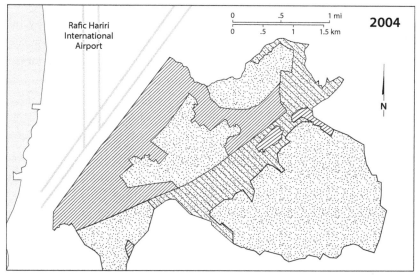

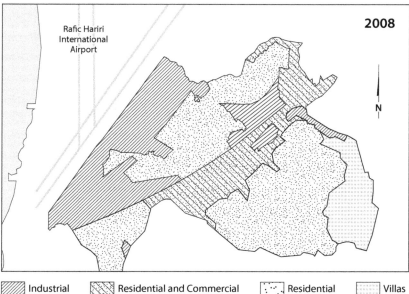

FIGURE 20. The 2004 and 2008 zoning schemes, showing the 2008 expansion of the residential zone in Sahra Choueifat and the introduction of a villa zone, Zone V, on the hilltop. Source: Adapted from DGU Zoning Maps, 2004 and 2008.

2008 law was the law's designation of Choueifat's hilltops as "villa areas" (for single-family houses), meaning one would need a large piece of land to build a small house (Figure 21). Zoned D in 2004, these hilltops were recast as Zone V in 2008.

What was critical about this change was not only that it further reduced allowable floor area ratios, to 0.5 of lot size from 0.75 in the area's former Zone D, but also that it instituted new regulations in these areas. As shown in Figure 22, zoning for the town's hilltops transformed them from being "scenic areas" (with the possibility of developing restaurants, cafés, and other commercial activities), to being strictly private zones—basically, gated communities where only one family per plot was allowed. Zone V was also expanded to incorporate some areas that had formerly been located in Zone D, which had once been equally exclusive, but which were now subject to tougher regulations. Indeed, if the same 1000-square-meter plot of land given as an example in the previous section were located in Zone V, its owners would have been allowed to build only one structure: a 500-square-meter, two-floor, single-family house (villa).

Again, in planning terms, such regulations may all sound normal. Typically, density, height, and infrastructure provisions are justified as means of conserving and redistributing resources, facilitating industrial production, protecting green belts, and preserving the ecology. However, in Choueifat and Sahra Choueifat, these practices also signal a completely different set of meanings and practices. Here, these tools are also being used by religious-political organizations to order the present geography in anticipation of future wars and violence.

As mentioned, both Hezbollah and the PSP are major political parties that double as paramilitaries. Central to their respective zoning strategies, therefore, are paramilitary urban strategies and the spatial imagination of how present urban development may play a role in wars yet to come. The creation of weapons tunnels, the domination of hilltops, and the ability to distribute militias in space are all key elements of these imaginary geographies. In effect, then, the attempt to turn Choueifat's hilltops into a "beautiful villa area," where development was explicitly limited to "only one family per residence," represented a tactical effort by the PSP to ensure that no other party could create a dense settlement there from which to attack PSP areas below. Beyond this concern, the PSP has been interested

FIGURE 21. Change in zoning for hilltops designated Zone D in 2004 and Zone V in 2008. Source: DGU, compiled by the author.

	Zone	Type	Minimum Plot Area after Parcelization (m2)	% Surface Exploitation	Maximum Allowed Built-up Area	No. of Floors	Maximum Height (m)
2004	Zone D	Residential	1200	25	0.75	3	9
2008	Zone V	Villas	1000	25	0.5	2	10

2002 Zone D regulations	2008 Zone V regulations
60% of the outer shell should be built out of natural stone.	Only one family per residence is permitted.
60% of the roof is to be covered with red tiles.	75% percent of the outer shell should be built out of natural stone.
Functions allowed include gas stations, car services, commercial enterprises, exhibition rooms, cafés, and restaurants.	A pyramid-like, red-tiled roof should cover 75% of the area.
Commercial activities should not be more than 50% of the ground-floor area.	At least 10% of the site should be planted with trees, and leftover spaces are to be covered with grass (gazon) or similar kinds of material.
	In case of violation of any of the above regulations, prior approval of the director of the DGU should be obtained.
	No piloti (pier) supported floor is allowed.
	The permit application should include site maps that indicate the location for the green areas and the trees. The number of trees should not be less than one tree per 40 m², and planting according to the approved site map is considered a necessary component of obtaining the residency permit.
	Industrial and commercial activities are not allowed.

FIGURE 22. Changes in hilltop zone regulations. Source: DGU, compiled by the author.

in preventing the settlement of Hezbollah-affiliated populations in other areas of Choueifat, where their presence might lead to these areas being bombed by Israeli warplanes in the event of a future war on Lebanon.

In summary, then, the 2008 zoning law represented an admission by the municipality that Sahra Choueifat was becoming an extension of al-Dahiya. But by writing more restrictive provisions for development of Zone T′, the PSP was able to ensure that new housing there would be less affordable than that which was already being built. This might "slow" development and bring in residents of a "different bī'a."

Ecochard's Shadows

In addition to the various parties directly involved in negotiating Sahra Choueifat's zoning lacework, older shadows were also present in the landscape, delaying resolution of the plan's development and creating additional uncertainty with regard to planning efforts. In particular, these reflected the layout of Sahra Choueifat's ghost road grid, existing on paper yet not fully executed on the ground and the decades-old reservation of land for a proposed peripheral highway around Beirut. Throughout the process described above, these transportation-related set-asides remained on the books. Some factions now hope that changes made in 2006 to the Lebanese law covering eminent domain will lead to these projects being cancelled. This would release the set-aside property for alternative development. But it would also reconfigure the entire pattern of urbanization in the area, as future developments would no longer have to reflect their presence. Such a condition would significantly alter the lacework of urbanization—although its precise impact cannot be known.

The long-standing proposal for a peripheral highway has been aimed at enabling drivers to circulate from one area of Beirut to another without having to pass through the central city. It was decreed in 1961, but it has never been built. The layout of a road grid in Sahra Choueifat was likewise contained in Ecochard's Master Plan for Beirut's suburbs, and its exact layout was decreed through legal steps taken between 1963 and 1977. However, it, too, was never fully implemented. Nevertheless, legal construction in Sahra Choueifat has had to take this ghost infrastructure into account in terms of setbacks and alignment. For the most part, Ecochard's road grid can today be traced as a series of voids between buildings. Parts of these voids were widened and paved in 2012, as an "exception" when religious-political organizations lobbied the municipality to improve the de facto roads, given that "it has been impossible to implement Ecochard's plan," according to a conversation I had with a municipal official in June 2017.

As I saw during a visit to Sahra Choueifat in 2017, flags of religious-political organizations now delineate this de facto road that was supposed to be the peripheral highway as it traverses Sahra Choueifat, parallel to the Old Saida Road. This landscape of flags shifts from Haraket Amal flags in the southern part of Sahra Choueifat to Hezbollah flags in the north. A joint Lebanese Army–Hezbollah security checkpoint was recently erected on the road (right next to the AA complex) as part of an increased security measure in the area. The checkpoint further marks the boundary of al-Dahiya and gives one the feeling of entering a military zone.

Interestingly, although the plots through which the proposed highway would pass have been left undeveloped, fifty years on, the government still has not paid for the land. The same is true for the land designated for the local street grid. As a result, owners of these areas have been unable to sell, mortgage, or develop their holdings, as they await an official decision on the status of the area's public road infrastructure.

The positions of various religious-political organizations on whether the peripheral highway should go forward or be halted are complicated. This is particularly true for Hezbollah. For example, in the adjacent Hayy el-Selloum area, construction of the proposed highway would result in the eviction of many Hezbollah and Haraket Amal supporters, who live in houses and apartment buildings built informally on lands designated for the highway.[32] However, Hezbollah is interested in building the highway through Sahra Choueifat because it would tighten the connection between Sahra Choueifat and al-Dahiya and provide a direct link to southern Lebanon.

The PSP, by contrast, has long fought the construction of the peripheral high-way through the area. One planner I talked to said the PSP and Choueifat residents had two main concerns: that the new highway would solidify the area as part of Shiite al-Dahiya, and that it would cut Druze Choueifat off from the airport. This second reason is likely related to military strategy. During the civil war, some weapons used by the warring militias were supplied through the airport, and the PSP would like to ensure that Hezbollah (and Haraket Amal) are not able to cut off access to it. For this reason, stretches of the four-lane highway "will always be a junkyard," as one PSP official told me, "and Sahra Choueifat's children will always be playing on its ghost lanes that are never to come."

The PSP is likewise not supportive of the construction of the Sahra Choueifat road grid outlined by Ecochard. This position was voiced to me by Choueifat municipal personnel on several occasions. When I asked a municipal officer in 2017 why the road network had not been implemented, he responded, "because of some politics." The municipality and affected landowners are thus waiting for the revised eminent domain law to take effect because they believe it would nullify all planned government infrastructure schemes for Sahra Choueifat—not only the planned highway but also the area's planned formal road grid.

The situation behind the eminent domain law is complex. The 2006 amendment to the existing law would limit to three years the time allowed to the government between ordering land acquisition for public use and beginning the appropriation process.[33] It would further limit to ten years the period allowed between the land appropriation and the start of construction on the proposed project. After ten years, if the government has not commenced construction, affected landowners may seek to reappropriate their plots. Before passage of the 2006 revision, Lebanon's eminent domain law contained no such required time frames. This is why blueprints for the peripheral highway and the Sahra Choueifat road grid, conceived in the 1960s and 1970s, still haunt the geography of Sahra Choueifat and restrict the development of large areas there. The new law might "unfreeze" these areas by nullifying these proposals, thus further scrambling planning and zoning provisions for the area. However, the new law has gone largely unimplemented due to lack of funds and political willpower, a result of the political gridlock that has gripped Lebanon since 2007. It remains to be seen —pending further negotiations—whether it will ever go into effect.[34]

Many planners I interviewed who hold modernist planning aspirations are against the 2006 changes to the eminent domain law. According to one of the most prominent: "This is unacceptable planning. Some people have already built their buildings taking into consideration Ecochard's road grid. Now, if this becomes nullified, what happens to the visual order of the street and place? We will lose alignment and end up with zigzagged streets." The fight over the shadows of old planning schemes, especially Ecochard's legacy in contested peripheries, thus adds yet a further dimension to the spatial processes of lacework that have shaped the urbanization of areas like Sahra Choueifat over time.

Dirty Planning

After all the political maneuvers to shape zoning plans for Sahra Choueifat, planning officials still had to draw lines on maps. This work took place after the initial plan that Mr. B worked on failed to be implemented. One such planner is Mr. I, who explained to me the lacework of zoning. When I visited with Mr. I, his office was overwhelmed with stacks and rolls of maps. Some, he said, had been there since he arrived at the firm more than twenty years previously, and there were traces of spider webs between the folds of some of the maps in unattended piles.

In our first meeting, Mr. I talked for five hours about his aspirations in planning practice and his painting and cooking hobbies. He sketched for me his ideal zoning map—a series of concentric circles of *imtidādāt* (degrees of urbanization), which provided a stark contrast to the concept of lacework that he used later to describe his work in Sahra Choueifat. He talked at length about his vision for an area like Sahra Choueifat, but initially avoided discussing what had ended up on current maps.

You have an industrial area on one side [Sahra Choueifat] and a dense settlement with a large unemployed and uneducated work force on the other [Hayy el-Selloum]. What is the planning logic to do? Create jobs for the unemployed people of the residential area in the industrial and agricultural areas. You separate the two zones with a large green area, which will act like the lung for the area, purifying the air coming from the industries and providing a green space for the residents of the settlement. It would have been a great plan, do not you think so?

As he was describing his ideal plan for the area, I considered how different this was from what had actually emerged: a checkered map of residential and industrial zones and a population on the verge of another round of displacement. What might have happened if Mr. I's vision had been implemented?

As he saw it, a quest for profit and the spatiality of the sectarian order had destroyed his dream for Sahra Choueifat. Two hours into my second meeting with him, Mr. I looked at me and asked, "But why did you choose to study Sahra Choueifat?" He continued:

You have been getting good planning education in the U.S. I was finely educated in the French planning system in Canada. I have to be blunt: the planning case of Sahra

Choueifat is *'amaliyyi wiskha* [a dirty operation]. . . . For me, working on Choueifat was a nasty and dirty job. While working on the project, I kept getting nasty, threatening, and insulting phone calls. My only strategy was to pretend that I did not speak English or Arabic. People from the municipality, landowners, and political parties would even show up unannounced at our office door. The director would say to them, "Here is the planner, but he is Canadian and does not understand any language besides French." They would then struggle, trying to talk to me in French, and eventually they would get up and leave, tired of trying to communicate with me.

He also described the difficulties and physical threats he had encountered working on the Choueifat plan. For example, because the area was intertwined with the informal settlement of Hayy el-Selloum, residents there on several occasions had thought the purpose of the planning team was to evict them. Mr. I said that he and his team were attacked twice on site by people wielding sticks. Such intimidating behavior continued until an official from Hezbollah intervened to explain to the residents that Mr. I was not there to demolish their houses but to develop a planning scheme that would help them stay.

Planners working for private companies, as Mr. I did, were not the only ones who were physically threatened, so were public planners at the DGU, who were predominantly women at the time. Gendered dynamics were an additional, crucial factor in these threats. Thus, Mr. I described how men who had an interest in the planning of Sahra Choueifat (municipal officials, representatives of religious-political organizations, landowners, and developers) would walk into Ms. G's office at the DGU and start banging with their fists on her desk, threatening her. He then added, "When they came here, they did not dare to bang on my desk. . . . But yes, men banging, threatening the planning ladies of the DGU to get it their way in Sahra Choueifat, that was a common strategy." After many such physical threats over planning issues, Ms. G resigned.

As he talked about his experience in Sahra Choueifat, and Choueifat in general, Mr. I kept repeating the word "dirty." For him, dirty planning meant subjecting planners to all sorts of threats and political pressure to make it impossible for them to do the jobs for which they were trained. He then explained how these threats were all part of a calculated exercise by the various religious-political organizations to shape the area.

In the beginning I was also including Sahra Choueifat in my master plan proposals. But I was eventually disgusted to work on it. They kept telling me, "*Estez* [Sir], don't propose ideas for this area. In this area, you just 'draw' what we—all the involved parties—agreed on. . . ." Can you believe it? I was not allowed to envision or plan anything for the area. How am I supposed to have a full vision for Choueifat if I am not allowed to think on this part of it [Sahra Choueifat]? I eventually gave up working on it and just labeled it whichever way they wanted. After that, I did not follow up with what was going on there. I proposed schemes for the other areas of Choueifat, and I left this area "blank" for them [the religious-political organizations] to fill it in.

My interviews with Mr. I took place after the eruption of violence in May 2008. He talked openly about the dirty process of planning that was so opposite to the planning ideals he believed in and hoped to practice. At one point, while asking about my choice to study Sahra Choueifat, Mr. I said: "I advise you to pick another area where you could study planning. If you want to look at a good planning job that I did, why do you not look at Miziara for example? Here, let me show it to you." Miziara is located in a picturesque mountainous area in the Zgharta district in north Lebanon. On another occasion, Mr. I pulled out a zoning map and photographs of Miziara. "Here, why don't you study the planning of this village? This is planning you can learn from, a neat and logical master plan," he said. He then went on to explain the beauty of working on Miziara, in contrast to "dirty" Sahra Choueifat. However, Miziara was not a contested frontier of a fast-urbanizing city like Beirut.

Talking Technical

During interviews, several planners insisted on trying to show me what good planning could be away from the "dirty" job they were forced to engage with in contested territories. They did this by referencing other projects and *talking technical*.

The approach of Ms. F was not very different from Mr. I's approach. A planner who had been in charge of Choueifat, among other projects, at the DGU, and a very influential figure there, she obviously did not like my "investigation" of Sahra Choueifat, and she was hostile to me every time I visited the DGU offices. As she commented during the one brief interview she granted me:

Sahra Choueifat is like any other place to plan; if you want to understand planning, you *do not need* to study that place in particular. See, as a student of planning, you first have to know the institutional makeup and the "standardized" legal process of how we do planning here. Have you seen the contracts we sign with the private companies and the clients for example? . . . You have to familiarize yourself with those. Sahra Choueifat or another area, they all require the same "standard" procedure. In preparation for your visit, I printed these contracts for you. Check them out.

She handed me an envelope with a stack of papers and ended our meeting. I was confident that the package contained material about Choueifat, the site I had told her I was working on. But when I opened the envelope later, to my surprise,

I saw that Ms. F had chosen to print for me the legal documents for the planning of Qornet el-Hamra, Zakrit, Deir Tamich, Mazraʻit Yashouʻ, Habbous, Beit el-Kikko, Ain ʻAr, Nabay, and Qornet Chahouane, in the al-Matn district east of Beirut. When I called to remind her that I was working on Choueifat, she said: "I know. I provided you with a sample. Choueifat is no different, it is the same."

The areas for which Ms. F had provided me with information were far from Beirut. Many were, like Miziara, mountainous villages, not even urban settings. It was obvious that Ms. F did not want me looking into the planning of Sahra Choueifat. She chose to "educate" me instead on how the DGU does planning in a standard way across space and time, with no difference between a city and village. However, the areas I was interested in were inhabited by a mix of sectarian groups, whereas each of the ones she chose to show me was inhabited by a single religious group, and the main religious-political organizations in the overall area were Christian.

Initially during my interviews with the planning technocrats, I was keen to turn the discussion to the politics of planning practice. Like Ms. F and Mr. I, however, these planners would often suggest that I look somewhere else to learn about what "good planning" was about in Lebanon. They also often hastened to move the discussion from a political question to a technical one. They would thus delve into the details of a plan, a design, or a policy—talking technical about an area or a policy that was different than the one I was asking about.

The lack of direct response to my questions was disturbing. Eventually, however, I started to discern a pattern. I soon realized that what was actually happening in these engagements was quite revealing. Talking technical was a technique that allowed the different actors to communicate and be productive across political dividing lines while avoiding the elephant in the room—the politics shaping the major planning decisions in peripheries transformed into frontiers. In these contested frontier areas, the lacework of planning practice was much less about expert knowledge and planning technicalities than about balancing the calculations of religious-political organizations with regard to their social and military roles in wars yet to come. In fact, these national and regional subjects were being discussed on a much higher level behind closed doors by political party leaders, developers, funders, ministers, and members of parliament. It was thus very often not up to planners to develop the vision that would be reflected on the blueprint.

In her discussions of the "will to improve" and development programs in Indonesia, Tania Li describes how "questions that are rendered technical are rendered nonpolitical."[35] Talking technical in Beirut's public and private planning offices, however, was not just an attempt by bureaucrats to render political issues technical. It was also their way to discuss the politics of planning in areas like Sahra

Choueifat without naming actors, practices, and techniques. Thus, by attempting to illustrate the difference between his work on Miziara and on Sahra Choueifat, Mr. I was trying to communicate to me the possibilities and limitations of planning in contested areas. When I was told that a particular question was "technically difficult," what a planner really meant was that it was politically messy.

Another way of talking technical in relation to my work on Sahra Choueifat emerged over the issue of land prices. A few of the planning technocrats and officials I interviewed maintained that land prices dictate land use, an attempt to establish a market logic that would explain the lacework of zoning. Real estate market logic is certainly a big part of the picture here—as much as political and military concerns. And at one point I decided to follow this lead. If the lacework of planning was a product of an economic rationale, I asked, how did land prices explain the ten rounds of zoning changes that had so far taken place? To address this issue, I interviewed various planners, economists, officials, landowners, and real estate brokers about how land prices had fluctuated over time. I focused my questions on the price differential between industrial and residential sales. In response, people drew me graphs and tables and wrote down complex economic equations that they claimed provided the rationale for differential land pricing. However, only a few of the stories were consistent. For example, one real estate economist told me that high demand for residential land made residentially zoned land more expensive and lucrative than industrial land. Another planner told me that due to the scarcity of industrial land in Beirut's peripheries, industrial zoning was more profitable for landowners. "The two main industrial zones around Beirut, Dora and Mkalles, are saturated, so Sahra Choueifat's industrial zone was in demand," Mr. I said. Others, as mentioned previously, talked about price-fixing in the area.

Yet other interviewees were keen on linking Sahra Choueifat's land prices to a national socioeconomic discourse. As one engineer and his economist friend told me:

The bird's-eye view of the low-income Sahra Choueifat buildings—despite it being a formal area—has major repercussions on national tourism and flows of money into the country. Do you think foreigners greeted with this unruly sight of Sahra Choueifat as they approach Beirut from the air would still invest in Lebanon? . . . Prices should make it unprofitable for low-income residential developments here in order to protect national tourism and foreign investment.

These disparities in stories about land pricing made it clear that talking technical was actually a mechanism used to justify competing claims, predominantly sectarian and socioeconomic, to the spatial production of peripheral frontier areas like Sahra Choueifat. This discourse becomes more prevalent when discussing urban planning. Those I spoke with often felt an urge to provide me with a logic that could explain Sahra Choueifat's tangled zoning lacework. Yet, there was rarely any mention of environmental crises or the new rounds of displacement that some families had to endure.

The Spatiality of Hezbollah

To sum up what I have been describing, lacework zoning is the product of the intertwined logics of urbanization, neoliberalism, and militarization. These are the forces that are shaping peripheries such as Sahra Choueifat into frontiers within the spatial and temporal logics of future wars. But as I have also implied, Sahra Choueifat's particular transformation from a peripheral agricultural space to a primary frontier of growth and local and regional violence must likewise be understood as reflecting its production as one of Hezbollah's "spaces of resistance." This project must be interpreted in relation to such larger regional and transnational conflicts as Israel's ongoing colonialism, Western imperialism, the ongoing war in Syria, and more recently, ISIS's rise to power in the Middle East and its fighting against Hezbollah and its allies in Syria. Interestingly, this in turn entails reflecting on how religious-political organizations (Hezbollah, in particular) have engaged with the Lebanese government's postwar neoliberal economic policies, such as the decision to grant monetary compensation to war-displaced families, which provides important lessons for the future of postwar reconstruction in Syria.

Within the contemporary discourse on "alternative" actors (such as NGOs and religious charities) and neoliberalism, there is a tendency to view organizations like Hezbollah as either local agents of a world capitalist system (whether celebrated or condemned) or entities that are entirely outside that system. In Turkey, for example, the infusion of Islam into the neoliberal state has led many scholars to argue that Islamic religious-political organizations have become agents of neoliberalism.[36] However, other Islamic organizations (one of which is Hezbollah) have been theorized as operating entirely outside the capitalist system.[37] Such actors are assumed to "announce to society that something 'else' is possible,"[38] although this kind of hope has been tapering with Hezbollah's involvement in the Syrian war.

In line with this perceived dichotomy, it was unusual to hear either scholars or Lebanese local communities describe Hezbollah's spatial practices as neoliberal, especially in the period before the initiation of project Waad, the Hezbollah-led reconstruction of Haret Hreik after the July 2006 Israeli war on Lebanon. The organization has often been characterized (and indeed, portrays itself) as a provider of services for the poor—an Islamic welfare NGO.[39] Hezbollah has also taken a vocal stance against policies considered Western and imperialist that often aligned with neoliberal projects,[40] and it has been active in the landscape of what Michael Watts has defined as "revolutionary Islam."[41] Increasingly, however, discussions have raised the question of Hezbollah's role within a neoliberal regime. Principally, these discussions have pointed out that the organization has been a major benefactor of the rollback of Lebanese state programs. Thus, Mona Fawaz shows how Hezbollah's top-down approach to project Waad benefited from the Lebanese government's privatization policies, arguing that "the current neo-liberal policy turn that delegates social services to non-state actors may witness and even strengthen the role of actors [other] than those expected by market proponents."[42] Hezbollah, indeed, has used the delegation to private entities of responsibilities that were supposedly public to keep control of its strongholds.[43] Across the world, non-state actors are today operating their own neoliberal regimes of what Ananya Roy calls civic governmentality, where the "urban subject is simultaneously empowered and self-disciplined, civil and mobilized, displaced and compensated."[44]

The case of Sahra Choueifat extends these arguments. It shows, I argue, that Hezbollah's role in the development of the area is neither that of a neoliberal regime tool, emerging within the neoliberal rollback of the state, nor that of an alternative nonstate organization carving its niche outside the capitalist system. Clearly, Hezbollah and the neoliberal economic order are not antithetical. Indeed, the possibility of a Hezbollah stronghold in Sahra Choueifat can only be understood in terms of its engagement with the neoliberal economic order (among whose policies are the operation of free markets and the privatization of welfare). Hezbollah has thus used land and housing markets, opened up investment for unsubsidized developers, worked with Lebanese government policies addressing the war-displaced, and engaged closely with the private planning companies that do most of the public planning in Lebanon. It has also participated in shaping building and zoning laws.

Rather than merely locating Hezbollah as either within or outside the neoliberal economic order, the transformation of Sahra Choueifat thus shows how what came to be seen as Hezbollah's spaces are in fact produced by the continuities and discontinuities of neoliberal economics with practices of religious affiliation, sectarian construction, service provision, resistance ideology, and militarization. Consequently, Hezbollah's intervention in housing and real estate markets in Sahra Choueifat rendered the area an extension of al-Dahiya, and like the rest of al-Dahiya, Sahra Choueifat was bombed during Israel's July 2006 war on Lebanon. Such practices have become even more entangled with Hezbollah's involvement in the Syrian War, which is increasingly being described as a sectarian war. As a result, areas like Sahra Choueifat (and al-Dahiya in general) have emerged as regional frontiers of the war in Syria, and indeed, Sahra Choueifat was targeted by an ISIS suicide bomber in 2014.

Instead of thinking of religious-political organizations as actors that are either inside the state or outside it, inside the market or outside it, it is important to recognize how these actors weave in and out of many such processes as they shape territories and construct otherness. This weaving creates a process of lacework that folds space in layers upon layers, and twists time in ways that collapse teleological notions of future, present, and past—thus creating labyrinths of simultaneous closeness and difference, coexistence and segregation, home and displacement.

Whereas Chapter 2 of this book examined doubleness as a framework to explain the spatial and temporal logics of territorial contestation in the immediate southern peripheries, where already existing urbanization meant that new construction replaced ruins, this chapter has expanded that discussion outward in space and used lacework as a framework to explain the urbanization of Beirut's second-tier peripheries, which are also peripheries of al-Dahiya, from agricultural land to a patchwork of residential and industrial areas. Examining lacework as a process, logic, and outcome reveals the contested spatial practices through which second-tier frontiers take shape as Beirut's and al-Dahiya's urbanization pushes outward.

In times of peace, lacework is produced by religious-political organizations that are interested in urban growth and profit but also in the use of space to gain advantage in anticipated future wars. They have come to use zoning tools and planning policies both as ways to achieve urban growth and as tools for negotiating conflict. The end product is a landscape in which areas for industry and housing may overlap and where roads may never be finished. Nevertheless, in the case of Sahra Choueifat, the lacework process has also allowed for the housing of poor, war-displaced families in an area close to the city.

This housing has been constructed largely by developers affiliated with and supported by Hezbollah, using financial mechanisms that take into account both these families' expected government compensation packages and their need for minimal down payments and lenient payment plans. However, the channeled markets and other real estate strategies that allowed such development also resulted in the creation of a Shiite enclave in what used to be Druze territory. This, in turn, resulted in zoning wars in times of peace—which then erupted into real battles in 2008, where dozens were killed on the new demarcation lines between Shiite Sahra Choueifat and Druze Choueifat.

The case of Sahra Choueifat thus shows how the ongoing practice of urban planning in frontier areas of Beirut relies on the development of innovative techniques to continuously balance a spatiality of political difference in order to keep a war at bay. At the same time, it also shows how planners, as technicians of mapping, end up deeply entangled and professionally compromised by this process. By drawing the contours of this lacework, they become agents of a practice that folds within it grave human health issues, environmental crises, segregation, and violence. Such outcomes stand in stark contrast to the common view of urban planning as a field that may be called upon to solve such problems, not create them. Planners emerge as the technicians of the war yet to come.

CHAPTER 4

A BALLOONING FRONTIER

MY FAMILY lives on the fourth floor of a ten-floor apartment building in Doha Aramoun[1] (Figure 23). Our apartment, like many in the area built with initially extra-legal floors during the civil war, used to have a sweeping view of Beirut's International Airport and the Mediterranean Sea—but not anymore. Since 1993, the year in which we moved, the beautiful meadows that once separated our building from the sea have been filled month after month, year after year, with new construction. Nowadays, our windows look out on a crowded landscape of concrete buildings, which have appeared like popcorn—instantaneously, haphazardly, and of varying construction quality.

In 2009, our last glimpse of the airport and the sea was being sealed off by the most recent of these structures. An engineer from the municipality told me that had the buildings in our area followed the law, our view likely would not have been blocked. However, developers commonly increase the size of their projects during construction through a practice known among developers, the engineer said, as "ballooning."[2] A building might thus be built to the layout approved by the municipality and other planning agencies, but the contractor would "blow up the plan like a balloon," increasing its dimensions, and hence the total built-up area of the building.

In 2010, we witnessed this process firsthand. Looking out our window at a neighboring building under construction, we saw concrete columns rising high in the air, indicating that the developer was planning to add extra, unpermitted floors. Then, a few days later, two columns appeared on the sidewalk overnight. Steel and concrete beams soon followed, connecting them to the main structure. These moves indicated that the developer planned to extend the building not only upward but also outward into the legally mandated 3-meter setback from the property line. This could conceivably translate into a 50 percent increase in both built area and profit, which he would gain by encroaching into space set aside for the public benefit.[3]

In Lebanon, it is usually futile to try to uphold the law in the face of profit, political connections, and corruption. After-the-fact legalization is also always a possibility.[4] Nonetheless, a number of families in our building tried to stop the new building from ballooning beyond its permitted size. Their first step was to petition the municipality and other public agencies. After they delivered their petition, the local police did show up a couple of times. But on each occasion, the authorities left after a brief chat with the developer, with no apparent result.[5] What the building officials apparently knew was that the illegal construction would continue, while the families' complaint would become entangled in bureaucratic maneuvering. And sure enough, concrete slabs were soon poured, and the expanded space morphed into rooms. During meetings with the families, officials then made statements such as, "Done deal—it is already built. You cannot change it now"; and, "Have mercy on the man [the developer]. You are affecting his livelihood. Everybody builds like this here. Just let it go." As construction continued, the signatories to the petition were also pressured to drop the case.

Events turned, however, six months into the process, when the signatories solicited the help of a high-level government employee affiliated with the Sunni Future Movement. Two days later, we woke up to the sound of bulldozers destroying the concrete skeleton that had illegally extended the building. These were add-on elements, and thus their destruction did not affect building safety. Nevertheless, this action of de-ballooning was surprising, considering that Beirut is a city where legalizing illegalities, instead of removing them, is a common practice. Over the next year, the developer then struggled to smooth the building's surfaces—cutting the protruding steel and dressing the façade with stone to hide the fact that the unpermitted extension had been sliced off. After the dimensions

FIGURE 23. View of Doha Aramoun from Bchamoun. Source: Author, 2015.

of promised apartments had shrunk in size (and certain units had been eliminated entirely), a number of buyers abandoned their purchases in the building.[6] Thus, in 2011, even as apartments were selling at a frantic pace in Doha Aramoun, an Apartments for Sale sign still hung on the building.

The above story reveals some of the informal building practices in a city where government agencies rarely uphold building laws as a matter of public interest. The implementation of the building law in Lebanon is uneven, and this case was no different. However, it is also about the fear of the sectarian other that has gripped areas like Doha Aramoun since May 2008, when battles were fought between an alliance of the Sunni Future Movement and the Druze Progressive Socialist Party (PSP) on the one hand and the combined Shiite Hezbollah and Haraket Amal on the other. At that time, families were displaced and people killed. And against that backdrop, the adjustments to the ballooning building's size revealed how all spatial production, even the limits of informal construction, must now be negotiated within the complex territorial logic of religious-political organizations. Thus, the main reason why our neighboring building was de-ballooned was that its developers were Shiite and connected politically with Haraket Amal and Hezbollah in an area that has been constructed since the end of the civil war in 1990 as a predominantly Sunni area.

When our building's residents initially raised their concerns about the neighboring building, no religious-political organization from the opposite political camp seemed willing to interfere in such a small-scale "neighborhood matter." A Druze PSP affiliate, for example, made it clear it would not take on such a minor

fight in an already tense area. Instead, this case required an appeal to a high-ranking Future Movement agent to enforce the building law. However, this agent's real concern had less to do with enforcing the law than with limiting the expansion of housing for Shiites in a Sunni periphery. The building law thus served as an arbiter of conflict—but only post-factum, after friction had already surfaced.

For almost three decades, between 1976 and 2003, the area of Doha Aramoun had been controlled by the Syrian Armed Forces (SAF).[7] At that time, construction illegalities were widespread and mostly straightforward. It was thus generally possible to add six supposedly illegal floors to any apartment building if the SAF approved and received a share of the profit or of the space. This form of informal construction was just a way of doing business. For example, this had been how the building we lived in had been built. With its ten floors, it towered over one of Doha Aramoun's hills, and was only fully legalized after the end of the war.

By 2009, the conditions governing construction of our neighboring building were far different, however. Following the withdrawal of the SAF from the area, the local political vacuum was filled by competing religious-political organizations that operate both inside the state and outside it, including Hezbollah, the PSP, the Future Movement, and a number of rising Sunni extremist entities. All have an interest in gaining control of the area, a territorial interest that was exacerbated after the clashes of 2008. Their multiple ambitions have created a complex terrain of overlapping powers and territorialities, as they wrestle for control of a strategic area. As a result, the contours of extra-legal construction must now be negotiated not only within a corrupt government system but also with a constellation of religious-political organizations, according to their honeycombed jurisdictions and in light of their strategizing for wars yet to come.[8]

Strategies and Tactics of Ballooning Frontiers

In addition to being a building practice, ballooning is also a useful metaphor for understanding the general processes of contested territorial expansion in Beirut. As illustrated in the case of our neighboring building, ballooning requires room—space and land—to occupy and the right political and economic conditions to enable it over time. Ballooning is thus not endless but is bound by both internal and external structures. However, it is also through ballooning that Doha Aramoun has been transformed from a distant periphery into a contested frontier under pressure from religious-political organizations, primarily the Sunni Future Movement, the Shiite Hezbollah, and the Druze PSP.

In the sectarian mapping of Lebanon, ballooning has ultimately translated into the expansion of Sunni Beirut, and later Shiite al-Dahiya, into what used to be Druze (and Christian) territory.[9] On the building level, ballooning describes a process of extra-legal construction. But on the urban level, it is not seen as an inherently legal or illegal process—or a positive or negative one for that matter. It is, rather, experienced differently by people positioned differently in relation to it. In the years immediately after 2008—as past, present, and future wars loomed—the process of ballooning was also being negotiated and contested on multiple scales. This ultimately makes it possible to interpret the battle over the size of our neighboring building as emblematic of the larger contestation over Beirut's peripheries as frontiers concurrently of urban growth and wars yet to come.

To ground these concepts in the terrain of metropolitan Beirut, this chapter will investigate two competing spatial and temporal logics that have enabled the ballooning of west Beirut and peripheral al-Dahiya toward Doha Aramoun. These are the strategies of capital projects and the tactics of filling in the blanks. According to Michel de Certeau, *strategies*, on the one hand, are practices that are dominated by calls for "the economy of proper place," as defined by those in power (experts, state agents, developers, etc.).[10] *Tactics*, on the other hand, are the everyday, clandestine ways that the weak make use of the strong, lending a political dimension to everyday practices. De Certeau has described strategies as the *science* of space making, and tactics as the *art* of spatial practices. But I will also use the terms here to discuss the two scales of space making inherent in ballooning.

Technically, a capital project is a "large-scale project entailing major expenditure," and it can be driven by either public or private interests.[11] Given the amount of capital, labor, resources, and time needed, capital projects are thus, by definition, strategies of those in power. State-led capital projects may include physical infrastructure like highways and sewage networks and large-scale master-planning initiatives. During the time period under consideration in Doha Aramoun, such interventions were primarily the work of one faction within the Lebanese state—the Sunni Future Movement of Prime Minister Rafic Hariri—and were made possible through foreign aid from Kuwait and Saudi Arabia. Such projects were part of the Lebanese government's spatial management of the increased pressure of urbanization, but they were also part of an attempt to transform Doha Aramoun into an acknowledged "Sunni periphery."

In contrast to the strategies represented by capital projects, filling in the blanks involves the tactics of completing or occupying space that has been left empty. Technically, the choice of how to fill such a void is informed and limited by existing institutional structures. However, *tactics* here does not refer solely to the practices of the weak but also to the practices of those who are not in power at a given moment. In the case of Doha Aramoun, filling in the blanks thus refers to incremental practices of urbanization that have taken place without government assistance. Existing quite apart from Sunni-directed capital projects, these incremental practices have simultaneously led to the transformation of Doha Aramoun into a perceived "Shiite periphery."

I borrow the *filling in the blanks* term from Druze PSP leader Walid Jumblat's geopolitical analysis of how Doha Aramoun has emerged in the last few years as a frontier of urbanization, militarization, and sectarianism. He described this process in a speech to followers at a closed meeting, details of which were subsequently leaked to the media. Seeking to avoid further sectarian violence between Druze and Shiites, Jumblat was attempting to gain support for a strategic realignment with Hezbollah—a realignment that was largely opposed by his followers, who had just fought a war with Hezbollah during which lives were lost, people kidnapped, and towns occupied. However, Jumblat was arguing that a new geography was emerging that the Druze minority needed to contend with:

Demarcation lines still exist . . . but we do not want them to be demarcation lines anymore. There is a mixed way of living between us and the Shiites in Choueifat, Deir Qoubil, and Aramoun. . . . The Shiite reality imposed itself with demography, monies, Iran, Africa. They buy land and *fill in the blanks. Empty spaces are not going to remain blank* [emphasis added].[12]

Within this logic, contrary to the intention of largely public capital projects, the tactics of filling in the blanks involve private initiatives that occur at multiple scales: for example, on the urban level through the construction of parallel private infrastructure networks, on the level of the town through the operation of land sales, on the neighborhood level through minority brokerage, on the apartment level through individual sales and purchases, and on all levels through the circulation of rumors about these geographies.

The strategies of capital projects and the tactics of filling in the blanks are not always distinctively different. Indeed, de Certeau does not hold the two in constant polarity, and neither do I present them here as antithetical. As power dwindles, for example, de Certeau argues that strategies become more like tactics.[13] And in the case of Doha Aramoun, both strategies and tactics are being used by already powerful entities competing to extend their spheres of control. Whether the tools they use look more like strategies or tactics depends on the relative position these actors occupy in relation to each other on the public-private spectrum.

Temporally, these two components of ballooning do, however, envision different futures. The strategies of capital projects rely on a planning logic that assumes a future of predictable urbanization. Indeed, decades-long government initiatives are conceived as providing the infrastructure that renders that future possible. Wars do not feature in this imagined future. As is characteristic of planning practice in general, the future here is always assumed to be one of progress and development, which is likewise imagined to be the common future for all inhabitants. Filling in the blanks, however, deals more tactically with a future that is imagined as contested and unpredictable, where urbanization, contestation, and war warp into each other. The temporality of filling in the blanks is thus fragmented, contained, and ad hoc.

Defined by such juxtapositions, ballooning thus implies constant negotiation within the overlapping logics of urbanization, militarization, and the production of sectarian order. The outcome is an interlaced, nested geography of a thousand frontiers, where wealth and poverty, hope and fear, neighborliness and estrangement, militarization and everyday lives, Sunnis and Shiites, empty and built spaces, beautiful views and environmental degradation, women in bikinis on mixed-gender beaches and bearded men in white coexist—albeit uncomfortably. And as building laws and political alliances change to reflect this contingent reality, the urbanization of Doha Aramoun has evolved as a patchwork of better-off areas with walled-in villas and fancy condos (Figure 24); middle-income, moderately dense areas, like the one my family lives in; and poor, almost slum-like neighborhoods, where many residents lack security of tenure in their apartments (Figure 25).[14]

FIGURE 24. An upscale neighborhood in Doha Aramoun in 2009. Source: Author, 2009.

Capital Projects: Interpolating the State

The image of Doha Aramoun as a space of plurality and coexistence dates back to the 1950s when it was a summer destination for well-off Beirut families. Before the 1950s, Doha Aramoun's largely open lands and forests had been owned by Choueifat's Druze and Christian families. Due to their poor soil quality and distance from centers like Choueifat, however, these lands in Doha Aramoun were initially considered *arḍ būr* (infertile) and of little or even no value for agricultural purposes. In fact, these lands were considered of so little value that local stories abound of Choueifat landowners bequeathing holdings there as punishment to their least-favored sons.[15] However, in 1954, Beirut International Airport opened in adjacent Khalde, and soon emerged as the leading air hub in the Middle East. This changed everything, transforming Doha Aramoun into a potentially profitable area for real estate development.

As Beirut's economy prospered during the 1950s and 1960s, developers sought to profit from investing in the hills around Beirut, which offered a green landscape, moderate climate, and views of the Mediterranean Sea. Seen as a summer retreat for Beirut's wealthy Sunni and Christian families, Doha Aramoun was subsequently developed as part of a parcelization project by CIL (Compagnie Immobilière Libanaise Sal), one of several real estate companies in the business of producing high-end, Western-style suburbs for Beirut's well-off.[16] A few villas testifying to this former status still dot the landscape.[17] For a brief moment, Doha Aramoun flourished, and was even home to a number of local politicians and international ambassadors.

The upheaval caused by the establishment of the state of Israel and the emergence of Palestinian resistance in Lebanon soon translated, however, into local and regional battles that rocked Beirut.[18] And eventually, Lebanon plunged into its fifteen-year civil war in 1975. As war raged in Beirut in the 1980s, many inhabitants of west Beirut, mostly Lebanese and Palestinian Sunnis, sought to escape the fighting by moving and settling in Doha Aramoun.[19] This pace accelerated between 1986 and 1990 when the bombing of west Beirut reached its peak.[20]

This war-induced migration transformed Doha Aramoun's landscape from small, low-lying buildings to tall, concrete ones—a development pattern facilitated by the illegal building practices condoned by the SAF, as mentioned earlier.[21] Starting in 1988, the SAF deployed in the southern suburbs of Beirut, and established a major military position in the Aramoun hills, with smaller posts all over Doha Aramoun.[22] Based in ruined or unfinished buildings, Syrian soldiers were then a constant presence, and became the area's de facto rulers.[23]

Such urbanization trends grew even stronger with the post–civil war reconstruction boom after 1990. At the time, Doha Aramoun's uncontrolled urbanization was seen in a favorable light, because developers were making large profits, especially when they were able to exceed the allowable built-up area. At the same time, Doha Aramoun provided affordable suburban housing for people who were being priced out of municipal Beirut, or who were being forced out by postwar reconstruction projects and changes to rent-control laws. People moving to the area celebrated their ability to afford larger apartments with views of the airport and the Mediterranean Sea. As one measure of how fast things were changing, one 1997 report claimed that 82 percent of Doha Aramoun's residents had lived there for less than ten years, and more than 60 percent of its buildings had been built within the last ten years.[24]

However, the area did not have the existing infrastructure to handle such urban growth—not in terms of sewage and water service, electricity, or roads. Each new building had to provide its own well, septic tank, and ad hoc connection to the road network. Soon this led to streets flooded with sewage, with a smell that was often unbearable. Meanwhile, the road network was fragmented and difficult to navigate. The underlying reality was that whatever infrastructure did exist had been built in the 1950s for a completely different planned future: that of a pristine, wealthy, low-density suburb. Thus, although the earlier parcelization scheme gave the area a spatial order on maps, in reality, driving around Doha Aramoun requires intimate knowledge of a maze of dead-end streets (Figure 26).

This pattern of urbanization went unchecked for more than a decade before the postwar Lebanese government intervened. Rolled out in the mid- to late 1990s, a series of large-scale capital projects were directed at water, sanitation, and

FIGURE 26.
Parcelization map
for Doha Aramoun.
Source: Choueifat
municipality, 2014,
adapted by the author.

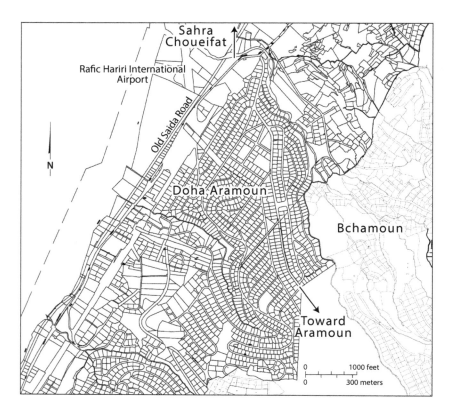

road infrastructure to address problems associated with sudden, uncontrolled urbanization. However, most of these projects were post-factum interventions that attempted to "catch up with Doha Aramoun's unplanned urban development," as one planner told me.

The projects also came hand in hand with what Druze inhabitants commonly refer to as the "Sunnification of the area." Thus, while Doha Aramoun was largely an unplanned periphery, there was nothing natural in the movement of Sunnis to that area. When Rafic Hariri became the Lebanese postwar Prime Minister (and was crowned the "savior of Lebanon"), he simultaneously emerged as the leader of Lebanese Sunnis. And while his national reconstruction policies caused mass evictions from the privileged center of municipal Beirut, he simultaneously launched a political project to expand Sunni west Beirut to more affordable suburban areas. By 1997, 38 percent of Doha Aramoun's residents were from west Beirut.[25] Doha Aramoun (and later, neighboring Bchamoun) thus emerged as a stronghold for Hariri's Future Movement.

The vision of a Sunni Doha Aramoun was not entirely new. On the eve of the civil war in the early 1970s, the Sunni Grand Mufti Hassan Khaled moved to the area.[26] Some speculate that Mufti Khaled had moved out of Beirut to avoid political harassment from the warring Lebanese and Palestinian factions operating in the vicinity of his residence. Whatever the reason, his presence established Doha Aramoun as an important political node and a destination for Sunnis displaced by the Lebanese war.[27] It thus also altered the area's sectarian makeup. Indeed, shortly after Khaled moved to the area, Doha Aramoun received its first mosque. A number of Sunni religious institutions also moved there, including al-Azhar, the al-Bayan Institution for the Blind and the al-Huda School for the Deaf, and the al-Tarbiyah Institution for the physically challenged.[28] At the time, the pristine, "uncorrupted" terrain of Aramoun was seen as an alternative to the polluted, urbanized, and war-torn neighborhoods of Beirut. For example, in 1978, Social Welfare Institutions, the predecessor of Dar al-Aytam al-Islamiya, a major Sunni welfare institution, was already thinking of building in Aramoun. This included a proposal (with a detailed program and budget) for a "social town," "to counter the ills of the country."[29] These institutions eventually became the backbone for the Future Movement's social infrastructure (such as clinics and schools) and supplemented government spending on capital projects in the area.

Consolidating Doha Aramoun as a Sunni suburb and a stronghold for the Future Movement required massive investments in the area's infrastructure, especially as the ballooning of Beirut toward Doha Aramoun had driven the area's existing infrastructure capacity to the brink. Moreover, Doha Aramoun is also once removed from the city geographically, with al-Dahiya separating it from west Beirut. This had made it an unlikely destination for Sunni families whose lives were strongly tied to municipal Beirut, and the project of bringing it closer to the city required a network of new highways and upgraded infrastructure. At the time, investment on this scale was within the realm of possibility for the Future Movement, which largely controlled the Lebanese government. In particular, the Future Movement controlled government spending on such capital projects, through the Council for Development and Reconstruction (CDR). There is no doubt that the area's infrastructure needed upgrading. But as one municipal official told me, with this level of spending, "Rafic Hariri sealed the area of Doha Aramoun as a periphery for Beirut's Sunnis."

As a consequence of these infrastructure projects, by 2000, a common refrain among people living in the area was that "Doha Aramoun is the New Tariq el Jdidi." The reference was to a hardcore Sunni area of Beirut known for its support for the Future Movement and for the Hariri family. Indeed, although many of the middle- and low-income families who moved to Doha Aramoun from Beirut after the end of the war mentioned the presence there of "trees and fresh air" that had been lacking in their former crowded neighborhoods, the underlying reality was a shared vision of the area as an emerging periphery of Sunni west Beirut.

This could be readily observed by the time of the 2009 Lebanese parliamentary elections and the 2010 municipal elections, when most of the posters, flyers, and campaigners in Doha Aramoun's streets were for municipal Beirut candidates.[30]

Overlaying a Physical Infrastructure

Two state capital interventions—physical infrastructure provision and the National Physical Master Plan—were ultimately critical to the urban growth of Doha Aramoun as a Sunni periphery. Capital projects, expensive large-scale public works, are usually assumed to benefit an entire city or to span several geographic areas. However, in Doha Aramoun, the construction of local water and sewage networks—tasks that might normally have been the responsibility of the local municipality—were paid for with national funds and international aid facilitated by the Hariri government.

Designating the work as a capital project allowed the CDR to fund it via a basket of foreign aid and loans from Arab and other international donors who were pushing Hariri's political agenda at the time. This also meant that the project did not need to tap into money from the municipality of Choueifat, despite the fact that the municipality derives revenue from taxpayers in Doha Aramoun.[31] I heard on several occasions that the municipality—whose representatives are mostly Druze and Christian—was pleased not to have to spend money on Doha Aramoun. Central government funding also meant that the projects did not have to go through the bureaucratic grinder of municipal approval. Instead, the infrastructure upgrade projects arrived as if by parachute, as the result of state "development" intervention for an area deemed "in need."

As a result of these initiatives, however, residents of Doha Aramoun inhabited a construction site between 1993 and 2002. The CDR first commissioned telephone and electricity services in 1993 and then road upgrades and storm drainage work in 1996.[32] More recently, a partial sewage system was also installed via a CDR capital project, which reduced overflows in certain better-off parts of town. However, as is frequently the case in Lebanon, these public projects were not coordinated. Residents watched as roads were dug up and then patched, only to be dug up again before the work was finally completed in 2002.[33] And despite all this disruption, the area still does not have water infrastructure; my family's apartment, for example, continues to be supplied from a rooftop container filled by pumping brackish water up ten floors from a thirty-year-old well. Twenty-five years after we moved in, we still have undrinkable water in our faucets and must buy drinking water separately. Moreover, the water often runs out because the building's water system depends on the availability of electricity in a country where power outages are common.

According to planning officials at the CDR and the Directorate General of Urbanism (DGU), Doha Aramoun was extraordinarily challenging and expensive to provide with infrastructure because its urbanization did not follow "any logic." As Mr. Mohamad Fawaz, the former head of the DGU, told me: "This area is so haphazard that it posed a major challenge to engineering and planning brains. How to provide sewage to an area where each developer subdivided land *ʿalā zawqu* [each to his taste or benefit]?"[34] A solution was eventually devised, and reaching for some paper, he drew it for me: two straight lines at an angle, and then small lines connecting the different building lots to the two main lines. He then looked up and said: "This was our engineering solution. Not a network in the real sense of an infrastructure network. We provided two main sewage lines along the two main roads of Doha Aramoun, and then each building or group of buildings connected independently to these two main lines. This after-the-fact planning project was a waste of the government's money." From his point of view, investing in such a fragmented system was also significantly costlier than it would have been had the DGU been able simply to build a new system from scratch before the area was urbanized.

The transformation of Doha Aramoun into a not-so-distant periphery of west Beirut was solidified in 2002 with the opening of the two-by-two-lane, high-speed Beirut-Saida Highway linking Beirut to South Lebanon. This project was also paid for with aid money—in the form of a loan from the Arab Fund for Economic and Social Development (AFESD) and a grant from the Kuwaiti Fund for Arab Economic Development.[35] Construction of this highway had two aims: to link the town of Saida in the south with Beirut, and to provide direct access from Beirut to second-tier peripheries like Doha Aramoun and Bchamoun. Usually, large-scale public projects are slow to materialize, but this project was completed in two years. The break came when Prime Minister Hariri decided to reroute it to the east of the airport, and away from the Ouzaii informal settlement, where it was contested. After many years of political and communal resistance led by Hezbollah and Haraket Amal, its construction was thereafter fast tracked.[36]

As rumor has it (and as one high-ranking public official I interviewed told me), as Hariri's private jet was taking off from the airport one day, he looked down, pointed his finger, and told his aides: "The highway is going to pass right there; now you go figure it out." According to Mona Harb, the highway "visually and physically bypass[ed] the suburb."[37] And though it bypassed al-Dahiya, it created a new ring of "Sunni suburbs" for middle-class families looking for affordable housing near Beirut.[38]

Needless to say, the highway was critical to the ballooning of Beirut to the south. Whereas in 1995 it took my family at least an hour to reach Beirut (on rainy days, it sometimes took two to three hours), by 2002, it took only about twenty minutes to drive from Doha Aramoun to downtown Beirut. However, nowadays, fifteen years later, the ongoing expansion of Beirut and al-Dahiya toward Doha Aramoun and its vicinity has exceeded even the capacity of this new highway. Currently a trip to Beirut during a weekday may take up to an hour and a half.

Targeting Development Funds through the NPMP

As aid and government monies were being pumped into building sewage and road networks in Doha Aramoun, another capital project was in the making: the National Physical Master Plan for the Lebanese Territory (NPMP). This effort to reorganize the entirety of Lebanese national territory was also initiated and supervised by the CDR. However, the research and proposal for the NPMP was the work of a joint venture between Dar al-Handasah, a private Lebanese urban planning firm, and the French planning firm IAURIF (Institut d'Aménagement et d'Urbanisme de la Région Île-de-France).[39]

At the time I was engaged in archival research at the CDR in 2010, the agency's planning unit was actively distributing glossy books with colorful maps that provided an overview in Arabic, English, and French of the newly approved NPMP. Although the books were being freshly distributed, the NPMP had actually been finalized in 2005. However, it had not been approved until 2009.[40] Reasons for the delay had included the assassination of Hariri in 2005, the July 2006 Israeli war on Lebanon, and the sectarian clashes of May 7, 2008. Nonetheless, the mere approval of a national master plan, more than fifteen years after the end of the war, after several failed attempts, was viewed as a tremendous accomplishment. It thus generated excitement in the planning community, and was accompanied by discussion forums in universities and research centers.[41]

The NPMP mainly focuses on land use. Nonetheless, the booklet describing it expresses the hope (at least among those who produced it) that the ordering of space could address or resolve social crises—namely, sectarian strife and the country's uneven geography of wealth and poverty. Specifically, the NPMP's final report states that "*land use planning*" should "*promote the unity* of the country, economy, society, and territory"; "*alleviate discrepancies of development* between regions, but in the framework of a new, objective and modern conception of *balanced development principle*"; and "*look for a rational use* of the country's limited resources" (emphasis added).[42] This view that a physical plan might be able to correct social issues is not new. It reflects a resurfacing of the deterministic modernist belief that the physical reordering of space could, by definition, bring social change.[43] But just how might the NPMP's ideals of unity, spatial justice, and balanced development be translated onto a map?

One detailed aspect of the NPMP was particularly surprising to me. This was that it names Aramoun and its vicinities—including Doha Aramoun and the Druze part of Choueifat (explicitly excluding Shiite Sahra Choueifat and Hayy el-Selloum)[44]—as one of three new and national target areas for imminent development.[45] The report thus joins these areas conceptually to three already existing national development projects: Solidere for Beirut's downtown, Elyssar for Beirut's immediate southern suburbs, and Linord for its northern suburbs. Interestingly, the NPMP refers to Aramoun and its vicinities as the "southern terraces of Beirut," and it identifies them as being located in the District of Aley, which is commonly understood to be under the control of Druze religious-political organizations.

The report then focuses on physical solutions to problems related to the development of the Aramoun target area. Among these problems, it calls out property, infrastructure, and building law as targets for reform:

This area seems to be an obligatory extension area for the agglomeration of Beirut towards the South. It is important to equip this area with adequate road network and infrastructures, allowing a *coherent urban planning*, which is not currently the case, due to the configuration of the authorized housing estates, the lack of infrastructures, the illegal connections to the highway, etc. . . . All of this requires *land consolidation, infrastructure funding and construction regulation* [emphasis added].[46]

I became curious about the process that had led to highlighting the previously mundane periphery of Aramoun as a priority for state development funding by calling it out with a thick red line on the final map (Figure 27). In the larger picture, Aramoun did not seem that different from other fast-urbanizing areas around Beirut, such al-Hadath, Kfarshima, and Hazmiyeh. What made it stand out? And when I searched through the NPMP, other than the paragraph quoted above, I could find little explanation for putting this area at the forefront of government attention. In fact, in its entire 227 pages, the NPMP mentions Aramoun only twice.

A further curiosity was that in the early version that I retrieved from the CDR's archive, Aramoun was not identified as central to the NPMP's vision. Instead, it was highlighted in yellow and tagged only as a potential zone for urban development (Figure 27). Conversely, no other areas were highlighted in that manner, and so, in effect, it represented a category of its own. What this meant was that just two years earlier, the area had clearly been identified as an exception but no specific plan had yet been worked out for it.[47] This most likely indicated a political struggle over how to address the inclusion of Beirut's southern peripheries beyond al-Dahiya. It also showed the presence of a desire to inject funding into up-and-coming Sunni areas with remaining Druze constituencies.

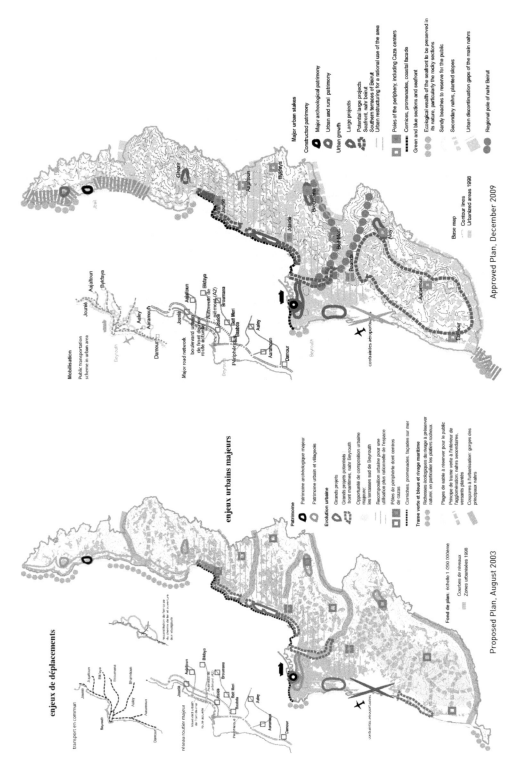

FIGURE 27. The National Physical Master Plan. Left: The proposed plan, showing Aramoun as a "major urban design opportunity: the south terraces of Beirut." Source: Council for Development and Reconstruction, National Physical Master Plan of the Lebanese Territory, Proposal Phase, 2003. Right: The final plan, showing Aramoun circled as a "potential large project." Source: Council for Development and Reconstruction, National Physical Master Plan of the Lebanese Territory, Final Report, 2009.

As I was to discover, the operative logic here was sectarian *balanced development*. This was perhaps best explained to me during one of my interviews with a high-level planning and political official in 2010. "You know very well why [the area is included]," he said. "This is the planning process of *baydat al-qabbān* [planning by touchstones]." This same logic was reiterated to me more recently, in 2016, by a CDR official as an indication of how planning "is done." According to this logic, then Prime Minister Hariri was seeking to inject more government funding into Doha Aramoun as a destination for Sunnis, but he wanted to make sure that the other major sectarian communities were benefiting too. Hence "planning by touchstones," which meant providing each main sect with a major urban development project in Beirut's peripheries. Thus (aside from the Solidere project in Beirut's central financial district), the government proposed to invest in the Elyssar project in the Shiite southern peripheries of Beirut, in the Linord project and its proposed extension in Beirut's Christian northern peripheries, and now, in a project in the "southern terraces of Beirut," as a Sunni emerging area with a Druze base.

Such a divided planning strategy is not new in Lebanon. Eric Verdeil, for example, discusses how the 1986 master plan, also prepared by IAURIF, "was criticized for its implicit acceptance of the political de facto order of the war," and so created "regional centers that matched with the militia in each"[48] (Figure 28). No doubt, a major effort went into preparing the 2009 NPMP and getting it approved within the entanglements of the Lebanese political system. But it seems to have been driven *in times of peace* by the same strategies that had shaped the 1986 master plan *in times of war*. Thus, while the 2009 NPMP's goals were to promote unity, spatial justice, and balanced development through rationalization of resources and modernization of planning,[49] in effect the plan has boiled down to an exercise in dividing up development funding between the country's major sectarian groups, reproducing a segregated sectarian geography.[50]

In Doha Aramoun, the NPMP has represented yet another capital project through which the Future Movement was able to interpolate the state into the urbanization of the area and reinforce a sectarian approach to the organization of its territory. However, this did not go unnoticed by rival political groups. Unhappy with the dominance of the Future Movement in the NPMP through the CDR, Hezbollah heavily criticized the end product as a lopsided exercise in physical planning, which did not take social issues into account. Hezbollah also indirectly accused the CDR of using government resources to benefit Beirut and Tripoli, commonly seen as predominantly Sunni cities. Such critiques have since rendered the NPMP simultaneously a tool of pacification and conflict, development and neglect, environmental protection and sectarian segregation, inclusion

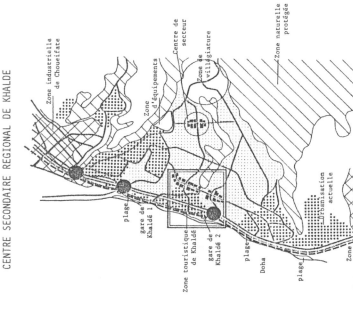

FIGURE 28. Left: The 1986 IAURIF Master Plan for Beirut and its peripheries, showing the proposed four regional centers, which coincided with the militias' geographies in the 1980s. Source: Cahiers de l'IAURIF, "Liban: Retour sur Expérience," no. 144, 2006. Right: A close-up of the proposed Khalde Regional Center. Doha Aramoun and vicinities are designated as "protected natural landscape." Source: Projet de Schéma Directeur d'Aménagement et d'Urbanisme de la Région Métropolitaine de Beyrouth/Mission Franco-Libanaise d'Étude et d'Aménagement de la Région de Beyrouth, 1986.

and exclusion—so that in itself it has become a site of contestation over different imagined futures for the built environment.

Overlaying a Social Infrastructure

The role of the state in ballooning west Beirut toward Doha Aramoun was accentuated by the Future Movement's provision of social services in the area. These were paid for by an assortment of NGOs associated with the Hariri Foundation, and were intended to ease the transition for Sunnis coming from west Beirut to Doha Aramoun and neighboring areas.[51] Such social service provision was in many ways a reinvigoration of Sunni welfare institutions established in the area in 1978 and 1980, which I have previously described. For example, in 1999, the Hariri Foundation opened a nonprofit health clinic on Doha Aramoun's main road. Part of a forty-clinic Health Directory initiative that the foundation was engaged in across Lebanon, it was intended to serve low- and lower-middle-income families.[52] This was followed in 2000 by the founding and funding of the Nazek Hariri Center for Human Development. Named for the wife of the Prime Minister, this was an orphanage and health center that provided support for physically and mentally challenged people.[53]

The Future Movement, through the Hariri Foundation, also invested in institutions aimed directly at attracting middle-class Sunnis to Aramoun and neighboring areas. For example, Aramoun was to be the location of Hariri V, a prestigious, 23,000-square-meter school compound. This project, proposed by the Hariri Foundation, was slated to open in 2005, but its progress was halted in 2003 for financial reasons.[54] This delay also reflected the emergence of larger crises and contestations in Lebanon at the time, which were being strongly felt in peripheries such as Aramoun, as these areas transitioned into contested sectarian frontiers.

Filling in the Blanks: Between Neighborliness and Militarization

The transformation of Doha Aramoun to a sectarian frontier started in 2000 with a new wave of migration spearheaded by middle-income Shiites searching for affordable housing outside crowded al-Dahiya. This demand spurred another massive surge in construction in the area, which had also become more desirable once the Hariri-led capital projects had made it more accessible and had upgraded environmental conditions there. The arrival of Shiites in Doha Aramoun was facilitated by a variety of tactics that can together be described as filling in the blanks. In contrast to the top-down projects of the Sunni Future Movement, this mode of urbanization was largely formed though individual real estate purchases—both for land development and individual residences. These incremental tactics greatly contributed to Doha Aramoun's ballooning.

Initially, this new building boom was cast as a "natural" result of suburbanization. At the time, Doha Aramoun was celebrated for being a relatively affordable suburb of Beirut with a diverse makeup, and originally, sectarian difference was not regarded as a critical issue among Lebanese Muslims. That changed with the assassination of Rafic Hariri in 2005, which charged the political atmosphere, as fingers were pointed at the Syrian regime and its Lebanese ally, Hezbollah. Eventually, the political turmoil recast the Shiite influx as a direct challenge to Sunni hegemony in the area. This contestation culminated locally in the sectarian clashes of May 2008.[55] As street battles erupted in the area, bringing death and displacement, the local Druze minority and the Sunnis felt their territories were under threat of being taken over by Hezbollah and its allies.

Since Doha Aramoun and Khalde are crossroads critical to the control of Beirut and its peripheries, these areas saw some of the heaviest fighting in 2008. Each group had its own strategic concerns. For Hezbollah, control of the Khalde intersection is important both to defend against a future Israeli invasion of Beirut and to maintain a protected passage between Hezbollah strongholds in al-Dahiya, southern Lebanon, and the Beqaa Valley. Sunni groups, meanwhile, want to keep the connection open between their strongholds in Beirut and Saida (also in southern Lebanon). And for the PSP, retaining a foothold on the coast and access to the airport are issues of military survival, because both locations are key to maintaining access to supplies of weapons.

However, what became even more apparent with regard to the urbanizing logic of filling in the blanks was how space was allegedly used during the 2008 clashes. In particular, rumors circulated about the double functioning of the built environment in Doha Aramoun as a paramilitary infrastructure. Thus, it was alleged that Hezbollah affiliates had bought apartments in strategic locations around Doha Aramoun expecting a war to come, that these individual apartments had become sniper positions, and that these apartments were also networked in a paramilitary geography that allowed Hezbollah and its allies to dominate the battlefield. Nowadays, people from both sides assume that the landscape of individualized housing in times of peace will be aggregated according to sectarian affiliation in the coming times of war. Now that the window of any apartment may be conceived both as a window and a sniper position, the previous binary between housing and militarized space has been collapsed.

The sectarian clashes also brought a new geographic reality to Doha Aramoun, as demarcation lines drawn during that battle continue to be enforced to this day, almost a decade later. More significantly, the clashes crystallized the fear of the sectarian other, and this fear is now often conflated with or articulated as an anxiety over urban development. For example, in a 2012 newspaper article titled

"Doha Aramoun: A Concrete Jungle over the Remains of a River," author Ahmad Mohsen lamented the loss of the mostly natural landscapes the name Doha Aramoun used to evoke—the sea, airport, forest, and river.[56] And he described the current area as a place where people live in ghetto-like conditions, worried about poor building quality, while segregation and discrimination expand over both new and old neighborhoods like an "oil spill." Mohsen further consolidated and articulated fears of urbanization as sectarian ghettoization:

Construction is adulterated. Building happens overnight. Aramoun is not a city. Aramoun was originally a stronghold for wild animals. Suddenly, its development skyrocketed, and cement ate its forests in a light flash. Residents are afraid of two things: the fragility of its overnight construction and its acute demographic segregation.[57]

Mohsen's tense language highlights the way 2008 ushered in a new form of war, in which real estate transactions are intrinsically bound up with military speculation. War may thus be fought over land and apartment sales and through circulating rumors about housing projects that double as military posts. Doha Aramoun's urban growth since 2008 has thus been conditioned by a climate of fear and suspicion toward the sectarian other—Shiites, in particular. Talk of war now reverberates through living rooms, gyms, and grocery stores—and across dinner tables. And people have become acutely vigilant about the identity of anyone buying land in Doha Aramoun and intensely curious about the religious affiliation of their neighbors. In such conditions, seemingly everyday confrontations—a parking dispute, neighbors bickering, a flag parade, personal relationships—may now erupt into violence.[58]

Such changes may be of particular concern for Lebanon's Druze minority. Reflecting on the process of urbanization that set the stage for the 2008 clashes, Jumblat has explained (at the 2009 meeting described earlier) how the urban logic of filling in the blanks represents a local manifestation of a larger Sunni-Shiite war raging in the Middle East. This is being funded by global financial networks of politically motivated aid from such places as Iran, Africa, Saudi Arabia, and Qatar. He thus has identified Doha Aramoun as a frontier in a transnationally contested geography, which the Druze minority must now contend with. As he stated:

In this coastal area, there is a competition between the Sunnis and the Shiites. These are now Sunni and Shiite areas. We have to live with the Shiites. . . . Tell me what I could do . . . ? I am ready to buy land, but in some areas, their spaces and our spaces have become *overlapped and nested. We are the ones who sold our land* [emphasis added].[59]

Jumblat thus emphasized how land sales were a culprit in this changing geography. Indeed, it has frequently been Druze landowners and PSP officials who have facilitated many of the moves made in this contest. As in Sahra Choueifat, Druze landowners in Doha Aramoun have sold their land and enriched themselves as the ballooning of Beirut and al-Dahiya has made prices irresistible. Before 2008, land sales were considered to be mundane transactions without political significance. But now residents see how land sales may be mapped into a new paramilitary geographic reality.[60] Thus, even though, as the historical population of the area, the Druze retain control of its municipal government and services, the area's rapid urbanization has made them a minority in their own "hometown."[61]

It is in such contested, nested space, Jumblat further explained, that the PSP and the Druze should seek peace, not war. From the minority Druze point of view, it is a matter of self-preservation, since "any war with the Shiites is without a future/ horizon."[62] Moreover, it was largely because the Future Movement and the PSP were unable to secure weapons from international allies like the United States that they lost militarily in 2008. Jumblat has also tried to quell his supporters' anxiety about the Shiite other by positing the new figure of the radical Sunni ISIS (Islamic State in Iraq and Syria) sympathizer as the real danger. Nevertheless, the Druze minority have become increasingly vigilant about the manner in which the urban process of filling in the blanks is reshaping their built environment. And the result has been a subtle process of contestation and confrontation, as each group has sought to use real estate markets and selective infrastructure development to advance its position, producing an intertwined geography of urban growth and fear, development and war, and neighborliness and militarization.

A Parallel Infrastructure: Hezbollah's Telecom Network

On October 8, 2011, the newspaper *Al Joumhouria* reported the PSP's dismay with some Hezbollah-related infrastructure construction in Aramoun, including in Doha Aramoun. This was an important development because the PSP and Hezbollah had avoided any public expressions of discord since Jumblat's announcement of the strategic Druze political realignment in 2009.

The newspaper claimed that "the security meeting between the PSP and Hezbollah in Khalde was to voice the PSP's rejection of Hezbollah's excavations in and around Aramoun that aim to install a telecommunication infrastructure network in Aramoun and its surrounding areas." It then quoted one PSP official as asking: "Aramoun is neither Aita ash-Shaab nor Maroun el-Ras, and therefore what interest does the resistance [i.e., Hezbollah] have in Aramoun and its vicinities?"[63] Aita ash-Shaab and Maroun el-Ras are villages on the Israeli border with southern Lebanon, which were under Israeli occupation until 2000 and were key sites of resistance during Israeli's July 2006 war on Lebanon. What the PSP official was suggesting was that while a Hezbollah telecom infrastructure might make sense on the militarized border with Israel, it was not clear why it was justified in the more mundane geography of Aramoun and its surroundings.

Again, this debate is not new. As I mentioned in a previous chapter, the May 2008 battles were sparked by questions over Hezbollah's parallel telecom infrastructure near the airport. At the time, Hezbollah had claimed that this infrastructure was necessary to its ability to fight future wars with Israel, and that it had fought battles in Beirut and its peripheries against the PSP and the Future Movement to protect it. By contrast, the intervention of Hariri and the Future Movement in the urbanization of Doha Aramoun had been welcomed by the area's Druze residents, many of whom told me the "Sunni presence" was not alarming. Indeed, the construction of the Shiite figure as a threat, and the militarization of Hezbollah in general, are key to understanding why Hezbollah's infrastructure, but not the Future Movement's, was deemed illegal, provocative, and a precursor for war.

However, there are two additional reasons for the difference of views regarding infrastructure provision by Sunni and by Shiite religious-political organizations. The first is reflected in the fact that the Druze residents, officials, and journalists I spoke to used a discourse around service provision to justify their views. Thus, the Future Movement's interventions, on the one hand, are seen as investments in the well-being of the organization's supporters that also benefit other groups, including the local Druze and Shiite communities. Hezbollah's interventions, on the other hand, are seen as an encroachment because they produce an infrastructure of war that will not benefit other groups. Once, in response to an inquiry on this subject, a middle-aged Druze man who frequented the municipality looked at me suspiciously. "You know what?" he said. "At least Hariri installed infrastructure for his people when they started coming to Doha Aramoun—not like Sahra Choueifat that is a burden on the municipality." His comment referred to widespread feelings that Hariri had paid for his geopolitical project, while Hezbollah was placing the burden of "Hezbollah's people" on local taxpayers.

This view also has much to do with a perceived distinction between formal and informal development. In Doha Aramoun, the Future Movement's intervention has always been seen as formal, with an aim of development, because it largely came through public agencies like the CDR, which made its spatial practices seem legitimate and rational. On the other hand, Hezbollah's interventions are seen as informal because they happen outside the state. The fact that Hezbollah helped, for example, to provide water and power infrastructure in Sahra Choueifat mostly went unregistered in these discourses. This highlights how, in a contested geography, what may be seen as official or formal (versus unofficial and informal) may be largely a function of power relations at the time.

The second reason for the different view with regard to investments by Hezbollah and the Future Movement can be traced to the multiple scales that each entity considers when it envisions future wars. It was clear that Hezbollah's disputed network in the Aramoun area was intended to prepare that area for a paramilitary role in future local and regional wars. Telecom and radio are key to waging any war—in a way that a sewage network, for example, might never be. Taken this way, Hezbollah's network might make sense on the scale of the regional Arab-Israeli conflict. But on the local scale, this infrastructure was seen as a threat, because it passed through areas the PSP considered to be its territory. The May 2008 events had also shown that such paramilitary infrastructures might be mobilized in local conflicts.

Mining for Land Sales Gold: The Figure of the Real Estate Broker

At the heart of these debates on where and how infrastructure networks pass is a debate about property ownership. In fact, Hezbollah's domination of Doha Aramoun in 2008 was largely blamed on real estate transactions that facilitated Shiite geopolitical tactics of filling in the blanks. Not all involved parties see the pattern of real estate transactions in Doha Aramoun in the same light, however.

In this kind of research, interviewing real estate brokers or developers is a difficult, often unsuccessful, endeavor. Thus, like most brokers around Doha Aramoun and Choueifat, Mr. L avoided journalists and researchers, and he was suspicious of me. However, a common friend and PSP affiliate had called him, given him a synopsis of my work, and asked him to meet with me. Nevertheless, when I attempted to contact him, he did not answer his door or any of his phones for two days. Despite his initially positive response, he was clearly trying to avoid me.

I had learned about Mr. L's relevance to my research during a family dinner. When I described my study, I was told that my research about Doha Aramoun would not be complete until I met with the "commander-in-chief of land sales" in the area. After several attempts and some family pressure, he finally agreed to meet with me. The friend in common who introduced us told me that Mr. L feared that I was really a rival who had chosen to disguise herself to find out more about his deals. Apparently, Doha Aramoun was "a zone of real estate warfare," as one historian and long-time resident of the area put it, and Mr. L was worried other brokers would steal his deals.

Mr. L finally met me in his office in a recently constructed building in Khalde along the Beirut-Saida highway. He owned the building, and his office had shiny marble floors, big leather seats with intricate brown woodwork, and a display vitrine. This was the space of an upscale realtor. But it also did not feel like a working space. A cigarette in one hand, his neck, arms, and fingers ornamented with gold bracelets and rings, Mr. L displayed his wealth on his body. The lavishness of his office and his jewelry suggested a person who made large sums of money.

Needless to say, Mr. L was a controversial figure. He was from a Druze family, but because he had worked for so long at finding buyers for Druze and Christian land in the Choueifat–Doha Aramoun area, many people in the Druze community, and even in his own family, described him as a "disgrace." One of his relatives angrily said, "His money is *māl ḥarām* [immoral money]." According to this same relative, the PSP had tried to approach him on several occasions, asking him to "change his business practices, but to no avail. He only cares about profit."

I came into his office with lots of questions about how real estate markets operated in the area. But Mr. L had a different plan. He had prepared points for our meeting, which he asked me to write down so that I could better "understand" his work and "learn" from him. Mr. L started by explaining that what he did was a form of sales and trading. "I have connections with both owners of capital and landowners. I am a middleman who helps owners of capital find land for their investment, and landowners find buyers for their land. This is my trade." This way of explaining his job aimed at depoliticizing it, making it seem to involve only "marrying" capital and land, buyers and sellers.

He then moved on to explain how the global financial meltdown had had a positive impact on the real estate market in Lebanon. This could be seen in an increase in capital inflows and real estate investment. Increased demand had in turn led to a boost in land prices, particularly for properties with access to infrastructure and highways. In Doha Aramoun, specifically, the boom had been accompanied by a change in the building law, which now allowed a greater floor-area ratio and building height. This had resulted in an even bigger rise in land prices, which had made the area even more lucrative for investors. In answering my question as to whether this logic applied to areas like Doha Aramoun and Sahra Choueifat alike, Mr. L told me he was mostly concerned with Doha Aramoun. As for Sahra Choueifat, he said, "I do not do business in such areas." Clearly, he was signaling that there were deals that were worth his time and others that were not. Doha Aramoun was worth it; Sahra Choueifat, as a low-income area, was of no interest to him.

Thirty minutes into his monologue, I managed to ask one of the more sensitive questions from my list: What political considerations shaped the real estate market of Doha Aramoun? He confidently replied: "The market is not affected by religion or sectarian dividing lines. This is a diverse, mixed area." Mr. L then went on to explain that his business was based on the "mixed" nature of the area, and therefore the sectarian identity of land buyers was irrelevant to him and to the market that he both constructed and operated. He was firm in his answer and signaled to me that he did not want to discuss the question further. The interview dynamics soon shifted, however, when a person who works with Mr. L walked into his office. The conversation I was then party to went like this:

Mr. L: Sit down and let's have a cup of coffee. I am done with my meeting [*pointing to me*].

Person: No, I cannot, Abu Tony is waiting for me in the car.

Mr. L: What's his story? Did you manage to convince him to finally sell his land? We need to close this sale soon. The *hajj* is waiting for us.

Person: He has been reluctant.

Mr. L: Okay, we need a plan. How about we do this: tell him that I am leaving for Brazil in two days, and that I am going to stay there for a long time, maybe a month or two. If he does not close the deal before I leave, he will then have to wait for two months, and he might lose the sale since the *hajj* might buy somewhere else.

Person: Good plan. I think this will make him close the deal by tomorrow.

Later, as I considered this conversation, I realized it might be a fairly typical one for a real estate broker; such assertive sales techniques might be a legitimate way of doing business. However, what rang a bell for me were the names of the seller and the buyer—the reluctant landowner, Abu Tony, and the buyer, the *hajj*. From what I knew about names, Abu Tony was most likely a Christian who was still holding onto his land in the Doha Aramoun–Choueifat area. *Hajj*, by contrast, was a term designating a Muslim who had fulfilled his religious duty by making a pilgrimage to Mecca. The buyer was certainly, therefore, either a Shiite or a Sunni developer. The fact that Mr. L was eager to close this deal (and others like it) positioned him, as it did other real estate brokers in the area, at the center of a heated debate on the changing demography of the area—shifting, in this case, from its traditional Druze and (remaining) Christian makeup to a new population consisting of Sunnis and Shiites. This deal also clearly positioned Mr. L as a controversial figure with regard to the PSP, whose leader, Walid Jumblat, had been calling (whether openly before August 2009 or behind closed doors since then) for a halt to sales of land by Christians and Druze in the Doha Aramoun–Choueifat area.

While I was astonished by what I had heard, the two men conducted their conversation as if it were any other mundane business exchange. That Abu Tony was a Christian landowner who seemed reluctant to sell; that the *hajj* had the means to buy land anywhere, anytime, from anybody in Doha Aramoun; and more importantly, that Mr. L could use "scare" techniques against landowners like Abu Tony by threatening to deprive them of sales opportunities—all these things seemed irrelevant to Mr. L's practice. The conversation didn't even warrant an effort by Mr. L to censor himself in my presence, even after he had lectured me on how the marrying of capital and land was an objective, apolitical business. The spatial practices of Mr. L show how markets, fear, and sectarianism are mutually constituted in shaping these frontier geographies.

While some residents, politicians, and developers may view figures like Mr. L as key to the functionality of a market, allowing the development and sale of housing in the area, others—especially concerned Druze families—see such figures as "money-making devils" who are displacing them from traditional Druze territories by inflating real estate values. Along with other realtors, figures like Mr. L are seen as key facilitators of the "takeover" of these areas by organizations like Hezbollah. And these discourses are now becoming increasingly public, after having been long only whispered behind closed doors. News articles on the topic are also becoming more common, under headlines such as "Suspicious Land Sales and Housing Projects, the Residents Mobilize . . . Will Aramoun Sink in Hezbollah's Tsunami?" That particular piece, published in several forums, claimed that "[a]ccording to a number of observers, the recent months witnessed record numbers of land sales in and around Aramoun. Realtors played a negative role in persuading people and luring them by doubling the prices and exploiting their poverty and their need for money."[64]

Mr. L was probably quite aware of the discourses and controversies surrounding his business, but he was happily mining for gold in a hot market. It was in his self-interest to believe and make-believe that the market was mostly driven by the need for urban development and profit. Likewise, it was convenient to ignore the ways these practices intersected with the spatiality of fear, domination, discrimination, and minority politics—a process he contributed to on a daily basis.

The role of real estate brokers has been noted in relation to other contested geographies. In American cities, the practices of blockbusting and panic peddling (from the 1950s to the 1970s)—in which brokers encouraged white owners to list their homes for sale by exploiting fears of racial change—have been well documented.[65] So has the role that real estate brokers played in the transfer of land ownership from Palestinian farmers to incoming Jewish migrants before the formation of the state of Israel in 1948.[66]

While some parallels certainly exist, the case of real estate brokers in Beirut, however, is different. Both the American and Israeli cases display particular spatial-temporal contexts within which the image of the profiteering devil was established and linked to discrimination, segregation, and expulsion in relation to a clear ethnic or racial majority operating within an ethnocratic regime or ideology. However, in the highly calibrated sectarian system in Lebanon, it is difficult to clearly categorize the role that real estate brokers play in rearranging territories. Nonetheless, this case adds to the attempt to do that by bringing further attention to the pivotal role that such brokers play in the transformations of politically contested geographies.

Arbitrating Minority Geographies: The Municipality as Broker

Despite the controversy around individual agents, brokerage, as a spatial practice, may be the only leverage minorities have in shaping the geographies where they live. As a result, the Druze-dominated municipality has arguably also come to play this role. As one PSP-affiliated friend asked: "What ought a minority group do when stuck between two warring factions, each supported by whales of capital, with outstanding capacities to shape urban growth and politics?" His question intrigued me. I had never thought of my work in terms of understanding a minority geography. But having conducted research in the Choueifat municipality since 2004, I had indeed witnessed a shift in rhetoric and action over time (specifically, pre- and post-2008), and across space (specifically, between such areas as Sahra Choueifat and Doha Aramoun). Mr. K, a prominent municipal engineer, embodied this transition.

When I began my fieldwork in the municipality, researching zoning in Sahra Choueifat in 2004 and 2005, Mr. K rarely acknowledged my presence. He agreed to briefly speak to me only once, at which time he told me that the work his office did was purely "technical," involving building permits, quality control, and infrastructure provision. By defining his work in this way, Mr. K was able to avoid political questions surrounding municipal practices.[67] Back then, however, violence was not yet part of the landscape.

Mr. K's approach toward me underwent a drastic shift in the 2009 to 2010 period, however. At this later time, whenever Mr. K saw me in the municipality, he insisted on chatting about my work. Indeed, he acted as though he had nothing to lose or hide anymore, and he often let me know that I could request whatever documents I needed from him or ask him any questions.

One morning in February 2010, I passed by his office to ask his permission to look at a sample of building permits in Sahra Choueifat—a request that would have been impossible in 2004. While I was there, his office phone rang, and I heard his side of the ensuing conversation: "I am so glad you finally called us back, Hajj B [a well-known Sunni family name]," he said. "I have been trying to reach you for several days now." He continued, "You know *Estez* W's villa in Doha Aramoun? He wants to sell it. He is moving permanently out of there. We asked him to wait before putting up a for sale sign. We wanted to ask you if you are interested in buying it. It will make a perfect piece of land for development. You know we don't want the development to go *la-mīn mā kān* [to a random person]." In the political talk of Doha Aramoun, this meant that municipal personnel preferred that a Sunni, not a Shiite, developer buy the property.

I was surprised? to hear that Mr. W's villa was up for sale. Mr. W, a prominent Druze lawyer, had been my family's neighbor since we first moved to Doha Aramoun, and his was one of two remaining villas in our neighborhood. Why was he moving, I wondered? However, something else was striking about this revelation. It was during that phone conversation, when a municipal figure was trying to find a "suitable Sunni" buyer for "Druze land," that I realized that the municipality had itself become a broker in this contested geography. Although Mr. L was being condemned by Druze families for his brokering practice, brokerage was actually becoming a dominant logic among the Druze minority, as they sought to survive in areas that were emerging as frontiers of local and regional wars. The strategy was being driven in part by the fact that it was becoming impossible for Druze families to compete financially. As one landowner I interviewed lamented: "I need the money. I have to sell my land. I would like to sell it to a Druze person, but where are the monetary-capable Druze to sell to?! They do not exist and the few that have money seem not to be interested."

It seems all the municipality could do in the face of a demand for land from rich Sunni and Shiite developers was to play the role of arbitrator. This inherently meant picking sides and playing the role of broker—not in the municipality's public capacity, but through a mechanism of private placement. Thus, despite the public position of the PSP as an ally of Hezbollah post-2008, a continued anxiety around the presence of the Shiite in urban space had created a preference among the Druze minority for Sunni developers and residents.

Such a condition indicates how, among the Druze minority, the Shiite other remains largely constructed as uncivilized, poor, uneducated, masculine, and prone to large families—with certain individuals now also seen as wealthy, powerful, and ready to martyr themselves for territorial control. Such a discriminatory logic was repeated to me by a reputable reporter. Compared to Shiites, he said: "At least Sunnis are educated, have smaller families, pay taxes, are not interested in fighting, and just want to 'live' a nice life with money. Between the two, who would you pick to be your neighbor?"[68] "Picking a neighbor," within the local and regional Sunni-Shiite contestation in the Middle East, is the essence of the type of brokerage activity that Druze residents of Doha Aramoun see as key to their survival.

Our Building and Its Residents: The Changing Demography

Anxiety around who gets to be one's neighbor becomes even more elevated on the apartment building level, as residents move in and out in a hot real estate market. This anxiety is fueled by memories of the civil war, in which atrocities and displacement often came at the hands of people who had once been neighbors. Therefore, in the geographies of the war yet to come, fear is a constant. It is also a powerful motivator of discourse behind closed doors—at dinner tables, family visits, and get-togethers—where people exchange calculations regarding the particular sectarian geographies.

My family's building provides one such example. When we first arrived in Doha Aramoun, our building was unfinished. Most of the residents were Druze, and there were a few Sunni families. Although we had bought our apartment for $80,000, a significant amount in 1993 (about $165,000 in 2011 dollars), the building's shared amenities were incomplete. The developer had walked away from the project without painting its walls or installing an elevator, a water pump, or other equipment. This had apparently been a result of the devaluation of the Lebanese lira in 1986, due to war. After that, the down payments the developer had received began to lose their value.[69] The task of finishing the building then became a community effort, as families who had bought apartments there sought to make the structure livable. They also worked together to get the building legalized, given that it violated the safety envelope around Beirut International Airport imposed by international civil aviation agencies. For several years, the families in the building became a tightly knit community.

However, when real estate and housing prices started escalating (around 2000), one after another, the apartments were put up for sale. In particular, many of the Druze families (especially those who were not well off) sold their apartments for double what they had paid for them, and moved to cheaper areas farther from Beirut. Many of the incoming families were Shiite. In the process, life in the building changed, as neighbors became less familiar with each other.

Two incidents highlight this change in occupancy. After the May 2008 events, an Iranian family moved into an apartment on the building's second floor. The family members largely kept to themselves, and residents only caught glimpses of a man, seemingly the head of the household, as he came and went in a BMW with tinted windows. His wife, by contrast, who wore a full *niqab*,[70] rarely appeared; indeed, I saw her only once, very briefly, as she opened the door for her husband. This reclusive Iranian family became a center of speculation in the building, especially for one neighbor, Ms. D, a long-time stay-at-home mother who had perfected the skill of figuring out the whereabouts of everyone in the building and the surrounding neighborhood.

Ms. D had been living in the building since 1988. From a low- to middle-income family, she had been able to buy her apartment there only because of family support. The fact that Ms. D had not been able to map the daily life of the Iranian family caused her and a number of other neighbors some concern. But the man and his family might not have raised such concern if not for the known connection between Iran and Hezbollah. This family might have been like any other ordinary family that bought housing in the area. However, our new neighbor's private demeanor and car with tinted windows spawned all sorts of narratives, including that he had some sort of security function and had located to our tall building for paramilitary reasons. It was not until 2014, four years after they moved in, that the anxiety eased a bit, as residents started seeing more of the wife and children. Still, neighbors whispered how they allegedly saw this neighbor arriving one night in March 2016 with a bullet-holed jeep, arousing speculations that he was fighting with Hezbollah and Iran in Syria.

This anxiety over the identity of new neighbors arises with every apartment sale. One spring day during my fieldwork, as construction noise emerged from a resold apartment, Ms. D knocked on our door. She inquired whether I knew "about the religious affiliation of the newcomers." I didn't. She then asked, "Do you think they are Shiites?" Seeing a disapproving look on my face, she said, "You were not here in May 2008; we had to flee overnight." Finally, in 2012, Ms. D decided that she needed to sell her apartment and move back to Choueifat. A big for sale sign was hung from her balcony. Her asking price was $400,000. "Who is going to buy an apartment in this old run-down building for almost half a million dollars?" I exclaimed to my mother one day. But the ongoing stream of interested buyers proved me wrong.

In the end, a family issue intervened, and Ms. D was not able to sell the apartment. And since then, with the beginning of the war in Syria, the real estate market in Doha Aramoun, as in the rest of Beirut, has been stagnant. But if and when Ms. D does sell her apartment, the building will then have only five remaining Druze households, and three of these families currently live in Dubai. It is this anxiety around the changing *demography* of the area, a euphemism for sectarian-political affiliations, that currently infuses the logics of urbanization in Doha Aramoun, and that is fueled by rumors about these constructed geographies of fear. This is true from the stairwell of my family's apartment building all the way to the national master plan.

Talk of War: Rumors, Snipers, and Private Property

Rumors are indeed cyclical and productive; they organize spaces and reproduce violence. It is irrelevant whether these stories are real or not; they produce a geography of fear that shapes space and draws sectarian demarcation lines. Elsewhere, in São Paulo, Brazil, Teresa Caldeira has shown how talk of crime is all that is needed to "impose partitions, build up walls, delineate and enclose spaces, establish distances, segregate, differentiate, impose prohibitions, multiply rules of avoidance and exclusion, and restrict movements."[71] However, what is fundamentally different between talk of crime and segregation in São Paulo and future

FIGURE 29. Above: The Dagher and Kazan housing complex. Source: Author, 2011. Below: The complex is located along the Old Saida Road, overlooking the Rafic Hariri International Airport, the Beirut-Saida Highway, and the Mediterranean Sea. Source: Adapted by the author from Google Maps, 2017.

violence in Doha Aramoun is the relationship between safety and private property. In the case of São Paulo, people retreat to private properties for safety. In Doha Aramoun, private property is assumed to be a strategic resource for violence as private apartments and buildings are presumed to provide the structure for a paramilitary geography in times of war.

On one corner of the main road that leads to Doha Aramoun stands a large housing project identified as being built by two developers named Dagher and Kazan (Figure 29). In contrast to the large flats in the apartment building behind it, the apartments here are small, with tiny windows and balconies that overlook both the Old Saida Road and the airport, barely 500 meters away. During my research, many rumors were circulating about this project, which was then under construction. One rumor was that the developers were Hezbollah affiliates who had been able to acquire this strategic site through quasi-legal maneuvers. According to one person I interviewed, "What could be a more perfect position than this to gain control of the entrance to Aramoun, Bchamoun, and Choueifat—as well as the airport and Beirut—in the event of war? This housing location is perfect to position and distribute fighters and snipers." Another person said, "Who buys such a strategic land and then crams small 'tuna-can-like' apartments into it, instead of providing expensive apartments that could sell for hundreds of thousands of dollars?" The implication was that such density makes no sense as a housing development strategy but is related to military concerns. These were the same kinds of rumors that had circulated around the presence of the Iranian family in our building.

Having heard many such stories about the real purpose of housing being to create a militarized geography of snipers, fighters, and spies, I was curious about the municipality's position. One day in September 2010, I was engaged in a conversation on the politics of urban growth with an engineer at the municipal offices when we got into this subject with another of his visitors, a longtime Druze resident, landowner, and developer. Our chat had initially been about the recent municipal elections, which had brought in a new board affiliated not with the PSP but with another Druze party (according to a rotation agreement between the two Druze organizations). But then the two men told me that the new mayor's policy was deliberately to issue fewer building permits, and thus slow down work around the municipality. They then started talking openly about the general mood of anxiety in the town, which had been caused by Hezbollah buying land and building projects that were intended to dominate its major arterial roads.

Hearing this, I asked, provocatively: "If what you are saying is true, what is the municipality doing to stop the militarization of everyday life?"

"Nothing," the visitor responded. "The municipality cannot do anything!

Why do you think we could stop such activities? These spaces that we are talking about are private property. Private property is the means to take over the area."

Indeed, both men were convinced that individuals, supported by religious-political organizations, buy apartments during times of peace, and that these spaces are then transformed collectively in times of war into a paramilitary infrastructure. The tactics of filling in the blanks were implicitly designed to take over vital areas in the town, to dominate the airport, and secure the southern entrances to Beirut.

"You know this is especially true in Doha Aramoun," the visitor told me. "There are several strategic hills there that overlook the Khalde [Beirut-Saida] highway and the coast" (Figure 30).

"So these are true stories, not rumors?" I asked, skeptically.

"Our ears are on the ground. These worries are not baseless," the visitor tried to assure me. "I have to tell you that many Hezbollah members who control the housing market are going under the names of developers—like Dagher, for example. Have you heard of him?"

"Of course, I have," I said. The visitor was referring to the co-developer of the locally infamous Dagher and Kazan project.

It was at this moment that I realized that talk within the municipal offices and talk on the street were referencing each other, blurring the line between rumors and facts. And I realized that even I had assumed a role in that economy of fear, as I was swept up daily by reports circulating not only in the streets and at the mu-

FIGURE 30. The hills of Doha Aramoun as seen from Khalde's coastal area in 2017. Source: Author, 2017.

nicipal offices, but at my gym, beauty salon, and grocery store. I was also subjected to such stories and political analyses in the homes of my own family and of my friends. Indeed, such talk of war and rumors of militarization were largely inescapable. Subsequently, I also struggled with how to converse with people without further contributing to the spread of such talk. However, as Michael Taussig has pointed out, terror is mediated through narration, and that makes it difficult to write against it, especially in ethnographic work.[72] And as Allen Feldman has argued, writing about violence is often a political project and an exercise that aims "to locate narrative in violence by locating violence through narratives."[73] Nevertheless, I still tried to cast doubt on these rumors, even as I inquired about them.

During my conversation with the two men at the municipal offices, I also asked: "How come people tend to link private property with military strategies? Can you explain to me why, if I buy an apartment, a home to call my own, people tend to think of it as a part of a military strategy?"

"You are not able to believe it because you are not 'ideologically-committed' to a religious and political entity," the two men told me. "But if you are connected, politically and religiously, to an organization—like the 90 percent of Shiites who are affiliated to Hezbollah—then, yes, your house could become a node in a military strategy."

I had also heard numerous such stories after the May 2008 clashes. Acquaintances had more than once told me stories of how a neighboring "Shiite building" had been evacuated of women and children in 2008, and subsequently occupied as a paramilitary site, strategically overlooking Doha Aramoun, the airport, and the sea.

Such rumors and accusations about how religious-political organizations have militarized everyday life circulate in both directions. On January 13, 2011, a few days after Hezbollah and its allies forced Hariri's Future Movement out of the national government, multiple versions of a single, largely unverified report circulated through the media. I heard people discussing this report everywhere I went, and it was clearly initiated by an entity close to Hezbollah and its allies. The rumor-report stated that the Future Movement—after its loss to Hezbollah and its allies in May 2008—had completed its military and geostrategic readiness and preparedness for future wars. The report further detailed the "military plan" of the Future Movement in the event of a future war. Here is one version of it:

[I]n the Khalde region, the envisioned military strategy requires the training of "sabotage/vandalism" groups that would be responsible for placing and detonating bombs and explosives, as well as the geographic distribution of groups of moving snipers in the areas of Aramoun and Bchamoun in an attempt to cause a stir in these areas that *are considered vital for the extended operations of the resistance* [i.e., Hezbollah; emphasis added].[74]

As these rumors continue to circulate, and Doha Aramoun continues to balloon, many more Druze families like mine are considering moving out of the area. The rumors seem to cement the realization that what was once viewed as a peaceful periphery has now become a frontier of future war. Development in the area was initially facilitated by the Future Movement's strategy of capital projects. But the vision of it as an extension of Sunni west Beirut has now been challenged by the tactics of filling in the blanks, by which Shiites have sought to establish their own presence there through incremental land development and apartment purchases. Meanwhile, the Christians who once called this area home have long ago moved away, and the remaining Druze minority are left wondering what their future there will be.

An Evolving Frontier

Recently, as the war in Syria has raged on, a new set of rumors has begun to circulate around the presence and geography of radical Sunni groups. One cause of these rumors is the upsurge in sympathetic feelings among some Sunnis in Lebanon, including in Doha Aramoun, toward transnational, militarized, radical Sunni political organizations like al-Nusra and ISIS. These sympathetic feelings towards radical Sunni groups are, according to Jumblat, on "the rise due to the political developments in Iraq, Afghanistan, and Pakistan, which have repercussions on our context."[75]

Since the Future Movement and the PSP were largely defeated in the 2008 clashes, some people believe that these new paramilitary entities may be better able to stand up to Hezbollah in the future. Recently, media reports have also begun to surface concerning the presence of militarized sleeper cells operating out of Doha Aramoun's mosques in support of al-Nusra and ISIS.[76] One reporter told me that these groups convene during the night. And he talked about a large network for weapons distribution, as these groups prepare to become more involved in the wars yet to come, both regionally and locally. These rumors had already begun to feed back into political calculations, as witnessed by Jumblat's appeal to his followers in 2009 to shift their alliance to Hezbollah. His calculation then was that the Druze minority had less to fear from Hezbollah's "men in black" than from "men with beards and shaved mustaches" who "are the real danger to us."[77]

These rumors about Sunni radicalism are, moreover, causing equal anxiety among supporters of the Future Movement Sunnis, the Shiites, and the area's remaining Druze population. This anxiety has been augmented by the increased presence of Syrian refugees. Although the memory of the 2008 battles has largely receded into the background, the arrival of the Syrians is now seen as a new threat. After 2011, many Syrians began seeking refuge in Doha Aramoun's low-cost housing projects and abandoned structures, where several families may cram together into one apartment. And recently, Hezbollah and the Future Movement (along with Sunni radical groups) fought street battles against each other using the Syrian conflict and Syrian paramilitarized groups as proxies.[78] These battles provided a reminder of the lurking contested geographies of the May 2008 events.

This chapter has examined the ways in which the spatial strategy of capital projects and the corresponding tactics of filling in the blanks have transformed Doha Aramoun into an evolving frontier of sectarian conflict, as different religious-political organizations struggle to control Beirut's peripheries within narratives of past wars and expectations of wars yet to come. As a feature of this conflict, religious-political organizations have interpolated the state into the process of arranging these territories as destinations for their supporters, legitimizing certain spatial practices while criminalizing others. For example, the Future Movement's provision of utility and road infrastructure in Doha Aramoun through formal institutions of the Lebanese government was initially seen as a legitimate investment in the region. But Hezbollah's subsequent development of a parallel telecommunications infrastructure has been contested as a tool of war (just as its intervention in setting up infrastructure networks in poorer areas like Sahra Choueifat was seen as informal and illegitimate).

The case of Doha Aramoun also highlights the conditions inherent in a minority geography, where geopolitical survival means playing the role of broker between more dominant parties. In Beirut's southern peripheries, the minority Druze are thus positioning themselves this way in the Sunni-Shiite conflict, as their towns on the periphery of Beirut are being shaped into frontiers of local and regional sectarian conflict.

Meanwhile, this contested geography is simultaneously providing a profitable business landscape for all entities, irrespective of their sectarian affiliation. These entities include developers, landowners, and the municipal officers who often tend to turn a blind eye to profiteering. Instead their calculations are aimed at "dividing the pie" with representatives of other sects.

These processes of ballooning are, however, not always visible; nor are they representative of the concerns of all the people living in the area. Parked in Sahet el-Timthel (Statue Square), the commercial center of Doha Aramoun, one afternoon in December 2014, I closely examined the congested scene in front of me. As a steady stream of honking cars tried to push their way through the busy intersection, other vehicles were attempting to park, motorcycles were zigzagging about, and pedestrians were struggling to negotiate tortuous routes between cars, signs, and merchandise for sale. The crowd was extremely diverse—with Lebanese, Syrians, Filipinos, Sri Lankans, Sudanese, and Ethiopians among the nationalities present. Over the years, Sahet el-Timthel has grown from a few scattered shops into a congested commercial node. Buzzing with people from all walks of life, this section of Doha Aramoun felt like any other market in a bustling metropolis.

Yet, peeking through this mosaic of human coexistence was one important reminder of the logic underpinning its geography of war. On my left, amid dozens of parked cars, was the statue that gave the square its name. It had been erected to recognize local martyrs who had lost their lives in the civil war, and was inscribed with a list of their names. The statue is fenced and decorated with a few shrubs, and every December it is dusted, cleaned, and manicured in preparation for Aramoun's Martyrs remembrance day. However, that day, amid the cars, artifacts, signs, and billboards, it seemed to fade into insignificance. Partially standing out, however, were two large, adjacent posters—one of Kamal Jumblat (the founder of the Druze PSP, assassinated in 1977), and the other of Rafic Hariri (the founder of the Sunni Future Movement, assassinated in 2005) (Figure 31).

Doha Aramoun has continued to balloon, housing ever-increasing numbers of residents. Predictably, the capacity of its infrastructure, boosted through the

FIGURE 31. The martyrs sculpture in Sahet el-Timthel, surrounded by large pictures of the assassinated leaders Hariri and Jumblat. Source: Author, 2015.

capital projects of the 1990s, has now again reached its limit. Likewise, most open lands have now been developed through the logic of filling in the blanks— although the area's remaining villas are still being demolished one after another to make way for more apartments. By and large, the geography of Doha Aramoun, transformed into a war zone in 2008, thus reveals its status to be that of an everyday urbanizing periphery. But this is largely the result of the people who pass through it—laborers from all over the Global South who come to Lebanon to make a living and send remittances back to their families. Meanwhile, the fact that the square was transformed into a battle site in 2008 is almost entirely hidden; and the people who navigate its increasingly congested and crowded spaces remain largely invisible to the forces that have established Doha Aramoun as a frontier in the logic of wars yet to come.

CHAPTER 5

PLANNING WITHOUT DEVELOPMENT

"AN URBAN PLANNER IS LIKE A FASHION DESIGNER," Mr. I told me in January 2010. One of the main figures in the planning and zoning of Sahra Choueifat, he continued:

I now design a master plan like a fashion designer designs a dress. You see, there is no difference, not at all. In fashion, you ask me for a dress, I design it and tailor it for you. After you take it home, you can take off the ribbon, remove the ruffles, and shorten the sleeves. It is none of my business anymore. It is the same for urban planners like me in Lebanon. I do my job and give them [the religious-political organizations] a master plan. If, after that, they want to remove a road, add floors, transform a zone, destroy the entire concept, it is none of my business.

This was a striking admission. By comparing contemporary physical planning in Beirut and its peripheries to designing a garment that can subsequently be modified to suit any request, Mr. I was signaling his inability to practice his profession as he envisioned it. Specifically, his words implied a total lack of agency in the face of religious-political organizations, and his mounting distrust of the planning process in Beirut. They also folded within them an elegy for the expert training he had received, but which appeared no longer relevant.

Mr. I had previously spoken to me about jobs of "dirty planning" and the physical threats that came with them.[1] In his view, the planner working in the context of Beirut's peripheries had become a technician, in the service of a compartmentalized political order, rather than a valued, and independent, social reformer. Such a role did not, for example, allow practitioners to engage with the concept of public interest, despite its supposed centrality to planning discourse. According to Mr. I, this had not always been the case. There was a time in Lebanon when planners believed in the larger purpose of their work, which was to instill order, ensure progress, and promote peace. Mr. I's remarks thus signaled a major shift in planners' view of themselves.

I was still processing the political implications of a comparison between designing a dress and producing a zoning plan (and the difference between ruffles and roads), when I met another well-established planner, Mr. H, in April of that year. He, too, had been involved in plans for a number of Beirut's southern peripheries. When I asked how he approached zoning and building regulations, he responded: "Urban planning should be like jewelry design. You need to combine art and science to produce finely calibrated master plans."

He continued: "You are a planner, right? Can you believe how they are changing the street alignments?[2] Take the example of Sahra Choueifat. Have you ever seen a street in the United States where the buildings are not aligned? This is unacceptable!"

Mr. H's training was in modernist planning. And like Mr. I, he believed in the potential of his profession to shape social outcomes. But here he, too, was reduced to talking about street alignments. His focus on alignments in an impoverished area like Sahra Choueifat signaled a lost belief in his profession's ability to change the larger picture.

How can these approaches to planning—as fashion or jewelry design—be understood in relation to peripheral areas of Beirut that have been transformed into frontiers of violence since May 2008? In fact, both Mr. I's and Mr. H's outlooks are symptomatic of the current role of planners as technicians regulating the spatial logic of the war yet to come.[3]

After presenting and discussing case examples in the last three chapters, I will now step back to provide a genealogy of the debates and discourses that have led to this condition. Specifically, I will examine the changing views of experts in development and planning, both globally and locally, to investigate the shifting relationship between development and urban planning and its implication for the urbanization of Beirut's peripheries. In Lebanon, as in many other decolonized countries, it is important to begin this effort by reaching back to the nation-building era of the 1950s. But it is also important to interrogate the relationship between development and planning from the periphery, rather than the city center. Such a focus establishes the periphery as a critical spatial category for understanding spatial production.

In the 1950s, concerns over development, representation, and equality were originally part of a larger debate over how to address uneven development in the nascent Lebanese nation-state. In Beirut, such concern related to the uneven development of the city's peripheries—their poverty, informality, and unruliness. These qualities were initially seen as a primary source of social and political instability, and as expert planning discourse on the condition of these areas has changed over time, so has the approach to arranging their geographies. Especially with regard to the southern peripheries (as discussed in the last three chapters), the changing relationship between planning and development over more than six decades has contributed to the gradual transformation of these peripheries into frontiers of both exponential growth and sectarian violence.

Temporally, the discussion of this transformation must further recognize three key moments. These coincided with the conclusion of major episodes of urban conflict: after the 1958 uprising, which claimed the lives of at least 2000 and possibly as many as 4000 people; in 1983, in the midst of the civil war, when the country experienced a short-lived moment of peace before again descending into violence; and in 1990, when an agreement was finally reached to end the fifteen-year civil war. The post-conflict periods that followed these violent episodes were significant because they raised expectations of better times ahead, to be achieved by imposing order over chaos. Urban planning as a tool of spatial order and management of the future was used at all three moments to materialize that hope.[4] The three moments of hope, however, were spatialized differently, leading to the current condition of Beirut and its peripheries.

Understanding the shifting discourse of urban planning and development during these three moments involves following two interrelated threads. One concerns the incremental emptying of planning in Lebanon of its former socio-economic objectives. Broadly, there were three stages to this transition, as the practice moved from its original focus on development planning to planning *as* development and finally to planning *without* development.

The other thread concerns how this changing relationship has coincided with the transformation of Beirut's peripheries into sectarian frontiers. It is here that the Lebanon case relates to a larger debate on urban planning and socioeconomic development in cities of the Global South. Specifically, when planning loses its ethical basis in socioeconomic development—that is, in efforts to address social inequality, poverty, spatial justice, and the redistribution of resources (however problematic the pursuit of such policies may be)—it becomes little more than a tool for ordering space in the interest of those in power, devoid of the normative attributes of equity and social justice that are usually attributed to planning practice.[5] Thus in Lebanon, as the larger goals of poverty alleviation and resource redistribution have receded, urban planning has devolved into a series of practices that produce the spatiality of sectarian difference while facilitating continued, profitable real estate development. It is this shift that explains the disillusionment of both Mr. I and Mr. H. But what they have witnessed in Beirut is the further reality that in cities of conflict, planning without development exacerbates violence and diminishes the quality of everyday life, as peripheries are rendered frontiers.

The Intertwined Discourses and Practices
of Planning and Development

Beginning in the 1950s, shifting notions of planning and development have rendered ambiguous the questions: What is planning? and What is development? In particular, as discourse in these two fields has evolved, the two terms have now come to mean different things to different people. Socioeconomic development (not just physical development in the form of real estate, housing, infrastructure, and so forth) is generally considered one of the desired outcomes of urban planning. However, a survey of planning literature shows that the relationship between the two fields has rarely been clear.[6] And the intertwining of the two fields has been exacerbated by the fact that academic work in the planning field has never arrived at a common view of how to define, theorize, and practice planning.[7]

The view of development presented here comes from a planning perspective; it therefore does not engage with in-depth discussions of development as an extensive field of study in its own right. But from this broad perspective, development may be understood as an activity that seeks to design and implement programs of socioeconomic intervention that aim to improve people's living conditions. Planning, by contrast, can be understood as a set of philosophies and practices related to the organization of space, which are in turn guided by a set of temporal ideas regarding uncertainty, progress, and the future. Following Oren Yiftachel, planning (which may include urban planning, spatial planning, and regional planning) typically involves "the formulation, content, and implementation of spatial policies."[8]

In this definition, ideas and theories of time and temporality are central to planning thought and practice. This has been addressed in the work of key theorists, such as John Forester, who wrote that "planning is the guidance of future action."[9] Similarly, Rexford Tugwell argued that planning seeks "the utility of the future in the present."[10] As shown by the case studies in this book, however, this is not always how planning is practiced, especially in contested spaces. In other words, it is not always possible to subscribe to a teleological narrative of planning as a chartered trajectory of progress toward a better future, or even to assume that planning is inherently good. Planning must instead be assessed, according to Bent Flyvbjerg, based on a view that it is "simply a phenomenon to observe and engage with which may be good or bad in specific instances of planning practice."[11] The view presented here therefore joins with scholarship on the dark side of planning, which argues that planning outcomes do not always bring an improvement of life for many people.[12] Indeed, the repercussions of planning for broad sections of the population may be increased oppression, control, and violence; environmental degradation; and a worsening of living conditions.

Until recently, planning theory has also tended to focus on the concerns of the so-called developed world, while the study of so-called developing countries was mostly relegated to the field of development studies, with its focus on economic development. Although a number of cities in the Global South, like Cairo and Casablanca, were sites of planning experiments, these were European colonial experiments. Other cities of the Global South were approached as empty sites, where elements of rationality and order could be imposed on "clean slates" (tabula rasa).[13] Brasilia, built in the 1950s and '60s, was an instance of starting anew—in its case, inspired by the European CIAM model.[14] The planning versus development divide thus parallels that in urban studies, where urban theory "broadly focused on the West," and development studies "focused on places that were once called 'third-world cities.'"[15] Specifically, the field of modern planning is dominated by a predominantly Eurocentric approach, as manifested in "liberal states" where the division between what is public and what is private is assumed to be clear. As illustrated earlier, however, planning activity in Beirut has increasingly collapsed this public-private binary.

Being a Western-centric field of thought, planning practice and theory has typically faced a challenge when it comes to addressing situations outside the Western frame. This is evident, for example, in the categories used by the Association of Collegiate Schools of Planning (ACSP) to organize its activities, a process that typically includes defining "international development planning" as a separate track at association conventions. Specifically, according to the track description: "[m]any developing countries share attributes that create unique challenges for planning, such as their recent independence and nation-building efforts, their position vis-à-vis other developed countries in the global economy, similar demographic profiles and rates of urbanization, inadequate infrastructure, large indigenous populations and systems of land tenure, and their relationships with the large international institutions."[16]

These artificial divisions, however, eclipse the fact that the planning and development fields were developed in conjunction with one another. And it is in this sense that the two questions *Where?* and *When?* highlight two critical dimensions that join them as regulatory regimes aimed at controlling territory (in space) and managing its future (in time). Clearly, a spatial problematic is essential to both fields. Space (and particularly territory, as area controlled by a certain group) is where both development and planning operate—albeit with different tools. Indeed, it is the control of space that makes both projects possible, physically and materially. Yet, as the relationship between the two fields has shifted, so has their approach to space and territory. Thus, eventually, in Beirut (as in many other cities of the Global South), urban plans became the blueprints for development, and it has been exercises in mapping that have allowed experts to not only shape space but also to project a certain idea of time.

Fundamental to both planning and development are teleological notions that assume a future of social change and progress. Yet the two discourses have a different relationship to time and the future. Development discourse is largely open-ended and timeless; nations, regions, and cities are thus conceived as being engaged in an endless quest for development. Planning, by contrast, is concerned with establishing a time frame for action, to make the task of development manageable. While development may propose a future, planning is tasked with figuring out how to order an unruly present to achieve it. Thus, planners are assumed to have the "ability to control the future through action guided by rationality and centralized authority."[17]

In expert debates in war-torn Lebanon, the notion of planning time traditionally brought hope. Such an attitude was clearly articulated by Mohammad Fawaz, one of Lebanon's leading planners, in 1980. As the civil war raged, he argued that "the main dimension of [planning] is time. This dimension refuses impossibility, looking always to the future."[18] This belief that a future of development and planning, made possible through rational thinking, would always produce a better outcome was constructed as common sense with the modernization project of the Global North. It was in turn exported in the project of development planning for the Global South.

Development Planning

Across the world, the 1950s were the era of development planning, as state-led *developmentalism* defined a framework for government action in young, decolonizing nations. Emerging out of the French Mandate (1923–1946),[19] Lebanon was a target of such talk and an important regional center for development planning debates. From 1949, this movement was facilitated by the labeling of Lebanon and other young nations as "underdeveloped" or "developing."[20] Development planning thus came to refer to what Gillian Hart defines as "big D" development: "a post–World War II project of intervention in the 'third world' that emerged in the context of decolonization and the cold war"—as well as the rise of new forms of US hegemony.[21] This intervention project entailed charted "trajectories of development," that the Western powers—mainly Britain, France, and the United States—advised countries to undertake. Developing countries like Lebanon were enthusiastic and willing participants in these discourses. Indeed, throughout the decade, they hosted conferences and workshops on the topic, especially when these came with a promise of international aid money. In Lebanon, for example, the United States Operations Mission (USOM) published several booklets on its local development work.[22]

At the height of the Cold War with the Soviet Union, the emphasis on economic development was central to efforts by the United States and Western European countries to counter the global rise of Communist aspirations.[23] Class struggles were at the time threatening to disrupt the West's hegemonic order. And as part of big D development logic, poverty alleviation and economic development were seen as ways to stop these aspirations from taking hold in the informal peripheries of cities, which were seen as breeding grounds of discontent in developing countries. Thus, US President Harry Truman's containment policy at the beginning of the decade proposed that spaces of poverty become a main focus of international aid and development.[24] Simultaneously, developing countries were encouraged to establish comprehensive "development plans," centered on economic development and supported by Western expertise.

Initially, the geographic question—that is, the *Where?* question—was not seen as central to development in the Global South. Attention centered rather on the poor as a general social category. In particular, the focus of international development aid was on rural development and the realization of national infrastructure projects.[25] In the Global North, however, cities were the principal target of planning efforts, with master plans being used to radically reorder urban landscapes, guided by a belief in rationality and comprehensive social engineering developed during World War II.[26] In hindsight, the period is "viewed by many as 'the golden age' of planning, an era when planning was seen as a positive, progressive force, the means by which a government could deliver equitable and efficient development and contribute to the greater public good."[27] And the belief in urban planning did lead to a number of utopian experiments in the Global South. Notable among these were tabula rasa designs for the new cities of Chandigarh and Brasilia, which positioned spatial planning as the vehicle for realizing quests for economic growth and social change.[28] Predominantly, however, planning in the Global South was about economics, intervening in agricultural and industrial sectors, without a comprehensive understanding of how to order space as part of these programs.

In the view of 1950s development planners, space was just a container in which development might happen. It was not understood as being produced by socioeconomic and political relationships, which might equally facilitate development or underdevelopment. At the time, the ideas of the Chicago School of urban sociology—including environmental determinism,[29] human ecology, and teleological progress—were prevalent and accepted, and these tended to attribute the causes of poverty to the urban poor themselves. Such ideas were conjoined with racist discourses, such as the *culture of poverty*, essentializing the poor's racial and ethnic traits by labeling such individuals as immoral, dependent, and inferior.[30] Described as *urban ideology* by Manuel Castells,[31] these theories failed to understand the role of socioeconomic relations, primarily those of capitalism, on the structuring of cities. In particular, informal settlers, squatters, and homeless people were seen as parasites in otherwise perfectly functioning cities. And because they could not "make it" in a formal urban economy, they were seen as extraneous to cities that were trying to "catch up" with the West.

In general, planning at the time was based on a logic of environmental determinism bolstered by a teleology of modernization. Ordered physical space was thought to have the ability to shape behavior, ensure progress, and bring social change.[32] And, rather than being comprehensive socioeconomic interventions, spatial interventions mostly involved the top-down rearrangement of territory by experts to address "problem spaces." In fact, these interventions mostly focused on ridding cities of the poor through slum clearance. And as areas of physical poverty were cleared away, governments also engaged in experiments with affordable housing. In much of the Global South, the goal of such initiatives, however, was to curb discontent and stop the spread of Communism.[33]

Spatializing Containment in Lebanon

In Lebanon, Pan-Arabism and socialism were both important movements during the 1950s. They reached their peak when Syria and Egypt joined to create the sovereign United Arab Republic, which lasted from 1958 to 1961, under the charismatic leadership of Gamal Abdel Nasser, who had become president of Egypt in 1956. Pan-Arabism gave new prominence to socialist aspirations in the region's identity, as poorer sections of the Arab population, including those in Lebanon, saw it as providing hope for a better future.

The Palestinian cause also weighed on Lebanon at that time. The 1948 Palestinian exodus (al-Nakba), caused by the creation of the state of Israel, led to the establishment of refugee camps in surrounding Arab countries, and some of these camps were erected around Beirut. At the same time, squatter settlements were also growing on the city's peripheries, as rural migrants from the east and south of Lebanon sought work in Beirut's industrial and agricultural sectors. As urban underemployment and joblessness rose, these settlements and camps witnessed political turmoil and opposition to pro-Western government policies.[34]

The United States closely monitored this shifting landscape. In 1954, the United States Department of State received a dispatch from the US Embassy in Beirut stating that "population sectors most lacking in confidence and thus mostly likely to threaten stability include the urban workers and unemployed, the students and intellectuals, and the Palestinian refugees."[35] The dispatch focused precisely on labor-related urban politics, mentioning that "discontented city workers, having little to lose . . . constitute the major potential threat to political stability in Lebanon and may become a political force of important dimensions."[36] This memo framed the looming conflict as being driven principally by class divisions. However, the following year, a second memo framed it in both class and sectarian terms. It concluded that "the repeated clashes occurring in Beirut were symptomatic of the 'awakening social and political consciousness of the Moslems of Lebanon and the increasingly militant and aggressive character of their organization, coupled with the realization on the part of the Christians that they are fighting a losing battle as far as numerical strength is concerned.' "[37]

Since the time of the Truman administration, the United States had followed a policy in the Middle East of seeking to "contain" the rise of such discontent. On the ground, this typically meant the physical containment of the poor and their spaces. Such "spatialization" of the United States policy in Beirut, as elsewhere, took the form of slum clearance and housing provision in "trouble areas," in an attempt to restore calm by promising market prosperity and providing low-cost housing.

Constantinos Doxiadis's work in Lebanon clearly reflected this approach to space. In 1957, a year before the first major uprising in Beirut, USOM commissioned Doxiadis, a Greek architect and town planner, to address Lebanon's housing shortage. Specifically, he was charged with finding a way to accommodate urban squatters and circumvent a future housing shortage.[38] Doxiadis had established himself as an international expert, with projects in Latin America, South Asia, and the Middle East, and he eventually became the US government's housing expert of choice in countries where the United States was seeking to expand or maintain its sphere of influence. In contrast to more design-focused local architects and engineers, he was also promoted as a policy and program visionary.[39] Thus, the USOM Housing Division's major report on US intervention in housing activities in Lebanon between 1956 and 1958 (essentially a report on Doxiadis's work) defined the program's intentions as being to "alleviate this constantly increasing elementary part of the cost of living for the mass of the Lebanese people, in addition create improvement in workers' efficiency, increase political stability and at the same time stimulate the building materials and construction industries."[40]

Although the project was not pitched in sectarian language, the "trouble areas" that concerned both the Lebanese government and the United States were the squatter settlements, refugee camps, and poor areas in Beirut's south and north peripheries (for example, Tel al-Zaatar, Qarantina, Medawar, Shatila, Bourj el-Barajneh, and Ouzaii). These were all inhabited by rural Shiite migrants and (mostly) Muslim Palestinians. In response to this problem, Doxiadis's most well developed housing scheme was a design for the Mkalles housing project on a site adjacent to the famous Tel al-Zaatar Palestinian refugee camp and neighboring quasi-informal Dekweneh, which was mostly inhabited by Shiite migrants from southern Lebanon. According to Hashim Sarkis, "The proposed housing program was therefore seen as a necessary tool to help alleviate poverty and to provide adequate housing more equally over the whole country. The program was probably meant as a preventive measure as well, as a means to appease the urban poor, the potential rebels and revolutionaries drawn to the Pan-Arabist project."[41] Its overall purpose therefore was to reinforce the position of Lebanon on the side of the United States in the Cold War.

Crisis: 1958 Uprising

As Doxiadis and his design team were working on housing programs to improve living conditions and help curb the rising dissatisfaction among Beirut's lower-income residents, the city erupted in conflict in May 1958. The issue that sparked the uprising was the decision by Israel, France, and Britain to invade Egypt in 1956 to regain the Suez Canal after it had been nationalized by Egyptian President Gamal Abdel Nasser. The decision angered many pan-Arab sympathizers in Lebanon, and they eventually demanded that Lebanese President Camille Chamoun, a Christian, break his ties with the United States. When he ultimately refused, the result was the first serious war in post-mandate Lebanon, a moment of violence now known as the 1958 uprising.[42]

The 1958 uprising is understood today according to either of two sometimes overlapping narratives. One frames it as a class war between the poorer sections of Lebanon's population on the one hand and the country's feudal landlords, businessmen, and pro-Western policies on the other.[43] The other narrative sees it as a sectarian war, during which the Muslim population revolted against the Christians who then dominated the government.[44] While some historians argue that the second frame more accurately describes the fighting, others say it is inaccurate to describe the uprising as a sectarian war, because a number of prominent Christian figures supported it. The reality is that both narratives hold some truth because the poorer territories of Lebanon were mostly inhabited by people identified as Muslims.[45]

Eventually, as mentioned earlier, the uprising claimed anywhere from 2000 to 4000 lives.[46] It also prompted the first US military intervention in the Middle East, an enactment of the just-announced Eisenhower Doctrine.[47] The US Marines landed in Khalde, south of Beirut, on July 15, 1958, and stayed there through October 25, 1958. The crisis ended only after a new Lebanese President, Fouad Chehab, a moderate, who was the army commander, was elected to replace Chamoun.[48]

Throughout these events, Doxiadis continued to work on his housing program, and he continued to submit his housing reports. However, his projects never left the drawing board. The US military intervention on the side of President Chamoun had made any further involvement of the United States in local affairs unwelcome. In particular, President Chehab dissociated himself from Doxiadis, who was seen as Chamoun's foreign housing and planning expert and an agent of US political interference in the country. Doxiadis's project was subsequently abandoned. And in December 1958, the Lebanese government halted its commitment to the US Eisenhower Doctrine and its containment policies.[49]

Mapping Spaces of Poverty and Discontent

As president, Chehab was a modernist who took a national approach to curbing the violence. Since the uprising had been fueled by pan-Arab socialist sentiments, his answer stressed social welfare and economic development programs, and he eventually created an ensemble of social institutions to help the country realize this vision. Early in his presidency, Chehab was also a proponent of development planning, seeing it as a way to ease tensions and rally people around a national agenda.[50] Big D development promised a better future for everyone, irrespective of class or sectarian affiliation.

Chehab further hoped that development would reverse the trend toward urban sectarian politics and policies that had been characteristic of Chamoun's term. This position had been articulated in a US Embassy memo in 1955. It argued that "avoiding civil strife . . . would be only possible if the new generation of Lebanese can be imbued with such tolerance and patriotic sentiment that administrative skill and professional competence can replace confessionalism as the bases for the allocation of government positions."[51] Local influential politicians, like Raymond Eddé, likewise stressed such views. They believed that state development could promote a general economic prosperity that would displace networks of sectarian allegiance.

With this goal in mind, Chehab envisioned a strong state that might solidify national unity. If unbalanced development and stark class differences were the underlying causes of the 1958 insurrection, development could provide a vehicle to eliminate conflict by eradicating poverty and distributing wealth more widely. And, rather than performing spot interventions in the spaces of the poor, as proposed by Chamoun and Doxiadis, this would be a national project. To reduce the disequilibrium between Beirut and its peripheries, Chehab thus advocated policies that would strengthen the central state, with "the belief in the unlimited capacities of planning in solving all development problems."[52] Trusting in the abilities of technical expertise, Chehab believed that the issue "was only a matter of time."[53] To that end, in 1960 he hired the French consulting firm IRFED (Institut de Recherche et de Formation en Développement), led by Father Joseph Lebret, to conduct an extensive socioeconomic study of Lebanon. Father Lebret had worked in Latin America, and at a time when the world was being pulled between capitalism and socialism, he advocated a "human economy" in the service of people, not just capitalists. To stop the spread of Communism, and its anti-church views, this approach involved "humanized development," which "included comprehensive national and regional planning and was intended to associate the poor with the development process."[54]

The IRFED report, published in 1963, focused more on income inequality and poverty than on the spatiality of the sectarian order. According to Fawaz and Peillen, it "was the first official document to mention 'poverty' as a policy concern."[55] Among other things, it noted that poverty was widespread in rural Muslim areas, and it called for a decentralization of economic development. The IRFED report also pointed out that "the continuing acculturation of the Shi'a [Shiite] will not take long to make obvious the increasingly wide lifestyle disparities, which in turn will pave the way for regional revolts, anarchist social agitation by some groups, and the intervention by other groups in neighboring areas."[56] Still, the report's principal focus was class rather than sectarian inequality. And according to Irene Gendzier, it provided

the material evidence of growing economic disparities in this period, from the skewed patterns of regional development, which favored the capital and its environs in the Mount Lebanon area, to the most deprived areas of the north and south, with the intermediary region of the Biq'a offering a more diverse tableau of development. Within these parameters, inadequate housing, sanitation, education, literacy, and rural indebtedness and underdevelopment were commonplace in the less privileged zones.[57]

The IRFED suggested addressing these problems by creating ten *growth poles* across Lebanon.

In official discourse, Chehab focused on the "unbalanced development" aspect of this work, and ignored the idea that this condition was intimately linked to the spatiality of the sectarian order. It was clear then that while "Christian areas" (that is, urban and central Lebanon) were enjoying a level of economic prosperity, the "Muslim hinterlands" (that is, rural lands distant from the capital) were mostly being neglected.[58] Still, the experts' discourse maintained a strict nonsectarian focus on poverty alleviation, redistribution, and economic development of rural areas.

Gradually, however, this concern with balancing development emerged as a spatial problematic, both locally and globally. Thus, as prevailing economic imbalances were mapped spatially—the hinterlands versus the city, and the city versus its peripheries—development discourse took a spatial turn. This was a time when space came to be understood as a social product. And spaces of poverty were thus being defined as targets of development, and subsequently as targets of spatial intervention.

From Development Planning to Planning as Development

The second phase in the transformation of the relationship between planning and development in Lebanon began in the 1960s. This is also the time when both international development agencies and major players in the planning field started asking a new set of questions. Gradually, as the issue of *where* to achieve development emerged, a shift took place from development planning to *planning as development*. Planning as development involves a quest to locate and delineate the most appropriate territories for development intervention. The shift fully engaged spatial planning as a tool to make development possible, and vast amounts of resources were invested in experiments to figure out how best to plan spatially to develop economically. It was during this time that poor peripheries came to be seen as important targets of development proposals.

Globally, the pressures of urbanization in the 1960s were accompanied by social, cultural, and political movements for civil rights and social justice in the Global North, while ever more countries in the Global South were decolonized. In the Global North, the Western-centric planning field started witnessing what Oren Yiftachel has called a "paradigm breakdown" when "the conventional wisdom of land-use planning as 'working in the public interest' was being challenged" by people who accused planners of acting as the tool of dominant groups.[59] Among the Marxist critiques of planning and development were those of Samir Amin, David Harvey, and Manuel Castells and Alan Sheridan.[60] They criticized planning for its role in capital accumulation, dispossession, and local and global domination. Meanwhile, within the profession, attempts to answer such questions as "What is urban planning?" "What is a good urban plan?" and "What is a good planning process?" pulled in many directions.[61] Responses to this crisis of expertise took different forms, such as containment, expansion, corridors, sustainability, decentralization, and renewal; and new tools and techniques, such as systems analysis, mixed scanning, advocacy, incrementalism, and rational pragmatism, appeared.[62] As the grand schemes that had characterized the field before the 1950s were discredited, planning was declared to be "a distinct and tightly bounded subject, different from social and economic planning," and it was "institutionalized into comprehensive land-use planning."[63]

In the Global South, the location of planning and development interventions became an essential concern. In tracing the origins of planning thought (economic planning, primarily), John Friedmann showed how the 1960s were a time when spatial experts had "to make concrete decisions in which *the question of where* had to be answered" (emphasis added).[64] The international development apparatus also became more salient at this time. Thus, the United Nations started playing a more crucial role in "building international consensus on action for development" through a series of ten-year International Development Strategies.[65]

In the Middle East, meanwhile, Beirut emerged as a hub for international development expertise. At a 1962 conference there, a United Nations report reiterated the famous motto "Development is not growth, Development is growth plus change," adding that this social change was possible through "change in the built environment."[66] Putting these ideas together, the United Nations in 1962 began a campaign to promote development through change in the built environment, which crystallized the spatial turn in development studies.

As the 1970s approached, this spatial turn acquired an increasingly urban character. At the time, global systems of big D development were shifting to a focus on "basic needs,"[67] as state-led development came to be seen as expensive, unrealistic, and unattainable. Until that moment, development policymakers had focused on investing in rural-based sectors (agriculture, irrigation, and so forth). The principal reason for this was that entities like the World Bank conceived of rural development as a way to stop rural migration and "stem the tide of rebellions and revolution in the countryside of ex-colonies."[68] The correlate, of course, was that urban areas, which were seen as more well-off, were not designated as appropriate targets for development policies. But this all shifted in the 1970s. Under the banner of "basic needs," the World Bank, which could not initially justify investing or lending money to cities, started to finance slum-upgrading schemes. Justification for the new program area was that "if housing and access to water and sewerage facilities were improved, the poor could have their basic needs met and could be better participants in the economy."[69]

The implications of the shift from development planning to planning as development were not trivial. Most importantly, it gradually shifted the "location of poverty" to urban areas, and therefore mapped urban peripheries as targets for development interventions. The shift also had stark political implications. Whereas development planning placed emphasis on development as a goal (where spatial planning was only one tool among many), planning as development put the emphasis on *spatial planning as development in itself*. Henceforth, development was territorialized, and specific areas were delineated as sites of intervention. Moreover, these areas were typically seen as those of the poor, at a time when talk of class struggle still boiled in the alleyways of the impoverished. This shift may have resulted in what Ananya Roy described as "the quite clumsy ways in which these understandings of the urban pose the connection between 'big' development models and spatiality," ways that consist of the mapping of "'social' categories such as peasants . . . with 'spatial' categories such as the rural or the urban."[70] In the case of Beirut, for example, the poor and "uncivilized" rural-urban migrants were mapped to Beirut's peripheries (mainly to the east and south), which were deemed in need of development, and consequently planning.

In an attempt to target the poor, this shift of approach initially involved the continuation throughout the 1960s of clearance of older slums and poverty eradication approaches to informal settlements. In 1968, for example, representatives of the Catholic Church—which was as worried as the United States about the spread of Communism at the time—joined a United Nations convention in Beirut to discuss world development.[71] Various speakers at the event, discussed development strategies aimed at alleviating poverty and eradicating economic disparities between nations and within nations—all the while reminding individuals of the "ethics of giving."[72] Several documents on planning and development from that time, especially those published by the Catholic Church, mention the need for slum clearance in areas like Qarantina, an informal settlement and refugee camp at the north entrance to Beirut.[73] In contrast to the earlier phase, however, housing and slum clearance were not the sole focus of the project. Slum upgrading projects were turned into full planning schemes, as exemplified by Michel Ecochard's 1963 plan for Beirut.

It is also important to highlight the new apparatus of planning and development established at the time, which greatly raised the profile of the Lebanese architect and planner as an expert entrusted with the task of development. These architects and designers were the product of modern thought, and were trained to believe in the capacity of their expert spatial training to shape the built environment in ways that would produce desired social outcomes. It was therefore unsurprising that they would use this lens to approach the social and economic issues of development.

Spatial Experts and Their Institutions

The history of the planning profession in Lebanon is naturally of concern to this discussion. A constellation of institutions established in the 1950s and 1960s proved central to the evolution of development and planning in Lebanon. The first of these was the Planning and Development Council, initiated and endowed by the Ministry of Economy in 1953. It was followed, in 1954, by a separate Ministry of Public Planning.[74] Both had been preceded by the establishment of the Order of Engineers and Architects in 1951. Eventually, the tasks of the Ministry of Public Planning were divided up among a variety of different physical planning institutions. After he came to office in 1958, President Chehab also encouraged the establishment of the Directorate of Town Planning (later renamed the Directorate General of Urbanism [DGU]) in 1959. This network of public institutions, created around urban planning and design practice, placed the profession at the heart of the official development discourse in the country.[75]

It was also at this time that planning became a synonym for development—or *planning as development*, as I have called it. For example, in his 1962 keynote address at the Pillars of the Lebanese House lecture series, Mustapha Nsouli, then General Director of the Ministry of Public Planning, stated that development "is the tool for the population to improve their society and their social and economic conditions." And he continued, "in this age, planning and development are actually synonyms. If one is mentioned, the second comes to mind instantaneously. *The first is a tool, and the second is a goal*" (emphasis added).[76]

Planning as development brought increasing visibility to the architects and architects-turned-urban planners (mostly men) who occupied the front rows in forums and meetings convened to address issues of development and the built environment.[77] While experts from all sorts of disciplines had taken a role in issues of development and planning until then, this period in Lebanon witnessed the arrival of a new wave of foreign experts and foreign-trained Lebanese architects who dominated the discussion.[78]

This was not the first time that architects and designers had been entrusted with drawing up plans for Beirut. Among other efforts, there had been Plan Danger in 1931, Michel Ecochard's first attempt in 1943, and Ernst Egli's 1954 plan for Beirut, as well as a plan for Beirut devised in the 1952 to 1954 period by a group of Lebanese architects and planners.[79] These were mostly exercises in physical planning, focusing on circulation, thoroughfares, and allocation of functions—a series of pointed interventions in the landscape to facilitate urbanization. However, planning as development, during the second phase of Chehabist rule, placed the huge burden of development on architects-turned-planners, entrusting them also with solving social problems through the built environment.[80] Physical plans were thus expected to fix economic problems, avoid future conflict, and ensure smooth business and real estate transactions. Underdevelopment was to be mapped and zoned out of existence, while development was to be planned, spatialized, and territorialized.

Locating Development: Beirut's Peripheries

A key feature of planning as development was the identification of "trouble areas," which would become targets of development in a campaign to stamp out the roots of instability that had led to class and sectarian conflict in Beirut. These trouble areas were to be sites of urban planning intervention, through proposals to alleviate poverty, provide housing, create industrial jobs, and promote security of tenure.

One could argue that this shift to territorializing development aid in Lebanon derived from Chehab's decision to employ the French architect and urban planner Michel Ecochard at the same time that IRFED was working on a national development plan. Both experts were seen as part of President Chehab's development program,[81] and both believed in a strong role for the state in development and planning—albeit very differently. While the two experts overlapped in their work on Lebanon, they do not seem to have collaborated. As mentioned, IRFED was hired in 1958 to put together a national development plan. Its key report, submitted in 1963, included a socioeconomic survey and a proposal for growth poles situated in different areas of the country. However, the report and its recommendations were, for the most part, not implemented. According to Mohamad Fawaz, the government issued a decree on May 18, 1964, that set up growth poles based on IRFED's work across Lebanon, but the work was abruptly halted later that same year.[82] Ecochard was then commissioned in 1961 to propose a master plan for Beirut and its suburbs. He submitted his master plan in 1963.[83] A modified version of Ecochard's plan was adopted by the government in 1964.[84]

While Doxiadis's intervention had been about construction and containment in "problem sites," and IRFED had been charged with developing a comprehensive national approach focused on the underdevelopment of the hinterlands, Ecochard's plan firmly articulated the problem of the periphery. It focused specifically on how to reorder these areas to tame their unruly and unplanned urbanization and unruly and discontented inhabitants. According to Eric Verdeil, Ecochard was initially hired in 1960 to provide a slum clearance plan for Qarantina, located at the eastern entrance of Beirut, and then in 1961 to develop a master plan for a new government city.[85] However, true to his era and training, he expanded this to encompass a much larger spatial project: the creation of a master plan for all of Beirut and its peripheries. Furthermore, he was ultimately able to convince the relevant authorities of the utility of such an undertaking. A view of problematic sites in need of spot interventions was thus transformed into a large-scale approach to space embodying the larger shift in discourse from development planning to planning as development.

As growth in and around the city boomed, the 1963 plan focused on developing a transportation network, a new governmental district, and several entirely new towns. More importantly, it identified existing peripheral areas as the primary locations for spatial intervention. According to Marlène Ghorayeb, Ecochard wanted to develop a "'healthy city' next to an 'ailing city,'" and to "absorb" the unplanned growth of Beirut's peripheries. He also wanted to move away from what he argued was an outmoded earlier conception of "urban planning as alignments" on the municipal level to a more potent regional conception.[86] He therefore expanded the territory of his planned intervention, ultimately creating a zoning plan that would reorder all the city's peripheries, slowing their urbanization by means of new (low) land exploitation factors and new (low) allowable building heights.

Father Lebret of IRFED was against a project like this that focused on planning Beirut spatially and that would result in additional government expenditures in the capital.[87] He argued that Beirut had been privileged for a long time at the expense of other areas in Lebanon, and his agency had proposed rethinking this uneven national pattern of development and resource distribution. One could argue that although both experts were trying to address the key sites of discontent in the city and the nation (mainly its territories of poverty, manifest as squatter settlements in and around Beirut), they approached this socioeconomic and spatial problem differently. On the one hand, Father Lebret was interested in addressing the underlying reasons why these urban territories of poverty had emerged—that is, rural-urban migration due to the lack of jobs in the hinterlands. This was a commonly held belief among development-policy experts at the time.[88] Ecochard, on the other hand, believed in the power of spatial reordering to address issues of discontent and unruliness. Consequently, he saw a master plan for Beirut and its suburbs as an opportunity "to reorder the present state of the city and order its future."[89]

It is a testament to changing discourse that IRFED's work remains inscribed today only on the pages of three bound volumes, shelved mainly in university libraries. Meanwhile, Ecochard's vision still haunts the everyday spaces of Beirut's peripheries, and the effect of its development proposals and zoning maps can still be seen in areas like Sahra Choueifat and al-Hadath. Almost fifty years later, many plots in such locations continue to be held hostage to aspects of Ecochard's scheme that never materialized. But beyond this, one can argue that the enactment of Ecochard's plan, a move to reorder Beirut's peripheries by decree, combined with the shelving of IRFED's national-scale proposals, represented the moment when planning as development triumphed as the new logic for organizing territories in Lebanon. Yet in both schemes, the spatiality of the sectarian problem and how it intersected with these other development and planning schemes remained a background concern. Although sectarianism was a topic of debate at the time, the focus of discussions about the built environment was still the problem of how to order an unruly periphery.

Gearing Up for Civil War

While Ecochard was drawing his master plan to reorder Beirut, the crises in neighboring Arab countries and the ongoing Arab-Israeli conflict imposed their own logic on the geopolitics of Lebanon and its capital. The urbanization of Beirut also continued unchecked, as ever more people left rural areas to come to the city.[90] Between 1964 and 1968, the country witnessed dramatic social and political change tied to a confluence of issues: the escalation of the Arab-Israeli conflict and the eventual defeat of the Arab states, the Lebanese banking crisis, and the growth of student social movements.[91]

As political crises mounted, in the early 1970s the Lebanese government made a last-ditch attempt to implement a planning-as-development vision. At the time, Western experts were still being invited to hold seminars in Lebanon to impart lessons to local professionals on how to plan for urban development.[92] One result of these seminars was the development in 1973, by the Directorate of Town Planning, of a White Book that outlined a vision for the future of Beirut for the years 1985 to 2000.[93] The plan focused on decentralization as a solution to looming problems. However, this plan, like all the others before it, remained little more than a blueprint, as the country descended into conflict, violence, militarization, and unrest.[94] As Jad Tabet described it:

The White Book, published in 1973, was a mere statement of impotence. The spatial organization model of Lebanon was in crisis. With the new situation created after the 1967 war [in reference to the war between Israel and Egypt, Jordan, and Syria], the Arab defeat, the emergence of new regional games, and the entry of armed Palestinian forces in Lebanon, this model collapsed. Given the degree to which these dislocations exacerbated socio-economic disparities and collective grievances, it is not at all surprising that the failure of planning during the Chehabist Regime, a regime reputed after all for its ardent support of central planning in Lebanon, should coincide with the escalation of urban violence and civil unrest.[95]

Tabet's comments reveal that while planning as development was seen as a cure for social ills, the "failure of planning" to deliver on this promise was later positioned as a principal reason for the country's disintegration into civil war. Underlying such a claim was a modernist belief in the ability of planning to improve living conditions. Planning was associated with peace; its failure with war. It should not be surprising then that with the onset of civil war, fingers were pointed at planning. The approach to planning ahead of war, however, was never questioned. Hence, rather than assuming that a lack or failure of planning was the cause for the outbreak of violence, it might be more useful to ask why the government pursued certain strategies over others. In particular, why had it chosen Ecochard's approach of massively reordering and plowing through existing peripheral spaces of the poor rather than IRFED's more comprehensive system of national economic interventions? Equally important may be the question of which group of poor were targeted by planning interventions.

It was around the time of the White Book that debate also began to emerge on the spatiality of the sectarian order. Such concern reflected growing discontent among the poor. An important milestone here was the establishment in the early

1970s of the Movement of the Dispossessed (which eventually became Haraket Amal), by Imam Musa al-Sadr, who argued that Shiites had been deprived, neglected, and impoverished by the Lebanese government.[96] Despite the movement's original aspiration to reflect a secular class struggle and the fact that its founders came from multiple religions, it soon became a Shiite-based sectarian party. And in Beirut, it gained most traction in the southern and northern suburbs with their predominantly Shiite populations.

By the debut of the civil war in 1975, only a handful of published studies had jointly addressed the sectarian political order and its spatial problematic.[97] However, two field-based studies do stand out in this period. One is Fuad Khuri's study of the development of the Christian Chiyah and Shiite Ghobeiri suburbs.[98] The other, which challenged Khuri's findings, is Suad Joseph's study of the Armenian Tashnak party's role in Borj Hammoud.[99] At the heart of both works was a quest to understand the interrelation between sectarianism and class issues in shaping the city's peripheries. These two studies were symptomatic of the contradictory positions among social theorists at the start of the initial two-year phase of the war. These positions centered on the question: Was this a sectarian or a class war?[100]

On the one hand, Khuri argued that class was not an important factor in societal organization.[101] Therefore, it was not appropriate "to use the concept of class to study social structure in Lebanon. . . . Family and sect interests, not class interests, dictate the course of political rivalry."[102] Joseph, on the other hand, an advocate of contemporary Marxist views, argued that sectarianism was a constructed identity that disguised underlying class struggles.[103] Writing against discourse that treated sects as primordial, she argued that sectarian divisions should instead be seen as a political construct. Specifically, such a discourse allowed groups to gain access to resources, and politicians to stay in power, because access to resources and services in modern Lebanon had come to be mediated, since the 1960s, through sectarian agencies. In other words, true class struggle, based on economic interest, had been disguised, divided, and/or silenced through sectarianism.

This discussion would be cut short once the civil war started. But in the early phase of the war, it would continue to hold ground, because left-leaning parties organized cross-sect alliances during the first two years of the fighting.[104] However, these alliances eventually disaggregated into militias operating along sectarian lines.[105] Some scholars did continue to maintain that the conflict was based on class, not sectarian, interest.[106] But as the civil war evolved, sectarianism emerged as the predominant logic of violence, and killings along sectarian lines led to mass displacement. Thus, west Beirut gradually became predominantly Muslim, and east Beirut became Christian. For many, it was difficult to make sense of this sort of violence, however—especially those in the urbanist circles, who kept talking about the poor peripheries.[107] For them, the logic of the unruly peripheries was still the logic through which the city needed to be understood and acted upon. As the war progressed, sects were mapped to specific geographies, and sectarian identities, assumed to be unchanging, were fixed in time and space.

From Poor Peripheries to "Illegal Peripheries"

Even after the civil war devolved along sectarian lines, built environment experts persisted in their diagnosis of urban problems and violence. For them, the crisis of uneven development between the center and the peripheries (as well as the hinterlands) was assumed to be the underlying cause of the war (which had only turned sectarian after the fact).[108] Eight years after the onset of civil war, one could thus still hear Lebanese sociologist Samir Khalaf arguing that "virtually all the urban problems of Beirut stem from one fundamental source: unguided, uncontrolled, and unplanned urban growth."[109]

Mirroring these views, in the brief interludes of peace that punctuated the war (in 1977 and 1983), policies for the built environment were the first issues to be discussed. Yet planning and construction proposals were halted repeatedly when the fighting renewed itself. Initially, such efforts were still conceived in terms of national comprehensive planning, aimed at reordering the built environment in the interest of national unity. However, as the war years went by, both the discourse of development and the tools of planning were redirected by the government, and eventually by separate militias, to justify the elimination of trouble areas.[110] Among these were unwanted populations, like the Palestinians in their refugee camps, and informal settlements inhabited by "problematic" sects, such as rural-to-urban Shiite migrants. Such mapping of both poverty and sectarianism to the peripheries eventually resulted in a shift of view, from seeing these areas as "poor" to seeing them as "illegal." And by the time a lull in the fighting came in 1983, this shift had crystallized into constructing them discursively as a legitimate target of destruction.

During the war years, the first moment of peace had actually come in 1977. This had momentarily allowed physical reconstruction to be established as a national priority, pursued through international aid. Donors from Arab and European countries and the United States, however, asked the Lebanese government to dissolve the Ministry of Public Planning, refusing to hand reconstruction aid over to it. These groups reasoned that the ministry was powerless because of its inability to implement any of the development plans and projects proposed since its inception in 1954. As a result, the Lebanese government established the CDR as a new central development and reconstruction apparatus. With financial independence, it would be less entangled in government bureaucracy and would report directly to the Prime Minister. Yet the move basically amounted to one institution replacing another. Thus, despite the evidence of two years of war, the belief that development and planning could end or avoid conflict remained unchanged.

What did eventually change, however, was that during the 1980s, planning as development itself emerged as a tool of war. Prime examples were the urban policies of President Amin Gemayel, who took office in 1982. Gemayel's presidency followed some of the most gruesome years of the war, which included the Israeli army's invasion of Beirut, the massacres in the Sabra and Chatila refugee camps, and the mountain war between Druze and Christian militias. Of course, by then, the conflict had become a primarily sectarian one, and the Palestinian camps had emerged in the discourse of some Lebanese factions (especially right-wing nationalists) as sites in need of being disarmed and sterilized. Within such a climate of opinion, and as the leader of the currently most right-wing Christian militia, Gemayel issued a new building law and urban planning regulations known collectively as Law 10/83, decreed in 1983.[111] These policies aimed to "improve" the living conditions of the Lebanese (after what was then imagined to be the end of the civil war), while managing the problem of the Palestinian camps.[112]

Among other provisions, these laws provided the legal justification for destroying informally constructed buildings. At the time, their target was clear, since both the Palestinian camps and many Shiite-inhabited suburbs were considered informal.[113] However, the decree further mandated that urban planning regulations should supersede any other regulations regarding the built environment, including building laws.[114] To enforce this heavy-handed policy (even though such measures were not applied to other informal settlements), Gemayel sent tanks to Ouzaii, one of the main Shiite informal settlements, to clear it in the name of planning.[115] The year 1983 thus marked a second turning point in the history of planning discourse in Lebanon. By reinscribing west Beirut's poor peripheries as "illegal," planning law established them as a legitimate target for destruction at the same time that it disguised the sectarian motivation for such discourse.

Also in 1983, Gemayel began, through the DGU, a holistic planning project for Beirut, which eventually took the form of the Schéma Directeur de la Région Métropolitaine de Beyrouth (SDRMB). It was prepared by the French consulting firm IAURIF (Institut d'Aménagement et d'Urbanisme de la Région d'Île-de-France), which had already had experience in Lebanon.[116] According to Verdeil, however, although the plan was ultimately completed in 1986, the "planners conceived of the SDRMB as a technical and methodological experiment. They spoke about the methodologies of uncertainty: uncertainty because of the context of war, which made available data rare, less accurate, and subject to rapid change."[117] But by taking "uncertainty" as the only certain reality, the SDRMB ended up reproducing the very geography of war that had been created on the ground by sectarian militias.[118]

Despite this failing, the SDRMB still represented an attempt at a comprehensive development plan for greater Beirut that was pursued through the narrow lens of physical planning. However, between the project's start in 1983 and its finalization in 1986, Gemayel's power weakened, and the power of sectarian militias increased. This allowed the militias to take an active role in shaping the SDRMB through their networks of experts, businessmen, real estate brokers, and military forces. The proposals of the SDRMB thus largely resulted from demands by the militias to plan and zone areas according to their areas of influence, defined along sectarian lines. Indeed, the final scheme reflected the spatial distribution of militias' existing operations, areas of influence, militarization logic, and territorial ambitions in Beirut and its suburbs.

Like many of its predecessors, the plan ultimately remained ink on paper. It was, however, the last attempt to make a plan for the city that integrated west and east Beirut.[119] It was also a last attempt at planning as development before the signing of the Taif Agreement in 1989.[120] By inscribing sectarianism as a fact of everyday life, the Taif Agreement brought back the issue of balanced development, albeit of a different kind.

From Planning as Development to Planning without Development

The approach to balanced development in the post–civil war years has not been the same as that which followed the 1958 uprising. Balanced development nowadays is less about addressing uneven development and income inequality than it is about providing a balanced distribution of public monies to different sectarian-defined zones. It thus marks the third phase of the relationship between planning and development in Lebanon. One official I interviewed in 2010 (previously quoted in Chapter 4) described this process as "planning by touchstones." The phrase defines what I have chosen to call a logic of *planning without development*. Such an approach allows for localized planning through an allotment among religious-political organizations, which in turn reinforces or facilitates an ever-shifting division of urban space along sectarian lines.

It should be noted that such an approach is not confined to planning, but has become a generalized practice of government in all arenas.[121] Yet, as illustrated in the three case studies presented in the previous chapters, it has allowed militias and religious-political organizations to configure space in their own interests, not only through the "sticks" of militarization, violence, and forced migration but also through the "carrots" of housing development and social service provision.

Such an approach to arranging territory, however, explicitly recognizes these actors' anticipated role in the war yet to come. Thus, within these delineated zones, for the most part, socioeconomic development is left to sectarian actors. But the urban planning and economic development they achieve is now principally a disaggregating effort, no longer concerned with a vision of public action toward social justice and redistribution of resources. Consequently, this practice of planning has contributed to the transformation of Beirut's peripheries from merely poor, informal settlements to sectarian frontiers, characterized by exponential growth and periodic, violent confrontation.

The spatial logic of the war yet to come has exceeded the "utopia" of homogeneous living developed during the civil war through mass displacements and evictions along sectarian lines. By the war's end, in the 1990s, living in homogeneous regions and neighborhoods—one's *bī'a*—had become a common practice, a preference for many, and a dominant urban reality.[122] Moreover, the de facto rule of former militias turned religious-political organizations in many of these areas has been exacerbated by the Lebanese government's neoliberal postwar policies. Although neoliberalism does not fully explain the postwar geography in Lebanon, the end of the war did correspond with a shift in global political and economic systems. Starting in the 1980s, this brought the rollback of state services in the Global North and a push for structural adjustment in the Global South. The war's end also coincided with the dissolution of the Soviet Union and the project of Communism, eliminating some of the risks of intervention that had hindered the expansion of the Western global order.

In need of foreign investment, monetary aid for reconstruction, and loans, postwar Lebanese governments adopted neoliberal policies in their approach to a range of issues. These have included the privatization of downtown Beirut's reconstruction and the decision to give displaced populations monetary compensation, instead of providing them with comprehensive livelihood reconstruction programs. Thus, postwar policies and design interventions, like the Fund for the Return of the Displaced and the provision of shared public spaces in Beirut's downtown, intended to remix previously heterogeneous areas, did not achieve much remixing.[123]

At the same time that urban planning practice in Lebanon was struggling with how to approach planning in a postwar context, planning debates globally witnessed a turn toward fostering "community" and promoting "identity." Thus, earlier planning concerns for national and regional development have been replaced by a new emphasis on the well-being of self-defined communities that make their own choices about their lifestyle. This has resulted in the almost complete erasure of attempts at comprehensive development planning. Indeed, the global production of architecture and planning knowledge has shifted from designing "large-scale, metropolitan-wide, technologically rational and efficient urban plans" to "a conception of the urban fabric as necessarily fragmented."[124] In academic circles, this shift has been felt in a move away from discussing development, modernization, and the role of the welfare state to a discussion of postmodernism. And in policy circles, it has corresponded to a new emphasis on the right of populations to be unburdened by taxation and social welfare programs, to exercise the right to choose, and to be able to vote with their feet. This shift has had major repercussions in terms of access, marginalization, segregation, and urban citizenship. And today such policy fragmentation not only defines the geography of Beirut as a city in conflict, but also urbanization across cities in both the Global North and Global South, where many disadvantaged and marginalized populations have been left to their own devices in neglected slums and squatter settlements.

Aihwa Ong has introduced the concept of *post-developmentalism* to explain this shift in the spatial order. Post-developmentalism is different from developmentalism, Ong argues, because it does not treat national space as uniform political space. She emphasizes how, instead, "the neoliberal stress on economic borderlessness has induced the creation of multiple political spaces and techniques for differentiated governing within the national terrain." The neoliberal developmental spatial logic of "graduated sovereignty" thus favors "the fragmentation of the national space into various noncontiguous zones, and promote[s] the differential regulation of populations," making some sites "more 'bankable' than other developing regions." Therefore, according to Ong, "[t]he deployment of such post-developmental logic in effect produces a post-developmental geography—the multiplication of differentiated zones of governing across the national territory—that has specific political effects."[125] Development thus becomes first and foremost a geographic project, during which certain zones are either developed or neglected.

Although Ong focuses her analysis on "illiberal" countries like China, this concept may also be useful to understanding how Beirut's peripheries have become mixed territories of development and underdevelopment, where the state plays a role in the former, while its role in the production of the latter is rendered invisible. In Beirut, and Lebanon in general, territories are now delineated into zones, and it is only within selected areas of these fragments that "development" may be pursued. This approach to planning and development is principally negotiated by religious-political organizations to promote control of their respective territories. And inside these sectarian-delineated zones, a number of organizations have championed local socioeconomic development (such as Hezbollah's famous and extensive network of social services).

It is important here to recall that development in Lebanon was never a total project that covered the entire national territory and was then lost to sectarian conflict. Nevertheless, as I have shown in my discussion of the previous IRFED, Ecochard, and government projects, there was formerly at least an aspiration toward such a program. This was promoted by expert discourses and thought, even if it was never actually produced as an outcome. However, the neoliberal turn that coincided with the end of the civil war helped usher in a newly accepted logic of fragmentation and segregation along sectarian lines. And this logic of *planning without development* has been sanctioned by spatial experts whose role is now diminished to being mere technicians of this territorial logic.

The Loss of Development

Two last attempts at development and planning were made, in 1992 and 2002, before the country slipped again into sectarian clashes in 2008. In 1992, Prime Minister Hariri initiated work on Horizon 2000, which envisioned a thirteen-year reconstruction and recovery plan for "all" of Lebanon, specifically targeting the years 1995 to 2007.[126] The report was prepared for the CDR by two engineering and planning companies, Dar al-Handasah and Bechtel. It set two principal goals: to engage in a massive campaign to construct and reconstruct physical infrastructure, and to jumpstart the nation's financial recovery by doubling the gross domestic product (GDP)—a level of future prosperity the Lebanese government promised international development agencies. Yet, despite its ambitions, Horizon 2000 was merely a collection of physical projects that the government hoped would together instigate development. Indeed, it offered little more than a list of separate, sector-based projects (dealing with electricity, water, sewage, telecom, and housing), rather than a comprehensive development plan. Moreover, a few years into the process, a series of political and economic crises made it clear that Horizon 2000 was an impossible task. And since then, the spatial legacy of Horizon 2000 has principally been the privatized reconstruction of downtown Beirut, a task handled by Solidere. A few infrastructure projects were also completed as part of the plan. But its major initiatives remained ink on paper.

The second attempt at comprehensive national planning and development has been the National Physical Master Plan for the Lebanese Territory (NPMP), which I introduced in my discussion of Doha Aramoun in Chapter 4. This effort began in 2002.[127] The NPMP is, again, mainly an exercise in physical planning focused on land use. But this has not stopped it from being imbued with hope that it might finally bring unity and prosperity to Lebanon. And for the handful of remaining modernist planners in Lebanon, such a physical master plan has been seen as a way to at least stem the haphazardness of the building industry in Lebanon, irrespective of its development goals. As Mohamad Fawaz wrote:

[D]espite its not being a development plan like I had hoped . . . it is an important work because it establishes a general framework for urban planning. The NPMP is an important project. I give it priority over the development plan. *The establishment of a development plan is possible at any time.* However, practices that are physically shaping the built environment are generally impossible to revert. The longer Lebanon delays decreeing a master plan to organize its territories, the larger will be the damages that will be impossible to reform or fix on the national level [emphasis added].[128]

When it was approved in 2009, the NPMP was celebrated as a triumph for the state. The CDR, specifically, had finally been able to produce a national plan, and have it decreed as law, despite the turbulence of the times.[129] At the time, however, the CDR was considered an arm of the Sunni Future Movement, and other political camps soon attacked the plan for its lack of socioeconomic sensibility.[130] For example, Hezbollah, through its research center, the Consultative Center for Studies and Documentation (CCSD), slammed the NPMP for being a physical intervention and not a development plan. Thus, during a 2006 seminar organized by the CCSD, a Hezbollah-affiliated expert claimed: "this study lacks a future vision and an outlook for a role that Lebanon could play in 2030. With the absence of this vision and role, the intended comprehensive development plan ended up being no more than a physical master plan for a collection of projects, thoughts, and proposals that are suggestive by nature and does not oblige any ministry or public agency to abide by it."[131]

In reality, such critiques of the NPMP were not only about the elevation of physical over socioeconomic concerns; they were also about the spatiality of the sectarian order and public investment in maintaining the precarious balance of that order. In the same CCSD seminar in 2006, Hezbollah, through its experts, argued that the approved NPMP gave "significant weight to Beirut and Tripoli" (in reference to the Sunni areas), while excluding other areas. It claimed this would result in "ripples of poor areas surrounding" Beirut (in reference to Beirut's "Shiite peripheries"). The Hezbollah experts then demanded a true development plan, in which "'land organization' is only one aspect."[132]

In effect, such a critique was an indirect way of arguing that the fruits of the master plan had not been equally distributed among sects. Yet, in many ways, just such a sectarian allotment has been a critical aspect of the approved NPMP. It is, if anything, a materialization of planning with touchstones, because it provides each sect with a major urban development project in Beirut and its peripheries. Thus, aside from the redevelopment of downtown Beirut by Solidere, it has proposed the

Elyssar project as an investment in the Shiite southern peripheries, Linord and its proposed extension for Beirut's Christian northern peripheries, and the "southern terraces of Beirut/Aramoun" for a Sunni emerging area with a Druze base. Thus, like the 1986 master plan, the NPMP (although celebrated by some experts) accepts the de facto spatiality of the political order—a spatial exercise (of distributing monies along sectarian lines) devoid of a comprehensive development logic.

The Technicians of the War Yet to Come

It is within this context of planning without development that one can, finally, locate Mr. I's and Mr. H's descriptions of their approaches to planning as akin to fashion or jewelry design. And Mr. I and Mr. H are not anomalies among their planning peers; they are in fact two of the more respected experts in the city. But their descriptions underlie the difficulty of addressing a contested periphery turned frontier like Sahra Choueifat.

During my twenty-plus interviews with planners working in Beirut about their approaches to planning, I learned a great deal about urban planning practice. For the most part, my interviewees were respected urbanists with many long years of experience in Lebanon, and I am very grateful for their willingness to discuss difficult issues with me at times. At other times, most of our discussions were focused on the logic of traffic and vehicular arteries and on how a proper city should look, and of course, there was lots of talk about Solidere, Elyssar, Linord, and Hezbollah's reconstruction project, Waad. Only a handful of my interviewees were interested in discussing, for example, the newly approved NPMP. What this indicates is that these planners have largely become technicians of a regulating spatial logic of planning without development.

As one planner described his job to me, planning in Beirut has turned into a practice of innovating within the spatial logics introduced in the previous chapters of this book—doubleness, lacework, and ballooning—which are aimed at reconfiguring the borders and boundaries between different groups in the city and its peripheries. Alternatively, as another planner put it: "Our job is to manage everyday territorial conflict on blueprints and spreadsheets." And as a third asserted, this job involves developing "a set of balancing practices to keep a war away." Long gone are Ecochard's grand spatial schemes or IRFED's schemes for social and economic development, which, despite their problematic qualities, aimed at large-scale progress. In fact, as I have tried to show, planning the geographies of the war to come instead involves the spatial practice of patching new spot designations around Ecochard's old, finely tailored lines.

What was further striking to me during my conversations was that only a handful of my interviewees even mentioned development concerns. Even when

I asked about areas like Sahra Choueifat, few even raised such formerly paramount concerns as poverty alleviation, informality, precarious living conditions, lack of jobs, the inability of the middle class to access affordable housing, and the unequal distribution of resources between the city and its peripheries. The only discussions that involved talk of unequal distribution were related to the government's pattern of investment in physical planning across regions. In this regard, many of those I spoke to did openly assert that investment in public planning had been happening along sectarian lines, benefiting areas inhabited by certain religious-political groups, while ignoring others.[133] But even in public forums (media, workshops, and the like), there was almost no talk about development as a national priority.[134]

When I interrogated these discourses further, however, a different picture emerged. A number of planners, especially Mr. I and Mr. H, had provided nuanced accounts of their experience with planning in Lebanon, as these had shaped their positions and approaches. Thus, Mr. I, a planner in a private company contracted to engage in the planning of Sahra Choueifat for more than a decade, had described to me (as detailed in Chapter 3) the threats, abuses, and humiliations he had been forced to endure. After a while, I realized Mr. I was in fact a planning idealist who found himself in an unfortunate situation that is apparently common in Lebanon. A graduate of a prestigious North American university, he still believed in the power of planning to "beautify, develop, and improve" living conditions. However, all he could now talk about was the impossibility of doing this job in the city and its peripheries. He painfully recounted the many times when politically backed landowners, militiamen, and land developers had intercepted him when he arrived at his office, threatened his planning team in the field, and banged on drawing tables—all to demand changes to zoning and planning proposals for Sahra Choueifat. In the end, Mr. I had simply been instructed to draw lines as he was told to by religious-political organizations. His initial scheme for Sahra Choueifat included a vision for an industrial zone separated from an affordable housing area with a green belt; what ended up on his drawing board and on the ground, however, were overlapping zones of industrial and residential use that created a host of dangerous environmental and political conditions.

Mr. I's engagement with planning in Sahra Choueifat thus provided the context for his description of his current approach to the planning of peripheries as "fashion design." It also explained his view that changes to his plans by the clients (in this case, warring religious-political organizations) were, in his words, "none of my business." Mr. I had been transformed into a technician of the regulating logic of the war yet to come. He still practiced his planning ideals—but only in picturesque mountain villages far from Beirut's contested frontiers.

Mr. H had received a similarly hostile response when he had attempted to put forward alternative planning visions. He has vast knowledge and outstanding expertise in the field of planning, and we engaged in wide-ranging conversations on, for example, social justice and the ideal city. But when I asked Mr. H about Beirut's peripheries, he scaled back his discussion to focus on the failure of street alignments in areas like Sahra Choueifat—areas that had just witnessed a miniature civil war.

From Poor Peripheries to Sectarian Frontiers

In light of such interviews with local experts, it appears that postwar Beirut has witnessed a complete shift in planning logic: from planning *as* development to planning *without* development. What this ultimately signals is that planning has become an end in itself, an arrangement of territories without larger social purpose. Indeed, planning in the city has now been emptied even of those ideas of spatial justice that remained resilient during the most difficult years of the civil war. It has largely been this shift from a "quest for development," centered on issues of poverty and illegality, to an exercise in spatializing sectarian difference that has been responsible for shifting the discourse around Beirut's southern peripheries—from being "informal and poor peripheries" to being "Shiite neighborhoods," the new frontiers of sectarian conflict. This reformulation of the political consciousness vis-à-vis the periphery—its economy, marginality, and inhabitants—has also had major repercussions in terms of increasing levels of poverty, segregation, violence, and loss of environmental quality.[135]

In my interviews with planners, as I attempted to unearth the genealogy of the current situation, I also came to realize that spatial practices in Beirut may best be characterized today as a post-poverty discourse. Planning as an exercise in attaining—or at least aiming to attain—spatial justice is rarely discussed anymore.[136] And as a result, the importance of the peripheries as targets of "national development" has receded, to be taken over by conversations about the unequal sectarianized distribution of planning monies across areas affiliated with different religious-political organizations. In this mapping, Beirut's southern peripheries have come to be seen as zones inhabited by Shiites and serviced by Hezbollah and Haraket Amal. And according to this logic, the socioeconomic condition of the "Shiite peripheries" has been divorced from any larger debate over development and planning.

This condition applies, moreover, not only to Beirut's southern peripheries but to all areas seen as under the control of religious-political organizations.[137] Questions of who is in need of development, and what, where, and when this may be the case, have all been left to the discretion of the religious-political organizations in control of each area. These questions are thus no longer up for debate in expert circles. This was clearly illustrated by the withdrawal of Mr. I and Mr. H from any claim to a role when it comes to redistribution of economic resources or spatial justice.

One can further argue that in Beirut, this shift in the logic of governing the peripheries has flipped the long-established formula of development and planning. Thus, the practice of planning has replaced the question of development as the overarching framework through which to organize territories. Planning nowadays is primarily useful as a way to delineate zones and territories in which development is delegated to religious-political organizations.

EPILOGUE
CONTESTED FUTURES

BEIRUT IS NOT NEW TO WAR—indeed, the city has been a site of conflict for nearly half a century. However, in the last decade, the Green Line that famously divided the city during the 1975–1990 civil war has mutated. As hostilities continue, the city is now fragmented by hundreds of new "green lines" that have transformed its fast-growing peripheries into frontiers of local and transnational violence.[1] Present conflict alone, however, does not provide an adequate framework for understanding emergent patterns of urbanization in the city. This book has thus offered the concept of *the war yet to come* as a lens through which to understand how planning for future conflict is also responsible for the ongoing creation of frontiers in Beirut. Structured by past wars and in anticipation of new ones, this new condition involves more than battlefield logics or paramilitary maneuvering. It involves the calculated construction, in times of peace, of a spatial order of sectarian and political difference. Thus, this book has additionally sought to reveal the important role played by religious-political organizations in shaping urban planning and zoning schemes, land and housing markets, and the provision of infrastructure.

Going beyond local circumstances, this book has also sought to illustrate the fallacy of accepting established binaries in the study of post-conflict cities. In Beirut's peripheries, war and peace, arrested development and growth, coexistence and segregation, destruction and construction, home and displacement are intimately entangled. At the time of this research, these areas rather appeared as a checkerboard of conditions, where ruins were simultaneously the product of past and future conflict, where housing and industrial zones interlaced and overlapped, and where neighborhoods designated for upscale development existed side by side with abject poverty and environmental crisis. Since then, these geographies have only been further reconfigured by new cycles of violence and displacement that continue to redefine otherness and engender new forms and mechanisms of spatial segregation.

Lessons from Beirut's Ongoing Urbanization

The lessons of the war yet to come in Beirut may appear exceptional with regard to Eurocentric urbanization theory, which imagines cities of the Global North as the norm. But what if we rethink normative configurations of center-periphery, private-public, and the relations of space and time from the perspective of the Global South?[2] From this perspective, Beirut's urbanization may open new avenues for rethinking four main issues of concern to urban and planning theory: the changing relationship between center and periphery; the growing importance of complex nongovernmental actors; the spatial and temporal production of political difference; and the role of urban planning in producing contested, as opposed to harmonious, geographies.

With regard to the first of these, I have sought from the outset of this work to rethink the way cities in the Global South are normally perceived according to a dichotomy between a formal, prosperous center and marginalized, informal peripheries. As I have showed, however, Beirut's peripheries may themselves be considered centers within today's transnational landscapes of finance, conflict, and religious and political ideology. Specifically, I described how the urbanization of greater Beirut is currently being structured as much by the expansion of predominantly Shiite al-Dahiya (Beirut's southern suburb) as by the post–civil war redevelopment of Beirut's central business district. This has led to the expansion of both al-Dahiya and Beirut into areas previously claimed by other sectarian groups—which, in turn, has been interpreted by some as encroachment on the territories of the religious other and evidence of the "Islamization" of the Middle East, thus transforming peripheries into frontiers and leading to friction and new cycles of violence.

On the transnational level, Beirut (like many cities of the Global South) has typically been excluded from the mapping of so-called Global Cities and their "spaces of flows."[3] But space-making practices in Beirut's peripheries are in fact tied to real estate transactions, informed by religious ideologies, that originate in places as distant as Washington, DC; Sydney, Australia; and São Paulo, Brazil. And these transnational flows have influenced not just the growth of al-Dahiya. The post–civil war rebuilding of the Beirut metropolitan area has also relied on great amounts of Kuwaiti and Saudi aid to provide Beirut's emerging "Sunni peripheries" with infrastructure. Beirut's southern suburbs have likewise become such an important center in the Arab-Israeli conflict that large areas there were leveled in July 2006 as part of Israel's war on Lebanon. Now, in the latest iteration of regional conflict, other areas of Beirut's southern peripheries, like Doha Aramoun, have emerged as recruiting grounds and battlefields for ISIS-affiliated paramilitary groups. In other words, it is the juxtaposition of local and transnational processes that has helped to structure Beirut's geographies in anticipation of wars yet to come. And such relationships further complicate notions of what is central and what is peripheral.

Crucial to this reconfiguration of center and periphery have been the practices of religious-political organizations. But the actions of these groups in restructuring territory in greater Beirut are further symptomatic of a larger concern within contemporary urban theory. Across the Middle East and beyond, such complex nongovernmental actors are today seeking to reshape cities according to their own politics and ethics of space making. Understanding the operations of these groups in Beirut may, for example, provide insight into the practices of Fatah and Hamas in the Palestinian territories, the Muslim Brotherhood in Egypt, and the Sadr Movement in Iraq.

Such complex, hybrid organizations are not simply local but are embedded in the global circulations of finance, real estate, development and humanitarian aid, religious ideology, and conflict. In Lebanon, for example, Hezbollah is both a Lebanese political party and a transnational Islamic military organization, fighting regionally against Israel's occupation of Lebanon and alongside the Assad regime in Syria. Meanwhile, in its local capacity, Hezbollah is both part of the state, helping to provide services dependent on public funding, and part of the private service sector. In this latter role, its affiliates offer goods and services not available from the state, including affordable health care, free access to water wells, low-interest loans, and low-cost housing for families in need. Hezbollah thus cannot be said to stand outside the state and the market; yet neither can it be seen solely as a beneficiary of the shift of previously state-administered welfare services to the private sector.

As entities in both the public and private domains, such groups also create geographies that represent a complex articulation of religious-sectarian belief and for-profit development. This is why Hezbollah cannot be said to be antithetical to the neoliberal economic order. Yet neither can it be said to be a tool of that order. In fact, championing for-profit housing and real estate projects has been one of Hezbollah's key spatial interventions. Indeed, it has been the success of these efforts that has been decried as the encroachment of a religious other on territories previously claimed by Sunnis, Christians, and Druze, and that has been a principal cause of the transformation of Beirut's peripheries into frontiers. These competing logics illustrate how the geographies of the war yet to come are produced by both continuities and discontinuities between neoliberal economic restructuring and religious ideology, sectarian difference, and individual relationships to land and home ownership.

I have sought to provide a grounded perspective on how such organizations may simultaneously be engaged in projects of urban development, nation building, and the transnational construction of difference along nationalist, religious, and ethnic lines. This, however, has required grappling with the difficulty of studying spaces of conflict—both as real territories and imaginary constructs. At a time when cities are increasingly subject to contestation and violence, finding appropriate methods for conducting research in them has become central to the field of urban studies. My approach was to attempt what I have termed an *ethnography of spatial practices*. This involved investigating the material and discursive processes underpinning urbanization trends at multiple sites—from public offices, where master plans are continuously drawn and undrawn, to grocery stores and hair salons, where rumors circulate about the hidden purpose of particular building schemes.

Key to this effort was the method of "patching stories and maps" that I adopted, an approach that spoke directly to the difficulty of doing research in a divided city. In conditions of conflict, nothing can be taken for granted: sources disappear, alliances shift, networks disintegrate, sites erupt in violence, maps vanish, and archives are almost nonexistent. This meant juxtaposing field information with archival fragments, and assembling these patchworks of data in relation to popular discourses and rumors circulating in the streets. It was ultimately such openings and closures, however, that revealed the transformation of Beirut's peripheries into frontiers as they were arranged and rearranged over time by master plans, real estate schemes, political alliances, territorial struggles, discourses of fear, and talk of war. Ultimately, my field engagement illuminated how various religious-political organizations, in both a local and transnational quest for material and political advantage, have produced and reproduced uneven geographies of segregation, poverty, environmental degradation, and violence.

As a grounded, ethnographic perspective illustrates, the behaviors of such organizations do not fit neatly within private-public, state-market, or government-insurgency binaries. The religious-political organizations of Lebanon currently employ a variety of different capacities as they continue to play a critical role in shaping Beirut's expanding urban territory within a paramilitary logic of imagined wars yet to come. As the cases of Sahra Choueifat and Doha Aramoun show, what counts (in addition to controlling real estate and housing markets) is the religious-political organizations' ability, in the event of future war, to maneuver militarily by controlling strategic hilltops, secure transportation hubs (such as Beirut's airport), and protect access to weapons caches and shipments. Thus, conflict, in times of peace, is about the *construction* of the built environment, rather than its *destruction*. And such logic ultimately translates into the militarization of everyday life—as each street, building, and window is evaluated as an asset in a possible future of renewed urban warfare.

As wars in the Middle East are increasingly described as sectarian, Beirut stands as a paradigm for understanding the implications of this future. More broadly, it can also be seen as prefiguring the future of all cities where political difference—whether religious, racial, or ethnic—is assumed to be primordial and inherent. More hopefully, however, this book has also attempted to show how what is commonly referred to as "sectarianism" is itself spatially and temporally produced. Using an ethnographic lens to investigate the practices that shape sectarianism has helped to show its instability. People produce and reproduce the geography of the self and the other in part through discourses on such concerns as *bi'a* and demography. And this order of things may be continuously contested, reconfigured, and reproduced by shifting political alliances and changing opportunities for financial profit. Indeed, these passing forces crucially redefine what sectarianism means at any given moment. Sectarianism must thus be understood as an unstable regime of difference that is constantly being made and unmade.

Mapping these processes geographically has become of paramount importance to unfolding debates about religious coexistence in the Middle East. What might the establishment of a new geography of coexistence entail? Is it about standing still in time—with no way forward and no way back—where the future can only be imagined as unimaginably bleak? The three processes of urbanization I have investigated here—doubleness, lacework, and ballooning—indicate rather that new territories of poverty and frontiers of sectarian violence are constantly being negotiated on local, national, and transnational scales. These are nested geographies of conflict, not a hardened geography of walls. Thus, even though some new borderlines may seemingly be solidified through violent confrontations, such as those of May 2008, others remain tenuously defined, in flux, constantly challenged through subtle, everyday acts of spatial transgression. Such a honeycombed urbanization, while violent at times, does still hold within it the possibility of encounter and collaboration. It is ultimately within the cracks made by these ongoing shifts that neighborhoods, towns, cities, and nations can locate possibilities for hope in the otherwise dystopic geography of the war yet to come.

Inverting the Urban Future

In light of the potential just described, what I have sought to do here is invert the lens through which present efforts to arrange urban territory in the Middle East and beyond are viewed. In particular, I have sought to contrast the "yet to" of modernization theory with the "yet to" of the war yet to come.

The "yet to" of the modernization project has consistently envisioned a better future, one that will bring prosperity and development to all. Thus, urban interventions and planning schemes—the paramount tools of modernization—have long proclaimed the expectation of improvement, the hope that the restructuring of territory can bring a more productive urban order. At the same time, a number of scholars have criticized the destruction that modernization may bring to neighborhoods in the name of development, and in doing so have exposed the myth that the utopia of modernization is all inclusive.[4] In fact, the modern utopia can only be achieved by marginalizing and further impoverishing the racialized and gendered poor. Despite these critiques, the bright teleology of modernization remains, for the most part, a powerful narrative force motivating planning interventions.

The "yet to" of urbanization likewise continues to provide an imaginary of hope for much of the world's population. Thus, AbdouMaliq Simone has described how rural people continue to move to the urban fringe in anticipation that "the city to come" will bring them new socioeconomic and political gains.[5] Such a hopeful urbanism seems to promise the poor a future without poverty. Yet, some scholars have decried such ongoing "planetary urbanization" as containing the seeds of global crisis.[6] This position has perhaps been most drearily encapsulated in Mike Davis's description of a "planet of slums."[7] Nonetheless, every year millions of rural migrants continue to flood the peripheries of cities across the globe, believing they hold the opportunity for a better life.

The "yet to" of the war yet to come, however, recasts this urban future more bleakly. While modernization folds dystopia within an overarching utopic narrative of the future, the horizon of the war yet to come holds only the prospect of new rounds of violence and displacement. Nonetheless, such a prospect does not imply a stalled present. Rather, the anticipation of future war is critical to how the present is shaped. In the words of Paul Saint-Amour, "when the future appears foreclosed, anticipation loses its conditional relationship to that future: once seen as a fait accompli, a future event becomes a force in the present, producing effects in advance of its arrival."[8]

The spatial logic of the war yet to come, therefore, is about locking up certain geographies in the present for fear of the future, while continuing to create calculated openings for urban growth and real estate profit. Territorial restructuring may thus be seen by key actors as a way to manage, control, anticipate, and prepare for future conditions, such as terror, gang violence, and racial antagonism. In this way, the restructuring of urban territory through the establishment of multiple dividing lines may be seen to produce a temporal regime that, according to Achille Mbembe, "closes the future for some and keeps it open for others."[9] Indeed, the geographies of the conflict yet to come have led to the establishment of "states of exception," where laws are suspended for certain segments of the population and applied only to others.[10] Territories may thus be carved into some zones deemed "safe" and others deemed "unsafe," allowing openings for a select few while enforcing closure for the many. These geographies are characterized by intimate entanglements of mobility and immobility, lavishness and poverty, accessibility and detention, opportunity and destitution, legality and illegality—creating complex categories of differentiated citizenship.[11]

Reacting to these practices means questioning the continuing utility of spatial organizing tools, such as zoning plans, building laws, and real estate regulations. How does an anticipated future of war shape the interventions deployed in the name of these practices? What kinds of geographies do they produce? In particular, as the previous chapters have shown, the production of the geographies of the war yet to come relies heavily on the legal mechanisms of urban planning. This is not planning practice as typically framed in the disciplinary literature, however. There, planning and regulated development are hailed as pathways to a future of progress, peace, order, and prosperity.[12] But the logic of the war yet to come in greater Beirut challenges the very foundations of such a belief. Here, planning tools are utilized strategically to twist time and space to enable openings and delineate closures, and thus arrange territories in expectation of future violence.

This condition is perhaps nowhere better illustrated in the present research than in the 1996 master plan for Sahra Choueifat. Originally meant to provide a blueprint for the town's development over the next thirty years, it was subsequently changed at least eight times in the twelve years after it appeared. The current outcomes of such planning processes are "planned" spaces where industrial and residential zones overlap, where access highways will never be finished and playgrounds never built, where streets fail to align or were abolished after buildings they were intended to serve were built, where ruins remain because the land they occupy is valued for its role in ongoing conflicts, and where luxury overlooks destitution. Yet, these same areas provide the best housing option for many middle- and low-income people who cannot afford to live within the city proper. This is the reality of planning in Beirut and its peripheries today. By being simultaneously a tool of pacification, conflict, and development, what was once regarded as a mechanism of order and progress has facilitated the transformation of the city's peripheries into dystopias of environmental degradation subject to ongoing cycles of violence. Meanwhile, real estate markets have soared, creating wealth for the few and displacing the many.

Such conditions emphasize the need for new ways of understanding the temporalities of planning practice in cities in conflict. Instead of assuming that planning will always lead to a better future, it would be more productive to study how it actually functions on the ground. Such an effort will be essential if the practices of urban planning are to continue to be seen as contributing to a better future through the pursuit of such public values as wise resource management, spatial justice, redistribution of economic opportunity, and risk mitigation. I have illustrated the perversion of these values through my investigation of planning practice in Sahra Choueifat and Hayy Madi/Mar Mikhail. There, assigning projects to the "under study" category allowed parties to negotiate and trade political gains based on this strategic suspension of land-use control, while the seemingly endless splitting of zoning categories was used to institutionalize the presence of otherwise irreconcilable environmental conflict. Such practices express a desire to "stand still" and to keep areas "frozen in time," while at the same time facilitating large-scale, lucrative residential development; the proposals of a new National Physical Master Plan; and massive infrastructure investment.

Ultimately, the spatial map of areas and projects that are "standing still" or "moving forward" can only be understood as configured through an intersection of urbanization pressure, neoliberal economics, the military maneuvering of religious-political organizations, and the political quest to create a new geography of sectarian difference. In such a landscape, the fate of individual areas is being determined by the spatial outcome of the civil war, postwar economic and demographic restructuring, and the skyrocketing cost of land and housing as gentrification pushes into the city's southern suburbs. These uneven geographies are created by negotiation and contestation, power brokering, sectarian affiliation, and geopolitical alliances. They embody a territory of both hope and fear, where neighborhoods subject to toxic flooding adjoin wealthy enclaves with lavish views of the Mediterranean Sea.

One of the central findings of this book, expressed in its title, is that planning can be a tool of war as well as of peace. Rather than assuming that spaces of conflict emerge from an absence of planning, the case studies presented here show they can likewise emerge from deliberate processes that incorporate layers upon layers of contested planning exercises. Within this alternative planning regime, innovative techniques have been needed to create a spatiality of political difference, keep war at bay, and enable the powerful to continue to profit from ongoing urban growth. An investigation of Beirut's planning history shows this has been made possible by emptying the planning discourse of its former development logic. Over decades, this logic has been stripped away, until planning in Lebanon has become little more than an exercise in ordering space, a tool of power brokerage in sectarian battles. *Planning without development* has divided Beirut's peripheries into territories where the state has delegated its former development obligations, such as the provision of affordable housing and social services, to competing religious-political organizations. Planners have become the technicians of this new regulating logic, signaling in particular, a shift in their approach toward urban peripheries as territories of poverty.[13] Whereas planners in Beirut previously thought of peripheries as sites of development, poverty alleviation, and future progress, their conversations nowadays mostly focus on explaining the sectarian logic through which plans for such areas are drawn and negotiated, policies are designed, and resources are distributed. These conversations highlight their inability to imagine an effective role for themselves in these areas beyond the territorial reproduction of sectarian difference.

Yet, new movements are emerging through the cracks in this dystopian tableau, movements that may one day challenge sectarian-based political alliances and their geographies of fear. Thus, rather than concluding that planning practice exists everywhere in similar ways, or that principled planning is an impossibility in Beirut's peripheries, I would like to end by asserting that planning remains a powerful tool in Beirut. It has recently also become a practice around which alternative groups have rallied. One of these groups is Beirut Madinati (Beirut My City), a movement "of technocrats, young professionals, academics and progressive activists" that won 40 percent of the vote in Beirut's municipal elections on May 8, 2016.[14] Its affiliate, Naqabati (My Syndicate), meanwhile, won the presidency of Beirut's Order of Engineers and Architects in its 2017 elections.

Rather than taking modernist temporality for granted and assuming a teleology of progress, these movements are questioning whether the tools of planning, as attendant to more general processes of space-making, might be more useful as a way to transform social engagement and stimulate new imaginings of the future. In a contested city like Beirut, such activities might help move politics beyond the present logic of sectarian division. In particular, the participatory tools of planning might be used to craft new spaces of engagement and knowledge that will offer a different horizon for city residents, one that sees beyond the inevitability of new wars.

Such practices might also speak to the possibility of imagining a different future for spaces of conflict across cities of the Global South and North. They involve reimagining the scope and purpose of planning practice in places where differences may be so extreme that the future cannot always be imagined as peaceful or uncontested.

The "Yet to" of Global Conflicts

This study, therefore, is not only about Beirut and its contested future. Indeed, I have tried to present it in such a way that the conditions it describes can be imagined as extending even beyond other recent cities in conflict, such as Belfast or Medellin. The reality underlying this effort is that the imagined future in most places today—whether in the Global North or Global South—is one of conflict and contestation, characterized by fear of ecological crises, disease, terrorist attacks, and destabilizing population flows that in many ways anticipate what I have called the war yet to come.

At the present global moment, the future of all cities may be thought of as contested. And considering the range of challenges, it has become increasingly difficult to imagine a future of social change that is fully inclusive of a racialized, religious, ethnic, and gendered other. In the absence of a significant reconfiguration of thinking about living conditions, therefore, most urban interventions can be expected to simply define and redefine the contours of inclusion and exclusion. And such redefined territories will inevitably facilitate the circulation and mobility of certain bodies and objects, while arresting that mobility for many others.

On the South Side of Chicago, for example, an imaginary of "the gang violence yet to come" resulted in the establishment in 2011 of the Chicago Safe Passages program for public school children. This program, whose goal is to delineate safe routes for students across the territories of warring gangs, has been coordinated by the Chicago Police Department and the city's public school district and mediated by community leaders and church figures. Yet, rather than addressing the underlying causes of urban violence, the program assumes a violent future, and intervenes by rearranging territories to separate "safe" areas from "unsafe" ones. In so doing it thus unintentionally reproduces the discourse of an inherently, or "naturally," dangerous racialized other.

In the United States, it is also possible to look back to the response to the events of September 11, 2001. For the last decade and a half, the country has lived in anticipation of new attacks. Thus, a logic of what may be called the "terror yet to come" continues to drive the design and reconfiguration of urban spaces. As public agencies anticipate future events of the same nature, 9/11 now shapes how people experience space in all major U.S. cities.

The logic of the terror yet to come has become even more pervasive following attacks in cities from Paris to Baghdad and Mogadishu to Barcelona. The future is increasingly seen as reflective of violence yet to come, giving rise to a global restructuring of geographies and the truncating of rights of those deemed to be other, with widespread calls to erect walls, both literally and figuratively, to shut out unwanted populations. As people move through militarized public spaces, retreat to gated communities, and travel through fortress-like airports, everyday anticipation of violence, terror, and war is affecting daily life in cities across the globe. Hope remains, however, in the prospect that these logics of fear and exclusion will be widely contested, giving rise to movements that bring on new spatial and political imaginaries for more equitable cities and better futures, and reminding us that the future is yet to be written.

NOTES

PROLOGUE

1. Some estimates put the number of people killed close to 200,000. The population of the country in 1980 was estimated to be 2.6 million (United Nations, Department of Economic and Social Affairs, Population Division, *World Population Prospects*). Also see Global IDP, *Profile of Internal Displacement: Lebanon.*

2. Kassir and Fisk, *Beirut.*

3. Ibid. These protests climaxed in 1958 when Lebanon witnessed civil unrest.

4. Shiites and Sunnis are the two main Muslim sects. Druze are a minority religious group in Lebanon and the Middle East. Officially, in Lebanon, they are considered a Muslim sect. However, many Druze differentiate themselves from Muslims.

5. Krayem, "The Lebanese Civil War and the Taif Agreement."

6. In 1982, Israel waged a war on Lebanon, named Operation Peace for Galilee, during which Israel invaded Lebanon from the south; its army reached Beirut. This invasion resulted in Israel's occupation of southern Lebanon for eighteen years. In 2000, Israel withdrew from the area while keeping hold of the contested Shebaa farms. In addition to occupying southern Lebanon, Israel has waged several wars against Lebanon, including Operation Accountability in 1993 and Operation Grapes of Wrath in 1996, that resulted in hundreds of deaths and massive displacement among the Lebanese population.

7. The May 7 fighting officially ended on May 21, 2008, after the factions signed the Doha Agreement in Qatar, an accord that also ended a seven-month vacuum in the presidency that had started in November 2007.

8. This estimate is based on the number of refugees registered with the United Nations High Commissioner for Refugees (United Nations High Commissioner for Refugees, *UNHCR Syria Regional Refugee Response*). The World Bank estimates the number to be more than 1.5 million, indicating that refugees who arrived in Lebanon between 2011 and 2016 account for 25 percent of Lebanon's 2016 estimated population of 5.8 million (World Bank, *World Bank's Response to the Syrian Conflict*). In addition, according to the United Nations Relief and Works Agency for Palestine Refugees (UNRWA), in 2014, some 450,000 Palestinian refugees were registered with this agency, accounting for about 8 percent of Lebanon's population (UNRWA, *Where We Work*).

9. Harvey, "On Planning the Ideology of Planning."

10. Friedmann, "Planning in the Public Domain"; Beauregard, "The Multiplicities of Planning."

11. Yiftachel, "Planning and Social Control"; Flyvbjerg and Richardson, "Planning and Foucault"; Roy, *City Requiem, Calcutta*.

12. Faour and Mhawej, "Mapping Urban Transitions in the Greater Beirut Area."

13. Ibid.

14. Ibid.

15. Based on estimates by the United Nations (United Nations, Department of Economic and Social Affairs, Population Division, *World Population Prospects*).

16. Central Administration of Statistics, "Household Living Conditions in Lebanon 1997."

17. Verdeil, Faour, and Velut, *Atlas du Liban: Territoires et Société*.

18. The highest profile project of these is Beirut's Central District, which has been undergoing reconstruction by the real estate company Solidere. Elyssar and Linord, two grand but unrealized planning projects for Beirut's southern and northern coastal suburbs, respectively, have also been discussed at length. More recently, Project Waad, Hezbollah's large-scale effort to reconstruct Beirut's southern suburbs destroyed during Israel's July 2006 war on Lebanon has been the subject of several studies. For more on Solidere, see Rowe and Sarkis, *Projecting Beirut*; Makdisi, "Laying Claim to Beirut"; and Sawalha, *Reconstructing Beirut*. On Linord and Elyssar, see Rowe and Sarkis, *Projecting Beirut*; The Consultative Center for Studies and Documentation, *Alissār;* and Harb, "Urban Governance in Post-War Beirut." On Waad, see Fawaz and Ghandour, *The Reconstruction of Haret Hreik*; Harb, "Faith-Based Organizations as Effective Development Partners?"; Fawaz, "Hezbollah as Urban Planner?"; and Al-Harithy, *Lessons in Post-War Reconstruction*.

19. For more on these areas, see Hamadeh, "A Housing Proposal against All Odds"; Charafeddine, "L'Habitat Illégal de la Banlieue-Sud de Beyrouth"; Harb, "Urban Governance in Post-War Beirut"; Fawaz, "Strategizing for Housing"; and Clerc, *Les Quartiers Irréguliers de Beyrouth*.

20. By "formal" I mean that most buildings received permits from their municipality before their construction. This contrasts, for example, with the neighboring "informal" settlement of Hayy el-Selloum. However, as I discuss in Chapter 3, a number of buildings in Sahra Choueifat did eventually grow to violate their initial permits, rendering them informal. For a detailed discussion of the development of Hayy el-Selloum, refer to Fawaz, "Strategizing for Housing."

21. I will at times also refer to Haraket Amal, which is, after Hezbollah, the second most important Shiite religious-political organization in Lebanon. Haraket Amal, formed in 1974, was initially called Ḥarakat al-Maḥrūmīn (The Movement of the Dispossessed People). Hezbollah was created in 1982, when its leaders broke from the older group. The two entities, however, remain political allies.

22. Maronites, affiliated with the Catholic Church, are an important ethno-religious group in the Middle East and the dominant and most influential Christian sect in Lebanon. The 1943 pact that led to the country's independence in 1946 mandated that the President of the Lebanese Republic always be a Maronite. Religious-political organizations that identify as Maronites include the Free Patriotic Movement, the Phalange Party (Kata'ib), and the Lebanese Forces.

23. Arendt, *On Violence*, 9.

24. In 1997, the United States placed Hezbollah on its list of "foreign terrorist or-

ganizations." And ever since September 11, 2001, these listed organizations, including Hezbollah, have been targets for the US War on Terror, which has consisted of military, political, and financial operations aimed at curtailing these organizations' influence.

25. Graham, *Cities, War, and Terrorism*.

26. Harvey, "The Political Economy of Public Space"; Muschamp, "Architecture View."

27. These geopolitical events include the fall of the Soviet Union; the two Gulf Wars; the September 11, 2001, terrorist attacks in the United States; the emergence of a global War on Terror; mutations in the Arab-Israeli conflict; and the resurgence of the Sunni-Shiite conflict in the Middle East in multiple places.

28. The March 14 protests were credited with forcing the final withdrawal of the Syrian Armed Forces from Lebanon, in April 2005, after a twenty-four-year presence. Syria's presence was originally an effort to stabilize a deteriorating security situation in Lebanon that threatened Syria's interests in the region (Salloukh, "Syria and Lebanon").

29. For example, the Free Patriotic Movement subsequently joined the March 8 camp, while the PSP exited the March 14 coalition, repositioning itself as an intermediary between the two camps.

30. At the time, the two camps had been engaged in a seventeen-month political standoff, in which Hezbollah's ministers and its allies had left their seats in the government, accusing those who remained of being Western-backed and pro-American. Two days before the clashes broke out, the remaining, "amputated" March 14–only government had announced it had "found" a separate, parallel telecommunication network operated by Hezbollah, which was among other functions being used to monitor activities at the airport. The government declared the network illegal, and vowed to shut it down. Meanwhile, the March 14 camp discursively tied Hezbollah's actions to the assassination of a number of its leaders, including Prime Minster Hariri. The network in question was an underground wired telecommunication system linking Hezbollah's three strongholds in Lebanon: south Lebanon, the Beqaa Valley, and the southern suburbs of Beirut. Hezbollah argued that this network was key to its campaign of armed resistance against Israel's occupation of Palestine and frequent violations of Lebanese sovereignty. Hezbollah's leader, Hassan Nasrallah, therefore proclaimed it to be Hezbollah's moral duty to use force of arms to defend it.

31. Fawaz, Harb, and Gharbieh, "Living Beirut's Security Zones."

32. I owe this insight to Delia Duong Ba Wendel.

CHAPTER 1: CONSTRUCTING SECTARIAN GEOGRAPHIES

1. Makdisi, *The Culture of Sectarianism*; Picard, *Lebanon, A Shattered Country*; Weiss, *In the Shadow of Sectarianism*.

2. Nucho, *Everyday Sectarianism in Urban Lebanon*; Hafeda, "Bordering Practices"; Deeb and Harb, *Leisurely Islam*.

3. The CDR was established in 1977 to undertake Beirut's reconstruction after the first two years of the civil war. It is supposed to be responsible for capital projects that span several municipal boundaries. A second agency, the Directorate General of Urbanism (DGU), is responsible for preparing urban regulations and master plans for municipalities, and it reports to the Ministry of Public Works and Transportation. These two government agencies coordinate their activities through the Higher Council for Urban Planning, but

the jurisdictional boundaries between them have long been contested. For more on the role of these two agencies, see Chapter 5.

4. Feldman, *Formations of Violence.*

5. Tsing, *Friction*, xi.

6. These popular discourses included those in comic strips, where the expectation of war also became prevalent, as Ghenwa Hayek shows in *Beirut, Imagining the City.*

7. Anna Tsing also discusses how studying transient global connections ethnographically in zones of "awkward engagement" requires a "patchwork and haphazard" approach to research methods (Tsing, *Friction*, xi).

8. I was typically categorized as part of a sectarian group based on my family name and where I said I came from. These assumptions were made immediately and without asking me directly about my position on religion or politics.

9. I borrow this phrase from Edward Said's *Orientalism.* The intimate estrangement here is not about orientalist engagements with the East as Said discusses, but it is about spaces that are quite familiar yet remain unknowable and strange.

10. Feldman, "Ethnographic States of Emergency."

11. Harb, "Urban Governance in Post-War Beirut."

12. Caldeira, *City of Walls*; Yiftachel, "Social Control, Urban Planning and Ethnoclass Relations"; Robinson, *Ordinary Cities*; Roy, "Why India Cannot Plan Its Cities"; Watson, "Seeing from the South."

13. Simone, *City Life from Jakarta to Dakar.*

14. Roy and AlSayyad, *Urban Informality.*

15. Ghannam, *Remaking the Modern.*

16. Simone, "At the Frontier of the Urban Periphery," 464.

17. Holston, "Insurgent Citizenship in an Era of Global Urban Peripheries," 245; also see Chance, "Transitory Citizens."

18. Fawaz, "The Politics of Property in Planning."

19. Smith, *The New Urban Frontier*, 199.

20. Yiftachel, *Ethnocracy*, 108.

21. Weizman, *Hollow Land*, 173.

22. Gregory, *The Colonial Present*, 19; Graham, "When Life Itself is War," 144.

23. Gupta and Ferguson, "Space, Identity, and the Politics of Difference," 18.

24. Leitner, Sheppard, and Sziarto, "The Spatialities of Contentious Politics," 311.

25. Simone, *City Life from Jakarta to Dakar*, 40.

26. Ibid., 40–41.

27. Simone, *For the City Yet to Come*, 9.

28. Harvey, "The Right to the City"; see also Lefebvre, *Writings on Cities.*

29. I first developed this argument in Bou Akar, "Contesting Beirut's Frontiers."

30. Andary, "Bay' Arāḍin wa Mashārī' Sakaniyya Mashbūha wa Istinfār lil-Ahālī."

31. In Arabic dictionaries, *bī'a* refers to the external systems and conditions that govern the living conditions of beings. It thus defines the basic environmental framework within which humans live (constituted by the soil, water, and air) and which governs the relationships between humans and other elements of the system.

32. In its dictionary definition, *al-bī'a al-ḥāḍina* refers to the external conditions that shape and nourish the development of infants.

33. Drake and Cayton, *Black Metropolis*.

34. Robinson, *The Power of Apartheid*.

35. Boal, *Ethnicity and Housing*; Shirlow, "Ethno-Sectarianism and the Reproduction of Fear in Belfast."

36. Even before the civil war, many of Beirut's neighborhoods were largely segregated. The city was inhabited by different religious groups, predominantly Sunnis, Druze, and Roman Orthodox (while the majority of the Christians in Lebanon are Maronites, who follow the Catholic Church, the second largest Lebanese Christian denomination is Roman Orthodox, also referred to as Antiochian Orthodox, and its members follow the Eastern Orthodox Church). However, these religious groups often lived in distinct, homogeneous neighborhoods (Beyhum, "Espaces Éclatés, Espaces Dominés"; Davie, "Demarcation Lines in Contemporary Lebanon"; Khuri, *From Village to Suburb*).

37. Based on the ideas of Darwinism, such views originally enabled geographers to "scientifically" justify imperialism, colonialism, and racism (see Peet, "The Social Origins of Environmental Determinism").

38. See Abu Ammo, "'Awdat al-Lubnānī ilā al-Ghīttū."

39. Foucault, *The Birth of Biopolitics*, 31.

40. Abu Ammo, "'Awdat al-Lubnānī ilā al-Ghīttū."

41. Hadifa, "Durūz Sāḥil Jabal Lubnān 'Hunūd Ḥumr' Yantaẓirūn"; "Junblāṭ."

42. Such discursive formations are constitutive of contested geographies elsewhere as well. For example, the debate around immigration in the United States similarly uses a discourse of demography to stand in for an underlying racism. Demography is also central to debates surrounding the immigrant African figure in European cities. Also relevant are the racist discourses of the "culture of poverty" that have been used to mark African-American spaces, and that mirror discourses of *bī'a* in Lebanon.

43. See Harb el-Kak, "Politiques Urbaines"; Deeb, *An Enchanted Modern*; and Fawaz, "Neoliberal Urbanity and the Right to the City."

44. For example, on November 7, 2010, a prominent online news outlet contained an op-ed by a Choueifat municipal officer in which he reflected on a spate of robberies in Choueifat's neighborhoods, saying, "it is true that robbers have no sect and no religion, but the scale of the 'rude' invasions that the city and its peaceful residents are witnessing has not been seen before." You have to know only a tiny bit about local politics to grasp that the author is accusing residents of neighboring Sahra Choueifat and Hayy el-Selloum of these "rude invasions." He then goes on to say: "Due to the excessive number of these robberies, the 'public' is having their doubts now. Is it a planned attack? Is it intended? Are there 'groups' that are dispatched to make sure these robberies happen every day? Could it be pure chance?!" (Haidar, "Bayn Mārātūn Bayrūt wa-Mārātūn al-Sariqāt"). This report is only one of the many that get written every week.

45. Shaery-Eisenlohr, *Shi'ite Lebanon*, 41-45; Deeb, *An Enchanted Modern*, 13; Johnson, *All Honorable Men*, 145.

46. Larkin, *Memory and Conflict in Lebanon*, 69.

47. Fawz, "Al-Ḥadath."

48. Nasr and James, "Roots of the Shi'i Movement"; Cammett, *Compassionate Communalism*, 41; Ajami, *The Vanished Imam*, 189; Deeb, *An Enchanted Modern*, 47.

49. Khalaf, "Some Sociological Reflections on the Urban Reconstruction of Beirut."

50. Harb, "Deconstructing Hizballah and Its Suburb."

51. Wilson, "Architecture and Consciousness in Central Europe."

52. Olsen, *The City as a Work of Art*.

53. Schrecker, "McCarthyism," 1060.

54. This view of course excludes the presence of ultra-religious Sunnis, who existed in Lebanon even before the emergence of entities like ISIS.

55. "Highlights of Speech by Nasrallah."

56. Cammett, *Compassionate Communalism*, 89.

57. Bou Akar, "Contesting Beirut's Frontiers."

58. Nasr, "New Social Realities and Post-War Lebanon," 67.

59. Harb and Leenders, "Know Thy Enemy."

60. Traboulsi, *A History of Modern Lebanon*; Hourani, "Capitalists in Conflict."

61. The financial assets of these organizations vary considerably. While their funding mechanisms during the war involved a wide set of activities ranging from diasporic remittances to forced taxation and smuggling (see Nasr, "Lebanon's War"), the postwar financial transactions of these organizations are not clear. Numbers on the revenues of each organization are not available, and most of the information is anecdotal. When business tycoon Rafic Hariri was at the helm of the Future Movement, that organization was considered to be wealthy and was backed financially by the Gulf countries; more recently, reports speak of the organization's financial hurdles. As for Hezbollah, it is difficult to draw a comprehensive map of its financial activities and assets as its operations extend globally to countries in Africa, Latin America, and the Middle East. The PSP's wealth is smaller compared to that of the other two organizations. In the cases of the PSP and the Future Movement, there is a conflation between the wealth of the leader and that of the organization.

62. For a discussion on rethinking the role of non-state actors, see Davis, "Non-State Armed Actors, New Imagined Communities, and Shifting Patterns of Sovereignty and Insecurity in the Modern World."

63. Even after Israel largely withdrew from southern Lebanon in 2000, it continued to occupy a few strategic border villages and to violate Lebanese airspace, providing a rationale for Hezbollah's continued campaign of resistance. Hezbollah argued that this situation necessitated its right to make military decisions without informing the Lebanese government or army. However, this ability to separately determine conditions of war and peace has been a source of heated debate, especially since Israel's 2006 war on Lebanon, which was precipitated by a Hezbollah military operation against the Israeli army along Lebanon's southern border.

64. Weizman, *Hollow Land*.

65. Graham, "The Urban 'Battlespace.'"

66. Graham, *Cities under Siege*.

67. Feldman, *Formations of Violence*; McAdam, Tarrow, and Tilly, *Dynamics of Contention*; Martin and Miller, "Space and Contentious Politics."

68. Castells, *The City and the Grassroots*; Bayat, *Street Politics*.

69. Coward, "Urbicide in Bosnia"; Graham, *Cities, War, and Terrorism*.

70. Gregory, "In Another Time-Zone, the Bombs Fall Unsafely," 23.

71. Wedeen, *Ambiguities of Domination*; Elyachar, *Markets of Dispossession*; Ismail, *Political Life in Cairo's New Quarters*; Tuğal, *Passive Revolution*; Bayat, "Politics in the City Inside-Out"; Fregonese, "Beyond the 'Weak State'"; Hourani, "Lebanon."

72. Shirlow, "Ethno-Sectarianism and the Reproduction of Fear in Belfast"; Simone, *For the City Yet to Come*; Tuathail and Dahlman, "The 'West Bank of the Drina'"; Tuğal, *Passive Revolution*; AlSayyad and Massoumi, *The Fundamentalist City?*; Hackworth, *Faith Based*; Deeb and Harb, *Leisurely Islam*; Atia, *Building a House in Heaven*.

73. Lefebvre, *The Production of Space*; Harvey, *Social Justice and the City*; Castells and Sheridan, *The Urban Question*.

74. Castells, *The City and the Grassroots*; Bayat, *Street Politics*; Simone, *For the City Yet to Come*.

75. Fawaz, "Hezbollah as Urban Planner?"

CHAPTER 2: THE DOUBLENESS OF RUINS

1. See, for example, Mona Hallak's comments, which are quoted in Wright, "Beirut's Museums of War and Memories."

2. Whitmarsh, "'We Will Remember Them,'" 11.

3. Ide, "A Symbol of Peace and Peace Education."

4. Naharnet Newsdesk, "Lebanon Eyes Future for Famed Hotel Turned Civil War Relic."

5. My research engagement with Hayy Madi/Mar Mikhail goes back to 2004. At the time, as I interviewed the residents of housing complexes in Sahra Choueifat (discussed in Chapter 3), I learned that many of them had been channeled there from Hayy Madi/Mar Mikhail, where they had lived for two decades in ruined structures. I also discovered that a vast network of housing developers in Sahra Choueifat had established sales offices in the Hayy Madi and Mar Mikhail neighborhoods. As residents in Sahra Choueifat talked about their lives of displacement in Hayy Madi/Mar Mikhail, they also spoke about families and friends who were still living there, awaiting compensation so they too could move out. Following this lead, I went to Hayy Madi/Mar Mikhail to conduct interviews with some of those who were still living there, to better understand housing access among low-income, war-displaced families in postwar Beirut.

6. Stoler, *Imperial Debris*, 9.

7. Although adjacent, Hayy Madi and Mar Mikhail are different neighborhoods, separated by a major road. I consider them together in this book to illustrate the various processes that co-constitute their production as a contested area. However, I also at times highlight their differences, in order to reveal the differentiated logic of spatial production in each neighborhood.

8. For example, on June 1, 2007, shortly after the announcement of the establishment of the Hariri tribunal, a bomb was thrown at the Mar Mikhail church.

9. On January 27, 2008, supporters of Hezbollah and Haraket Amal clashed with the Lebanese Army during demonstrations in the area against repeated electric power cuts in al-Dahiya. Seven people were killed. However, since 2013, as al-Dahiya has become the target of car bombings related to the ongoing war in Syria, Hezbollah and Haraket Amal have been closely coordinating al-Dahiya's security with the Lebanese Army and the Lebanese Internal Security Forces, which have established checkpoints at the entrances and exits to the area (Naharnet Newsdesk, "Security Forces Complete Deployment in Dahieh").

10. For example, on April 15, 2012, the anniversary of the onset of the civil war, a protest against repeating the civil war took place there. On May 22, 2012, the area was the location of peaceful protests organized by the families of men kidnapped in Syria.

11. Khuri, *From Village to Suburb*.

12. For more information, see Fawaz, "Strategizing for Housing."

13. Ecochard's initial proposal "limited the building plots to a minimum of 1,000 square meters (10,764 square feet), of which only 400 could be used for construction. The number of floors was also restricted to three" (Khuri, *From Village to Suburb*, 191).

14. Mona Fawaz's work on the informal settlement of Hayy el-Selloum shows how Michel Ecochard's master plan for the southern suburbs made the practice of parcelization illegal by setting the minimum lot size at 2000 square meters, whereas the subdivided lots bought by rural migrants at the time were typically 150 to 200 square meters. Nonetheless, Hayy el-Selloum developed under laws made flexible by the client-patron political system in Lebanon (Fawaz, "Strategizing for Housing," 87).

15. The economic logic of these political choices needs further research, since Fuad Khuri did not clarify the ways in which the market was functioning at the time vis-à-vis land use, supply and demand, and property ownership.

16. Khuri, *From Village to Suburb*.

17. According to Khuri (ibid.), real estate transactions also fueled a pre-independence sectarian war in Lebanon. This took place in 1860 between Druze and Maronites, as Maronites used revenue from silk manufacturing and trade to buy land from Druze landowners.

18. The civil war formally started on April 13, 1975, in the bordering area of Ain el-Remmaneh.

19. It is precisely the difference in the logic of peripheral expansion into a "built-up landscape in ruins" versus into an "empty landscape" that I am interested in highlighting through my examination of doubleness in Hayy Madi/Mar Mikhail in this chapter, and lacework in Sahra Choueifat in Chapter 3.

20. This interview was conducted by Leen Hashem on October 3, 2011. I am grateful to Dr. Mona Fawaz at the American University of Beirut for sharing a recording of this interview with me.

21. A reference to Nabih Berri, the head of the Shiite Haraket Amal. Berri has also been the Speaker of the Lebanese Parliament since 1992.

22. In Lebanon, putting an area under study has become a planning tool to halt development until a political consensus can be reached. A more detailed discussion of these issues is provided in Chapter 3. Also see Bou Akar, "Contesting Beirut's Frontiers."

23. For more information on how the security measures of the different parties dissect the city, see Fawaz, Harb, and Gharbieh, "Living Beirut's Security Zones."

24. Bergman, "The Hezbollah Connection."

25. This section of my research thus relies mostly on nonparticipant observation and conversations with people in Hayy Madi/Mar Mikhail, along with eight open-ended interviews that I was able to conduct with individuals who did not live in the neighborhood but who were involved in making decisions related to spatial issues there.

26. Apparently, other people felt the same way about it. Thus the author of a text and photo essay titled "The April 13 war anniversary almost brought the war back. . . . War behind the Mar Mikhail Church," featured in the newspaper *Al-Mustaqbal* on April 13, 2007, the thirty-second anniversary of the start of the civil war, asked: "Is this a neighborhood of Beirut or a ghost town?" (Zarakit, "Dhikrā 13 Nīsān Ḥarb Kādat Tustaʿād").

27. For reference, the monthly minimum wage in 2010 was $333, and it was raised

to $450 in 2012. The average price per one square meter of newly built apartments in the vicinity (al-Hadath) was $1600 in 2012 (InfoPro, "Business Opportunities in Lebanon"). The average price per one square meter in Beirut was $3223 in 2012 ("Beirut Apartments Second Most Pricey in MENA"). In Lebanon, the US dollar is widely used as a currency. Since 1997, the exchange rate has been fixed at 1507.5 Lebanese pounds per US dollar. Real estate prices are often quoted in US dollar value.

28. I was never granted an interview with the mayor of Chiyah. I visited his office on several occasions to try to make an appointment and followed up with phone calls to no avail. An aide kept promising me an interview "to come soon," but it never materialized—probably to avoid talking about the very issues discussed in this chapter. For a comprehensive analysis of the role of the municipality in the development of Chiyah, see Farah, "Différenciations Sociospatiales et Gouvernance Municipale dans les Banlieues de Beyrouth."

29. One of the most influential postwar Christian religious-political organizations in Lebanon.

30. On October 31, 2016, Michel Aoun was elected President of Lebanon.

31. Nasr and James argue that by 1975 the Shiite population was possibly already the largest religious group in Lebanon (Nasr and James, "Roots of the Shi'i Movement," 12). They explain that although in 1948 the Shiite community in Lebanon constituted about 18.2 percent of the country's total population (behind the Sunnis and Maronites), on the eve of the civil war in 1975, they constituted around 30 percent of that population, "perhaps the largest community in the country." And between these two periods, the Shiite community's class position changed as they went from being a predominantly rural community dominated by a handful of elite families to a community that included "a new migrant bourgeoisie, a layer of middle-level salaried workers in the cities, an industrial proletariat in the suburbs of Beirut and a community of migrant workers in the Arab oil-producing countries." There are no government numbers available on the current size of the Shiite community, but the Pew Research Center estimates that 45 to 55 percent of the Lebanese population in 2009 was Shiite (Pew Research Center, "Mapping the Global Muslim Population").

32. Wehbe, "Living Sectarianism."

33. Farah, "Différenciations Sociospatiales et Gouvernance Municipale dans les Banlieues de Beyrouth," 379.

34. Drawing on information from interviews, Farah states that the project was intended to be a combination of residential and commercial activities, with a cost amounting to $5 million (ibid., 383).

35. Ibid., 383. "[R]egistered in the community" is my rendering of the mayor's phrase "inscrits a la commune."

36. This inability to vote in one's place of residence in Beirut's peripheries will be a recurrent theme in this book.

37. For a discussion of the difference in the housing strategies of the Maronite Church and Hezbollah, see Brundiers and Odermatt, "Analyzing Socio-Spatial Processes of Integration and Disintegration by Examining the Local Housing Market."

38. Al-Amin, "Fī al-Ḥadath"; "'Al-Baladiyya Mā Raḥ Tumḍīlak' . . . Hakadhā Tuwājih al-Ḥadath Bayʿ al-Arāḍī!"

39. The Ministry of Justice declared the proposal unconstitutional (Alaily, "Ba'd Mashrū' Qānūn Ḥarb").

40. Sfeir, "Ijtimā' Bkirkī 'Yuthmir' Iqtirāḥāt li-Ta'dīl Qānūn al-Milkiyya al-'Aqāriyya"; Alaily, "Ba'd Mashrū' Qānūn Ḥarb."

41. This process is comparable to yet different from the process commonly known in the United States as *blockbusting*. Blockbusting was a spatial practice prevalent before the civil rights movement in the United States. Real estate brokers would imply that racial minorities were moving into a previously white-only neighborhood, using this fear tactic to encourage white homeowners to sell their properties at a loss. They would then sell the properties with large margins of profit to incoming black and other minority populations (see, e.g., Aalbers, "When the Banks Withdraw, Slum Landlords Take Over"). Blockbusting, however, was supported by institutional racism that included redlining and homeowners associations' racial restrictive covenants. These processes were constituted within a history of slavery and racism and institutionalized at the time by a state ruled by a dominant racial majority. That is not the case in Lebanon where both sectarian groups share the government and where attempts to legally institutionalize geographic segregation along sectarian lines have failed so far (Alaily, "Ba'd Mashrū' Qānūn Ḥarb").

42. For a discussion of the political implications of the discourse of *bī'a*, see Chapter 1.

43. Harvey, *The Limits to Capital*, 347.

44. Smith, *The New Urban Frontier*.

45. Baabda is the town adjacent to al-Hadath where the Lebanese Presidential Palace is located. Since, by law, the Lebanese president must be a Maronite, it signifies the seat of the highest Christian government authority.

46. As I will describe in Chapter 3, the territory of the religious other in the case of Sahra Choueifat, to the south of al-Dahiya, has largely been Druze.

47. MTV, *Bi Mawdouiyeh—Land Sales in Hadath*, September 26, 2011.

48. Khalaf and Khoury, *Recovering Beirut*.

49. Nagel, "Reconstructing Space, Re-Creating Memory."

50. Pant, "The Impulse to Remember"; Huyssen, "Nostalgia for Ruins"; Sandler, "Counterpreservation."

51. Haskins and DeRose, "Memory, Visibility, and Public Space"; Sturken, "The Aesthetics of Absence."

52. Fawaz and Ghandour, *The Reconstruction of Haret Hreik*.

53. Guy, "Shadow Architectures," 76.

54. Coward, "Urbicide in Bosnia"; Graham, *Cities, War, and Terrorism*.

55. Coward, "Urbicide in Bosnia."

56. Fregonese, "The Urbicide of Beirut?," 317.

57. Stoler, *Imperial Debris*.

58. Buck-Morss, *The Dialectics of Seeing*.

59. Ibid.

60. Roy, "Praxis in the Time of Empire," 23.

61. Roy, "The Blockade of the World-Class City," 274.

62. Gill, cited in Roy, "The Blockade of the World-Class City," 274.

CHAPTER 3: THE LACEWORK OF ZONING

1. The process of lacework zoning is comparable to gerrymandering in the process of setting the boundaries of electoral districts in the United States. In both cases, the manipulation of the contours of inclusion and exclusion has significant political implications for the populations inhabiting these zones.

2. Municipal Beirut covers approximately 18 square kilometers (while metropolitan Beirut, which includes Choueifat, is estimated at 85 square kilometer). According to a Choueifat municipal official, Sahra Choueifat, including Hayy el-Selloum, covers approximately 7 square kilometers.

3. One of these hills, al-Qobbeh, commonly known as Doha Aramoun, is the subject of Chapter 4.

4. Hamadeh, "A Housing Proposal against All Odds," 80.

5. Kazzaz et al., "Rebuilding the Residential Sector of Beirut," 39.

6. About $41,000 and $50,000, respectively, in 2016 dollars. In 1993, the minimum wage was equivalent to $69 a month (Nasr, *Investor's Guide*).

7. For more on this, see Chapter 1.

8. A *hajj* is a Muslim person who has concluded his pilgrimage duty by visiting Mecca in Saudi Arabia.

9. Fawaz, "Strategizing for Housing."

10. Kazzaz et al., "Rebuilding the Residential Sector of Beirut"; Abed, "L'Agriculture Urbaine dans la Plaine de Shweifaat."

11. Sawalha, Reconstructing Beirut.

12. Bou Akar, "Displacement, Politics, and Governance."

13. Sawalha, *Reconstructing Beirut.*

14. Bou Akar, "Displacement, Politics, and Governance."

15. I developed this idea and some additional material presented in this chapter in Bou Akar, "Contested Beirut Frontiers."

16. Fawaz, "Strategizing for Housing."

17. These agreements stipulated that after ten years, if the buyer did not register the apartment, the developer could legally retrieve the apartment and sell it to a third party, without compensating the original residents. However, because most families did not face serious legal problems with the developers, they learned to trust the AA. Most residents have maintained this contract and have not registered their units, due to the high cost of this process. According to the World Bank, registration fees are close to 6 percent of the apartment appraisal, a large sum for many of these families (World Bank Group, "Registering Property in Lebanon)."

18. For more on *bi'a*, see Chapter 1.

19. *Price-fixing* is "the setting of prices artificially (as by producers or government) contrary to free market operations" (*Merriam-Webster Dictionary*). In the United States, price-fixing is a federal offense, and perpetrators may face criminal prosecution. Price-fixing is considered a violation of laws relating to business competition because it stalls the "free market" and excludes other businesses from competing against the price-fixers.

20. Such a rumor begins to make sense when examined in relation to new zoning laws passed after violence broke out in the area in 2008. Together with the ticketing system, the

easy installment plan, the self-provision of infrastructure, and the construction of social centers, price-fixing is an element of Hezbollah's spatial and economic strategy.

21. After the May 2008 violence, Walid Jumblat, the leader of the PSP, and Talal Arslan, the leader of another Druze political party, allied with Hezbollah, agreed that control of the municipality would be handed over to Arslan to avoid further conflict between supporters of the PSP and Hezbollah in the area. However, this ongoing agreement also stipulates a rotation in the mayor's cabinet between the two parties with each election cycle.

22. Verdeil, "Methodological and Political Issues in the Lebanese Planning Experiences."

23. Ibid., 5.

24. The negative connotation associated with *bid'a* possibly draws on certain Islamic traditions, where innovations in belief and practice, beyond what existed at the time of the Prophet, are considered to be wrong (Robson, "Bid'a").

25. An "under study" legal status may be assigned by the Minister of Public Works and Transportation after taking into account the opinions of both the concerned municipality and the DGU.

26. Fawaz, "The Role of DGU in Providing Low-Cost Housing in Lebanon."

27. For more information, see Chapter 2.

28. As mentioned, the approval of new zoning plans requires the signature of the Lebanese President, Prime Minister, and Minister of Public Works and Transportation. At the time of the 2008 approval, the Minister of Public Works was PSP-appointed, and the Prime Minister was Rafic Hariri, the head of the Future Movement. This was before the PSP changed its alliances in August 2009, reestablishing ties with Hezbollah a year after fighting the 2008 battles. Various people have justified the move by the PSP leader Walid Jumblat as a geopolitical one, designed to protect the Druze in areas like Choueifat and Doha Aramoun from more bloody conflicts with Hezbollah (see Chapter 4).

29. A typical floor-to-floor height is 3 meters.

30. This is given that 25 percent of the floor area will be allocated for circulation and common facilities.

31. There were other cases of mutating categories in the 2008 plan, such as the addition of a Zone C2; and certain elements of the 2004 zoning scheme were removed (such as Zone E2). But these changes are not as significant as the creation of Zone V.

32. Fawaz, "Strategizing for Housing."

33. Lebanese Parliament, "Ta'dīl al-Qānūn Raqm 58 Tarīkh 29/5/1991 Qānun al-Istimlāk."

34. In 2015, the law was opened to negotiation once again when a parliamentary representative of the Lebanese Forces, a Christian political party, proposed new changes (Lebanese National News Agency, "Al-Ma'lūf Qaddam Iqtirāḥ Qānūn Yarmī ilā Ta'dīl Qānūn al-Istimlāk").

35. Li, *The Will to Improve*, 7.

36. Tuğal, *Passive Revolution*.

37. Watts, "Development and Governmentality."

38. Melucci (1989), cited in Townsend, Porter, and Mawdsley, "Creating Spaces of Resistance," 812.

39. Fawaz, "Agency and Ideology in the Service Provision of Islamic Organizations"; Harb, "Urban Governance in Post-War Beirut."

40. Bello, "Globalization and Social Change."

41. Watts, "Revolutionary Islam."

42. Fawaz, "Hezbollah as Urban Planner?"

43. Fawaz, "The Politics of Property in Planning."

44. Roy, "Civic Governmentality."

CHAPTER 4: A BALLOONING FRONTIER

1. Officially, this area is al-Qobbeh, and like Sahra Choueifat, it is part of the municipality of Choueifat—not the neighboring municipality of Aramoun, as its common name might suggest. In Arabic, a *dawḥa* is a majestic and wide tree, capable of providing shade.

2. The engineer used the Arabic word *nafkh*. I later learned this word is commonly used to describe illegalities in building construction in Doha Aramoun and its vicinity.

3. Although the mandated setback restricts the use of part of a private building lot, its purpose is to maintain adequate access to air and light and provide space for utilities and sidewalks. By intruding into the setback, the developer was violating the public interest.

4. Krijnen and Fawaz, "Exception as the Rule"; Fawaz, "Exceptions and the Actually Existing Practice of Planning."

5. It is common knowledge that illegal building practices are often facilitated by quite straightforward and time-tested methods—among which are drinking cups of coffee with municipal officials. At such social events, favors, money, and goods may be given in exchange for turning a blind eye to illegal construction.

6. Many apartments in Lebanon are sold based on design drawings, before the buildings that will contain them are even erected.

7. The Syrian Armed Forces (SAF) initially entered Lebanon in 1976, during the first phase of the Lebanese civil war, and remained in Lebanon until April 2006. Over the years, their mutating presence had different purposes; however, their strong presence in Doha Aramoun and its vicinities after 1988 was principally due to the fact that whoever controls that area can militarily dominate Beirut's airport and secure access to the Mediterranean coast south of the city. For more on this subject, see Traboulsi, *A History of Modern Lebanon*; and Kassir, *Ḥarb Lubnān*.

8. While many perceive Doha Aramoun to be a nondescript suburban community, its history highlights its strategic military value. During the civil war (1975–1990), the area was a vital weapons-smuggling zone, linking the southern peripheries of Beirut to Syria by way of the Shouf and Jurd mountains. Equally important was that the area overlooked the strategic Khalde intersection. Khalde was an important military site throughout the twentieth century. For example, on July 9, 1941, Australian artillery and infantry cooperated in attacking the hills overlooking Khalde to destroy a wireless mast set up by Vichy France. In 1958, the United States Marines landed in Khalde to stop what the United States feared was a Communist-inspired uprising in Beirut. During the civil war, Khalde witnessed many battles between Lebanese factions. It was also the site of the critical 1982 Khalde Battle between the invading Israel Defense Forces and a coalition of Palestinian groups and the SAF. At that time, the area was heavily shelled, and a few buildings in Doha Aramoun still bear evidence of that conflict. Khalde was also where, on May 17, 1983, an infamous peace agreement was signed between Lebanon and Israel—an agreement that

never went into effect. Later, the SAF shelled Beirut from hills in the area, after redeploying there in 1988.

9. Most Christian families did not return to the area after their displacement during the civil war.

10. de Certeau, *The Practice of Everyday Life*.

11. *Oxford Dictionaries*.

12. "Junblāṭ fī al-Khalwa al-Durziyya."

13. De Certeau, *The Practice of Everyday Life*.

14. Although many apartments in Doha Aramoun are legal, the tenure status of many others remains vague. And questions of tenure are intertwined with calculations of who can afford to live where. As a result, most of the advertising targeting middle- and low-income families either has indicated that the apartment sellers hold a "green title deed" (colored blue today), or has remained silent on the issue of legality when the sellers have no deed.

15. Today, these individuals are considered lucky because their land in Doha Aramoun is worth millions.

16. Fawaz, "Notes on Beirut's Historiography."

17. As land prices have skyrocketed, most of these villas have since been torn down and replaced by denser, more profitable apartment buildings.

18. For example, in 1968, the Israel Defense Forces raided Beirut's international airport, destroying twelve passenger planes, allegedly as part of their battle against Palestinian resistance fighters in Beirut (Al Jazeera, "Timeline: Lebanon").

19. They were later joined by Druze families, like mine, who left the mountains for a setting closer to Beirut.

20. Ironically, some claim that a number of the bombs that hit west Beirut were fired from an SAF missile station in the Aramoun hills (Associated Consulting Engineers, "Master Plan Proposal for the Municipality of Choueifat").

21. Little has been written about the role of the SAF in the urban development of Beirut and its peripheries. Fawaz has alluded to its role, along with Hezbollah and Haraket Amal, in protecting illegal construction in Hayy el-Selloum in exchange for apartments or lower payment rates (Fawaz, "Strategizing for Housing, 127, 233). In Lebanon, people do not agree on how to characterize the former presence of the SAF, a foreign army, in the everyday life of neighborhoods like Doha Aramoun. The production of a geography of housing and public space within the context of a non-Lebanese military presence thus calls for further research and theorization.

22. Picard, *Lebanon, A Shattered Country*.

23. However, that did not factor into my family's decision to move to the neighborhood. Two decades after the SAF first entered Lebanon, its presence had become an unquestioned reality. Deemed to be the almighty apparatus of power and control in Lebanon (with an army of soldiers, spies, and affiliates and a notorious reputation for cruelty toward disobeyers), the SAF was feared and typically obeyed by every militia, party, gang, and businessperson in the country. Living for a decade in an apartment building between three such posts, my family constantly had to negotiate its way around armed SAF soldiers.

24. Associated Consulting Engineers, "Master Plan Proposal for the Municipality of Choueifat."

25. Ibid.

26. The Grand Mufti of Lebanon is the Mufti of Beirut, who also serves as the official representative of the Muslim community to the Lebanese state.

27. In Aramoun in 1973, Mufti Khaled held the first Sunni leadership conference, where the political representation of Sunnis and their position vis-à-vis the Palestinian resistance movement was discussed. The transformation of Aramoun into a focal point for Sunni religious leadership then continued through the first two years of the civil war (1975–1976). At this time, Khaled hosted a series of political summits at his home. Called the Aramoun Summits, these four meetings took place between May 1975 and January 1976, and provided an arena for discussion of issues among an alliance of groups, including Palestinian factions, then operating in west Beirut. The meetings were attended by representatives of religious-political organizations, political parties, and militias—but also by representatives of the foreign states then supporting or funding the alliance (Syria, Libya) and representatives of the other foreign entities involved in negotiations in Lebanon (for example, the United States and the Vatican) (Khaled, *Al-Muslimūn fī Lubnān wa Ḥarb al-Sanatayn*). As the civil war raged, in 1982, other key Sunni religious institutions (the most famous of which was Azhar Beirut) relocated temporarily to Aramoun. This transformed the area into a destination for Sunni religious scholars and students. (Private communication with N. Moataz, April 2014.)

28. Dar al-Aytam al-Islamiya, *Mujammaʿ Inmāʾ al-Qudurāt al-Insāniyya*.

29. Taleb and Saab, *Al-Mushāraka al-ʿArabiyya wa-l-Duwaliyya fī Inmāʾ Lubnān mā baʿd al-Ḥarb*.

30. This would have occurred because, as mentioned previously, Lebanese vote in elections in their place of origin, not according to where they live at the moment.

31. Choueifat is considered a rich municipality, in part because of the taxes it collects from the airport, industries, beaches and resorts, shopping centers, and up-scale residential areas that lie within its limits.

32. All projects were commissioned from the Zakhem Group. According to Zakhem's website: "The project comprised 27 kms of roads & stormwater drainage, drilling and equipping 6 wells, chlorination building & pump house, 3 reservoirs, 39.2 kms of ductile iron water pipelines, 25 kms of sewage pipelines. The rehabilitation of electrical and telecommunication networks were also carried out as part of the project. (US$10.71 million of the US$17.90 million project value relates to water & waste water networks and the related structures)" (Zakhem Group, "Business Activities").

33. Council for Development and Reconstruction, "Roads, Highways and Public Transport."

34. Similarly, in 1997, ACE reported that "Doha Aramoun does not have a sewage system, but there is a line 600 m long of 200 mm diameter that was installed by one of the residents. Most of the buildings have their own septic tanks" (Associated Consulting Engineers, "Master Plan Proposal for the Municipality of Choueifat").

35. According to the *Daily Star* (March 15, 2002): "The Kuwaiti Fund for Arab Economic Development . . . and the Arab Fund for Economic and Social Development . . . jointly covered 80 percent of the road's construction cost, which amounted to $6.9 million. The road can accommodate up to 5,000 vehicles (including trucks) per hour driving in each direction" (Kanafani, "South Now Has 'High-Speed' Link to Downtown Beirut").

36. Deboulet and Fawaz, "Contesting the Legitimacy of Urban Restructuring and Highways."

37. Harb, "On Religiosity and Spatiality," 277.

38. Although older maps suggest that there might have been a road already approved there in 1973, what matters here is the story more than the actual facts. The story emphasizes how the highway was effectively a Hariri project.

39. IAURIF has a long history of involvement in planning schemes for Lebanon, in times of both war and peace (see Chapter 5).

40. The NPMP was approved by the Council of Ministers on June 20, 2009. It was subsequently enacted through decree 2326, and published in the official government gazette on July 2, 2009. I was told by a CDR official that the decree covers only Phase I of the NPMP, which includes the general guidelines for land use, and that the more detailed element of the plan—Phase II, which includes the "target of development" areas—has not yet been made into a decree.

41. These included the City Debates at the American University of Beirut (AUB) in 2003, and a conference organized by Hezbollah's think-tank, the Consultative Center for Studies and Documentation (CCSD), in 2006 (Harb, *City Debates 2003*; The Consultative Center for Studies and Documentation, *Al-Khuṭṭa al-Shāmila li-Tartīb al-Arāḍī al-Lubnāniyya: Niqāsh fī al-Mabādi' wa-l-Khiyārāt*). These conferences were followed by a discussion with the director of the project, at the Lebanese University in 2010, and a forum at the Order of Engineers and Architects in Beirut in 2010 and another more recent forum in 2017.

42. Council for Development and Reconstruction, *National Physical Master Plan for the Lebanese Territory*, III-2.

43. Holston, *The Modernist City*.

44. It is important to note that there was no reference to Choueifat in the NPMP. Choueifat's absence is puzzling, because it is a city of the same size as Beirut, and it contains most of Beirut's international airport. However, visual material accompanying the written document showed that the "Aramoun targeted development zone" included the Druze part of Choueifat (to the east of the Old Saida Road), and excluded the now-Shiite Sahra Choueifat.

45. The three new proposed projects were Aramoun, Nahr Beirut, and the extension of the Linord project between Maamletein and Nahr el-Kalb. However, Aramoun's target area was vast in comparison to the other two projects.

46. Council for Development and Reconstruction, *National Physical Master Plan for the Lebanese Territory*, VI-17.

47. Instead, the 2003 proposal highlighted an adjacent smaller area, Khalde, as the target of future development. Moreover, Khalde remained central to the discussion in the NPMP's final report; Aramoun was highlighted only in the visuals, and rarely mentioned in the text.

48. Verdeil, "Methodological and Political Issues in the Lebanese Planning Experiences," 5.

49. Charafeddine, "The Lebanese National Master Plan."

50. For more on planning with touchstones, the 1986 master plan, and the NPMP, see Chapter 5.

51. In addition to the Hariri Foundation's series of NGOs and educational institutions, other Sunni groups have established a range of NGOs and welfare institutions. However, no data about these other institutions are available.

52. Cammett and Issar, "Bricks and Mortar Clientelism." The clinic was shut down in 2016.

53. A web page titled "Nazek Hariri," which was available in 2012 on Prime Minister Rafic Hariri's now discontinued website, described the Nazek Hariri Center for Human Development, which "is located on 20,000 square meters of hillside outside Aramoun, south of Beirut. The center is affiliated to the Institution of Social Welfare—the Islamic Orphanage 'Dar al-Aytam al-Islamiya.' The center was built and equipped through personal donations of Mrs. Hariri. It provides care and rehabilitation for about 1,000 disabled persons, the handicapped and mentally retarded, as well as the deaf, mute, blind and orphaned."

54. Coincidentally, I worked on the design of Hariri V while employed in a Beirut architectural office between 2000 and 2002. Despite the fact that Hariri schools are excellent, sectarian-diverse institutions, the four in operation are located in majority Sunni areas (Zokak el-Balat, Batrakieh, Tarik el-Jdidi, and Saida). Many of my Doha Aramoun and Bchamoun acquaintances, who are adamant middle-class Hariri supporters, send their children on buses to the Hariri schools in Beirut, despite the fact that they live in an area with many top-notch schools.

55. Some unverified news reports mention that the Sunni-Shiite contestation that culminated in 2008 actually dated back to 1996, when Operation Grapes of Wrath, an Israeli military operation against Lebanon, left 150 to 170 dead, scores injured, and hundreds of families displaced (see Luca, "The Alley Flag War"). However, this belief was not consistent with the views of those I interviewed in Doha Aramoun in 2004 and 2010.

56. Mohsen, "Dawḥat ʿAramūn."

57. Ibid.

58. On May 28, 2008, for example, the *Daily Star* reported on a fight between two Druze residents and a Hezbollah official over a parking space that resulted in injuries and a death ("Lebanese Soldier Killed in Gunfight in Dohet Aramoun"). Similarly, on June 16, 2010, *NOW Lebanon* reported on daily fights over flags in the area, as "the March 14 people were taking them down and the March 8 supporters were putting them back up" (Luca, "The Alley Flag War").

59. "Junblāṭ fi al-Khalwa al-Durziyya."

60. Al-Husseini, "Al-Qādimūn al-Judud."

61. As in other peripheral frontier areas, only "original" residents can vote in municipal elections. Thus, despite their swelling numbers, newcomers (even if they have lived there since the 1980s) are unable to bring about local municipal change. This was certainly one factor contributing to the outbreak of violence in Doha Aramoun in 2008. According to one municipal council member: "Only the 13,000 people whose origins are here are allowed to vote in the municipal elections, according to the Lebanese law. . . . The newcomers don't have the right to vote. There are people who feel they are being taken over by the newcomers, but in the end the vote is the same as always" ("Lebanese Soldier Killed in Gunfight in Dohet Aramoun").

62. "Junblāṭ fi al-Khalwa al-Durziyya."

63. Shahin, "Abʿad bi-Kathīr min Intiqād Taʿyīn al-Sayyid Husayn."

64. Andary, "Bayʿ Araḍin wa Mashārīʿ Sakaniyya Mashbūha wa Istinfār lil-Ahālī."

65. Drake and Cayton, *Black Metropolis*; Massey and Denton, *American Apartheid*; Seligman, *Block by Block*.

66. LeVine, *Overthrowing Geography*; Yiftachel, *The Power of Planning*.

67. Li, *The Will to Improve*.

68. This idea of "the Sunni" is based on the middle-class followers and affiliates of the Future Movement. It is a feeling that could change if Sunni extremism were to rise in Doha Aramoun.

69. The inflation index went from 95.4 percent in 1986 to 487.2 percent in 1987. It was 7.2 percent in 1983. See Makdisi, *The Lessons of Lebanon*, 55, 59; and International Monetary Fund, *World Economic Outlook Database for April 2006*.

70. A piece of cloth that hides the face, worn by some women as part of their hijab outfit.

71. Caldeira, *City of Walls*, 20.

72. Taussig, "Culture of Terror—Space of Death."

73. Feldman, *Formations of Violence*.

74. Although many of the websites that published this same report (by an unknown author) have removed it, a few versions could still be found on several websites online, including saidaonline.com ("Maʿlūmāt Daqīqa li-Maṣādir Amniyya") and the official Facebook page of Tayyar.org, the main website for the Change and Reform Block, one of the main Christian religious-political organizations, which is an ally to Hezbollah (Tayyar, "Utimm bi-Tishrīn al-Thānī Injāz Bināʾ al-Quwā al-ʿAskariyya").

75. "Junblāṭ fī al-Khalwa al-Durziyya."

76. See, for example, the rhetoric in Alshoufi's essay in the November 26, 2014, issue of *al-Akhbar*, "Doha Aramoun: Takfiri Imams and Terrorist Sleeper Cells" (Alshoufi, "Dawhat ʿAramūn: Aʾimmat Takfīr wa Khalāyā Irhābiyya Nāʾima").

77. "Junblāṭ fī al-Khalwa al-Durziyya."

78. "Khafāyā Ishtibākāt ʿDawhat ʿAramūnʾ"; "Intihāʾ al-Ishkāl bayn Lubnāniyyīn wa Sūriyyīn fī Dawhat ʿAramūn wa-l-Jaysh Yūqif ʿAdadan min Muṭliqī al-Nār."

CHAPTER 5: PLANNING WITHOUT DEVELOPMENT

1. For more on this, see Chapter 3.

2. Mr. H is referring to the amended eminent domain law approved in 2006. See Chapter 3.

3. Parts of this argument were developed earlier in Bou Akar, "From Poor Peripheries to Sectarian Frontiers."

4. Brooks, *Planning Theory for Practitioners*.

5. Fainstein, "Planning Theory and the City."

6. Friedmann and Alonso, *Regional Development and Planning*.

7. Beauregard, "The Multiplicities of Planning."

8. Yiftachel, "Planning and Social Control," 395.

9. Forester, *Planning in the Face of Power*, 3.

10. Quoted in Friedmann, *Planning in the Public Domain*, 11.

11. Flyvbjerg, "Phronetic Planning Research," 296.

12. Yiftachel, "Planning and Social Control"; Flyvbjerg and Richardson, "Planning and Foucault"; Roy, *City Requiem, Calcutta*.

13. Mitchell, *Colonising Egypt*; Rabinow, *French Modern*.

14. Brasilia is discussed in Holston, *The Modernist City*. CIAM is the French acronym for the International Congress of Modern Architecture. The first of these congresses was organized in June 1928 in Switzerland by Le Corbusier for twenty-eight European architects.

15. Robinson, "Global and World Cities," 531.

16. Association of Collegiate Schools of Planning, "Annual Conference Tracks."

17. Holston, *The Modernist City*, 46.

18. Fawaz, *Mabādiʾ Tanẓīm al-Mudun*.

19. The French Mandate formally ended in 1943, but the French remained in Lebanon until 1946.

20. Sachs, *The Development Dictionary*.

21. Hart, "Development Critiques in the 1990s," 650.

22. United States Operations Mission to Lebanon, *Lebanon: USOM Report*.

23. Rostow, *The Stages of Economic Growth*.

24. Truman's containment policy proposed curbing the expansion of Soviet influence by providing US economic and military aid to countries where communist sensibilities were on the rise. See Gendzier, *Notes from the Minefield*, 126.

25. For example, the US aid booklets from the time celebrate interventions in such areas as improving livestock breeding or crop yield (United States Operations Mission to Lebanon, *Lebanon: USOM Report*) and infrastructure provision (USAID, *Lebanon: History*).

26. Yiftachel, "Planning and Social Control."

27. Barakat and Narang-Suri, "War, Cities and Planning," 116.

28. Holston, *The Modernist City*, 60.

29. *Environmental determinism* is the belief that physical, spatial, environmental, and geographical conditions determine social outcomes. See Peet, "The Social Origins of Environmental Determinism."

30. An idea perpetuated by Oscar Lewis in his work on Mexican families in 1959 (Lewis, *Five Families*).

31. Castells and Sheridan, *The Urban Question: A Marxist Approach*.

32. Taylor, *Urban Planning Theory since 1945*.

33. Theodosis, "'Containing' Baghdad."

34. Sarkis, *Circa 1958*.

35. Cited in Gendzier, *Notes from the Minefield*, 197.

36. Ibid., 198.

37. Ibid., 191.

38. The fees for two thirds of his services were paid by the US government, while the rest came through staff and in-kind support provided by the Lebanese government (Sarkis, *Circa 1958*, 17).

39. For example, in Iraq in 1955, for his major project in the Middle East, Doxiadis was introduced as an "expert on housing and development, at a time when the Iraqis needed 'foreigners on policy and program,' since they had 'plenty of competent architects and engineers for design'" (Theodosis, "'Containing' Baghdad").

40. Lang, "Housing Activities 1956–1958," 19.

41. Sarkis, *Circa 1958*, 19.

42. Gendzier, *Notes from the Minefield.*

43. Johnson, "Class & Client in Beirut."

44. Salibi, "Lebanon under Fuad Chehab 1958–1964."

45. See Traboulsi, *A History of Modern Lebanon*, 134. The uprising took shape mainly in the mostly Sunni Basta neighborhood and its surroundings, as well as in the Druze Shouf mountains.

46. Picard, *Lebanon, a Shattered Country.*

47. In 1957, in a speech on the situation in the Middle East, US President Dwight Eisenhower outlined intervention policies that are now commonly known as the Eisenhower Doctrine. The doctrine advocated intervention in countries threatened by international Communism. In that regard, it was a continuation of the Truman containment policy of 1948, but it specifically targeted the Middle East region. As protests emerged in Lebanon later, Chamoun asked the US government to apply this doctrine to assist his government in putting down the uprising and to help him stay in power (Gendzier, *Notes from the Minefield*).

48. Ibid.

49. Beshara, *Lebanon.*

50. Tabet, "From Colonial Style to Regional Revivalism."

51. Gendzier, *Notes from the Minefield*, 191.

52. Tabet, "From Colonial Style to Regional Revivalism," 86.

53. Sharara, *Al-Silm al-Ahlī al-Bārid.*

54. Father Lebret's work was representative of social Catholicism, a movement that championed the redistribution of resources as an individual and communal project within a larger capitalist system (Verdeil, "Methodological and Political Issues in the Lebanese Planning Experiences").

55. Fawaz and Peillen, "The Case of Beirut, Lebanon."

56. Cited in Picard, "The Lebanese Shi'a and Political Violence in Lebanon," 197, and based on Khuri, *From Village to Suburb.*

57. Gendzier, *Notes from the Minefield*, 200.

58. Kassir, *Ḥarb Lubnān.*

59. Yiftachel, "Towards a New Typology of Urban Planning Theories," 33.

60. Amin, *Unequal Development*; Harvey, *Social Justice and the City*; Castells and Sheridan, *The Urban Question.*

61. Yiftachel, "Towards a New Typology of Urban Planning Theories."

62. Ibid.

63. Hall, *Cities of Tomorrow*, 355.

64. Friedmann, *Planning in the Public Domain*, 8.

65. United Nations, *The United Nations Development Decade.*

66. Ibid.

67. Hart, "D/developments after the Meltdown."

68. Goldman, "Development and the City," 56.

69. Ibid., 56.

70. Roy, *City Requiem, Calcutta*, 16.

71. The Church intervened in the debate on development to help dispel Commu-

nist sentiments, especially among the disadvantaged populations. In 1966, Vatican II, in cooperation with the World Council of Churches, established the Committee on Society, Development, and Peace, which in turn organized the World Cooperation for Development Conference in Beirut. (Father Lebret, the founder of IRFED, who died in 1966, served between 1962 and 1966 as special advisor to the Pope on development issues. This might explain why the conference was held in Lebanon [private communication with Eric Verdeil, 2013].) The conference sought to advise churches on "economic and technical aspects of certain issues of grave interest to them and to the entire human family." Economic conditions were central to the Church's anxieties (Munby, Vatican Commission on Peace and Freedom, and World Council of Churches, *World Development*, ix).

72. Munby, Vatican Commission on Peace and Freedom, and World Council of Churches, *World Development*.

73. Verdeil, "State Development Policy and Specialised Engineers."

74. In Arabic, the Ministry of Public Planning is called *Wizārat al-Taṣmīm al-'Aam*. While some people translate *taṣmīm* as "design," others translate it as "planning." I have followed the word choice of French scholars who work on planning in Lebanon and who argue that the names of Lebanese planning institutions were conceived in French (drawing on the name of the French planning institution Aménagement du Territoire), and then translated into Arabic (private communication with Eric Verdeil in 2013). In English, *aménagement du territoire* is "urban planning." It would be interesting to find out why *aménagement* was translated as *taṣmīm* (design) rather than *takhṭīṭ* (planning).

75. Ironically, the creation of these multiple entities with overlapping responsibilities spread the decision-making process for the built environment over multiple arenas, which created conflicts among the different public agencies.

76. Nsouli, "Design and Development," 11.

77. In 1964, the influential Development Studies Association was established, spearheaded by Hasan Saab (along with Charles Rizk and Zaki Mazboudi). The association would eventually organize thirteen workshops between 1964 and 1988, focused on development in Lebanon through times of peace and war. Their approach to development was a "humanistic" one. Their workshops were multidisciplinary, concerned with a variety of issues, ranging from education to defense. Nonetheless, economic development remained central to their mission. The urban dimension did not feature much in these workshops.

78. This period also witnessed the emergence of locally trained urban planning experts who started their careers by working closely with foreign experts; many were architects by training (Verdeil, "Methodological and Political Issues in the Lebanese Planning Experiences").

79. Al-Asad and Musa in association with Saliba, *Emerging Trends in Urbanism*.

80. Sarkis, "Dances with Margaret Mead."

81. Verdeil, "Michel Ecochard in Lebanon and Syria (1956–1968)."

82. Fawaz does not mention the reasons that led to terminating the work (Fawaz, *Inmā' Lubnān*).

83. Also in 1963, the first urban planning legislation applicable to the Lebanese territories was passed (Tabet, "From Colonial Style to Regional Revivalism"), the Ministry of Public Planning was overhauled to allow for decentralized administration of land, and the Higher Council for Urban Planning was created.

84. Ecochard did not sanction these modifications, yet in colloquial use the master plan still bears his name. See Verdeil, "Michel Ecochard in Lebanon and Syria (1956–1968)."

85. Ibid.

86. Ghorayeb, "The Work and Influence of Michel Ecochard in Lebanon."

87. Verdeil, *Beyrouth et ses Urbanistes.*

88. Goldman, "Development and the City."

89. Ecochard (1961) cited in Verdeil, *Beyrouth et ses Urbanistes,* 143.

90. Khalaf, "Some Sociological Reflections on the Urban Reconstruction of Beirut."

91. Sharara, *Al-Silm al-Ahlī al-Bārid.*

92. See Taylor, "Planning for Urban Growth." The first local question to the British experts in the published volume from those seminars concerned how to make economic planners more spatially aware.

93. *White book* is a general term used to describe an official report or document usually issued by the government. This may sometimes be a government proposal presented for approval by a legislative body.

94 The Directorate of Town Planning's proposal was made further impossible by powerful interests that advocated private profit over public utility. See Verdeil, *Beyrouth et ses Urbanistes.*

95. Tabet, "From Colonial Style to Regional Revivalism," 88.

96. Ajami, *The Vanished Imam*; Nasr and James, "Roots of the Shi'i Movement."

97. Among these was Khalaf and Kongstad's study of Hamra, which discussed sectarian affiliation but argued that it had not affected the way Hamra had urbanized as "a fusion of different ethnic and confessional groups without any apparent civil tension or urban strife" (Khalaf and Kongstad, *Hamra of Beirut*).

98. Khuri, "Sectarian Loyalty among Rural Migrants in Two Lebanese Suburbs"; and *From Village to Suburb.*

99. Joseph, "The Politicization of Religious Sects."

100. Nasr, "Backdrop to Civil War."

101. Khuri, *From Village to Suburb.*

102. Khuri, "The Changing Class Structure in Lebanon," 29.

103. Joseph, "The Politicization of Religious Sects."

104. The most important case was the Lebanese National Movement (LNM), led by Kamal Jumblat, which included parties from all sects. However, the main pillars of the LNM eventually disaggregated into several notorious militias, especially the Shiite Haraket Amal and the Druze PSP.

105. It is important to note here that many of the "trouble areas" in east Beirut were cleared in the first two years of the war (see Fawaz and Peillen, "The Case of Beirut, Lebanon"). The most famous of these involved massacres in the Qarantina and Tel al-Zaatar Palestinian refugee camps in 1976. Seen as the breeding grounds for the Palestinian resistance groups which had played a key role in starting the war, the camps were attacked and cleared early on by right-wing Christian militias. While the Christian militias framed their invasion in terms of national rhetoric (clearing Lebanon of the "troublesome" Palestinians), the massacres were also framed in sectarian terms as Christians killing Muslims, sanctioned by the Syrian regime (Yassin, "Violent Urbanization and Homogenization of Space and Place").

106. Odeh, *Lebanon, Dynamics of Conflict*; Johnson, *Class & Client in Beirut.*

107. Khalaf, "Some Sociological Reflections on the Urban Reconstruction of Beirut."

108. Traboulsi, *A History of Modern Lebanon*. This view was also related to who had been writing the history—basically leftists and socialists. For them, uneven development had always been a central issue. The sectarian order of development and its evenness was also absent from forums like the Development Studies Association.

109. Khalaf, "Some Sociological Reflections on the Urban Reconstruction of Beirut," 18.

110. Verdeil, "Methodological and Political Issues in the Lebanese Planning Experiences."

111. Amin Gemayel had previously served as an assistant to his uncle Maurice Gemayel, who established and headed the Ministry of Planning. Maurice Gemayel was a planning visionary, and he wrote numerous books and essays introducing his ideas for social and economic development. This exposure might have affected Amin Gemayel's beliefs in the ability of planning and building law to solve social issues (private communication with Eric Verdeil, 2013).

112. Nasr and Verdeil, "The Reconstructions of Beirut"; Fawaz and Peillen, "The Case of Beirut, Lebanon."

113. The core areas of the camps were originally built on land rented by the United Nations Relief and Works Agency for Palestine Refugees (UNRWA). As Mona Fawaz pointed out to me in a private communication, they were thus considered extra-legal (with no right to exist). However, as the camps expanded to accommodate increasing populations, the urbanization that came to surround them was mostly informal. See Fawaz and Peillen, "The Case of Beirut, Lebanon."

114. In addition to issuing a decree that superseded any other regulations (even those issued by the DGU), Amin Gemayel relied on the CDR to materialize his planning vision.

115. Fawaz and Peillen, "The Case of Beirut, Lebanon." In 1982, 5000 households from Ouzaii took to the streets to protest this uneven treatment (Cobban, "The Growth of Shi'i Power in Lebanon and its Implications for the Future," 148).

116. The first work by IAURIF in Lebanon had been an airport-related study in 1965. In 1971, they had also been hired as technical experts to develop the Master Plan for Beirut, with target years of 1985 and 2000.

117. Verdeil, "Methodological and Political Issues in the Lebanese Planning Experiences," 5.

118. Discussing the 1986 IAURIF attempt at a national master plan, Verdeil wrote: "the main legacy of this project is found in the involvement of IAURIF in the Lebanese scene. The experience, personal relationships, shared conceptions and methodology, and its knowledge of the country enabled IAURIF to be commissioned for important postwar reconstruction studies: the Demarcation Line, the Transportation Plan, the Coastal Environmental Assessment, and the Development and Reconstruction Plan for South Lebanon" (Verdeil, "Methodological and Political Issues in the Lebanese Planning Experiences"). This list by itself shows how interventions during and after the war became increasingly concerned with sectors and sections, shifting from an attempt to plan comprehensively in 1983 to a collection of self-contained projects.

119. Private communication with Mona Fawaz in October 2014.

120. The Taif Agreement provided the basis for ending the civil war in Lebanon.

121. Traboulsi, "Social Classes and Political Power in Lebanon."

122. However, it is also important to recall that, as discussed earlier, even before the civil war, many of Beirut's neighborhoods were not mixed.

123. Bou Akar, "Displacement, Politics, and Governance."

124. Harvey, *The Condition of Postmodernity*, 66.

125. Ong, *Neoliberalism as Exception*, 77–78.

126. MacKinnon, "Washington Report on Middle East Affairs."

127. According to a private communication with Verdeil in 2013, these efforts were started even before by IAURIF, which followed up on the NPMP for ten years, pushing it through all political hurdles in order to get it approved in 2009 (supported by allies inside the DGU and CDR).

128. Fawaz, *Urban Planning in Beirut*, 140.

129. The decree was issued for Phase I of the NPMP. Phase II is still just a proposal.

130. This was a time when the country was divided between the March 14 and March 8 political camps. The CDR was seen as a tool of the March 14 camp, while Hezbollah was in the March 8 camp.

131. The Consultative Center for Studies and Documentation, *Al-Khuṭṭa al-Shāmila li-Tartīb al-Arāḍī al-Lubnāniyya*.

132. Ibid.

133. Many interviewees also mentioned the environment and issues of sustainability. But I can only assume that this concern was influenced by the current global moment, in which most aid money to developing countries like Lebanon was being channeled toward projects that deal with the environment. Nowadays, the aid money is going toward coping with the influx of Syrian refugees.

134. In the process of forming governments, religious-political organizations always fight over what they call *service portfolios*. This is not, however, a fight over different visions of development, but over access to ministries with funds that can be used to lure voters to their candidates through investments in certain areas. For example, the Ministry of Public Works, which is the umbrella entity for most of the planning work in Lebanon (other than that of the CDR), is considered a key service portfolio through which client-patron relationships may be cultivated.

135. This shift, although it is in a different context, is similar to that Mustafa Dikeç identified in the transformation of Paris's *banlieues* from "neighborhoods in danger" to "dangerous neighborhoods," an alteration that had a number of repressive repercussions for the populations inhabiting these spaces (Dikeç, "Revolting Geographies").

136. This shift of focus could also be traced in terms of the knowledge currently being produced about Beirut (including this study). In the late 1990s and 2000s, there was a considerable amount of research on urban planning approaches to poverty, the poor and their informal spaces, and the exclusion of such concerns from projects like Solidere. But these topics seem to have been eclipsed today by debates focused more on sectarianism, infrastructure delivery, and the location of high-end developments.

137. For example, the development and planning of Shouf has been left to the PSP, the development of Doha Aramoun is being decided by the Sunni Future Movement, and the development of the Matn-Keserwan region is being decided by Christian religious-political organizations.

EPILOGUE

1. Bou Akar and Hafeda, *Narrating Beirut from Its Borderlines.*

2. Parnell and Robinson, "(Re)theorizing Cities from the Global South."

3. Sassen, *The Global City*; Castells, *The Rise of the Network Society.*

4. Berman, *All That Is Solid Melts into Air*; Holston, *The Modernist City*; Scott, *Seeing Like a State.*

5. Simone, *For the City Yet to Come.*

6. Brenner, "Theses on Urbanization."

7. Davis, "Planet of Slums."

8. Saint-Amour, *Tense Future*, 12–13.

9. Mbembe, "Chinua Achebe and the African Century."

10. Agamben, *State of Exception.*

11. Ong, *Neoliberalism as Exception.*

12. Brooks, *Planning Theory for Practitioners.*

13. Bou Akar, "From Poor Peripheries to Sectarian Frontiers."

14. Khouri, "Beirut Madinati."

REFERENCES

Aalbers, Manuel B. "When the Banks Withdraw, Slum Landlords Take Over: The Structuration of Neighbourhood Decline through Redlining, Drug Dealing, Speculation and Immigrant Exploitation." *Urban Studies* 43, no. 7 (2006): 1061–86.

Abed, Jamal. "L'Agriculture Urbaine dans la Plaine de Shweifaat, entre Politique Spatiale et Chronologie Différentielle des Pratiques dans l'Espace." In *Interfaces: Agricultures et Villes à l'Est et au Sud de la Méditerranée*, edited by Joe Nasr and Martine Padilla, 355–74. Beirut: Delta/IFPO, 2004.

Abu Ammo, Ruba. "'Awdat al-Lubnānī ilā al-Ghīttū." *Al-Akhbar*, November 16, 2010, 1271 edition.

Agamben, Giorgio. *State of Exception*. Chicago: University of Chicago Press, 2005.

Ajami, Fouad. *The Vanished Imam: Musa al-Sadr and the Shia of Lebanon*. Ithaca, NY: Cornell University Press, 1987.

Alaily, Ghadir. "Ba'd Mashrū' Qānūn Ḥarb, al-Zu'amā' al-Mawārina Yuṭālibūn bi-l-Shuf'a: Hal Nushāhid Wilādat al-Ṭā'ifiyya al-'Aqāriyya?" *Legal Agenda*, July 27, 2011.

Al-Amin, Rami. "Fī al-Ḥadath . . . Irtifāq wa Takhṭīṭ wa 'Unṣuriyya." *Al-Akhbar*, July 12, 2011, 1459 edition.

Al-Asad, Mohammad, and Majd Musa in association with Robert Saliba. *Emerging Trends In Urbanism: The Beirut Post-War Experience*. An Essay on a presentation made by Robert Saliba to Diwan al-Mimar on April 20, 2000. Beirut: Center for the Study of the Built Environment, 2001.

"Al-Baladiyya 'Mā Raḥ Tumḍīlak' . . . Hakadhā Tuwājih al-Ḥadath Bay' al-Arāḍī!" *IMLebanon*, September 26, 2016.

Al-Harithy, Howayda. *Lessons in Post-War Reconstruction: Case Studies from Lebanon in the Aftermath of the 2006 War*. Planning, History and Environment Series. New York: Routledge, 2010.

Al-Husseini, Ali. "Al-Qādimūn al-Judud . . . 'Hizb Allah' min al-Zāḥifin naḥw al-Quds ilā al-Qādimīn bi-Ittijāh al-Jabal." *Al Joumhouria*, July 7, 2012.

Al Jazeera. "Timeline: Lebanon—A Chronology of Key Events in Lebanese History," June 4, 2009. Accessed May 29, 2017. http://www.aljazeera.com/focus/lebanon2009 /2009/06/200961145224882101.html.

AlSayyad, Nezar, and Mejgan Massoumi. *The Fundamentalist City? Religiosity and the Remaking of Urban Space*. New York: Routledge, 2011.

Alshoufi, Firas. "Dawḥat ʿAramūn: Aʾimmat Takfīr wa Khalāyā Irhābiyya Nāʾima." *Al-Akhbar*, November 26, 2014, 2454 edition.

Amin, Samir. *Unequal Development: An Essay on the Social Formations of Peripheral Capitalism*. Translated by Brian Pearce. New York: Monthly Review Press, 1976.

Andary, Salman. "Bayʿ Araḍin wa Mashārīʿ Sakaniyya Mashbūha wa Istinfār lil-Ahālī . . . Hal Taghraq ʿAramūn bi-Ṭawafān ʿḤizballah'?" 14march.org, October 15, 2011.

Arendt, Hannah. *On Violence*. New York: Harcourt, 1970.

Associated Consulting Engineers. *Master Plan Proposal for the Municipality of Choueifat*. Beirut, 1997.

Association of Collegiate Schools of Planning. "Annual Conference Tracks." 2015. http://www.acsp.org/page/ConfTracks.

Atia, Mona. *Building a House in Heaven: Pious Neoliberalism and Islamic Charity in Egypt*. Minneapolis: University of Minnesota Press, 2013.

Barakat, Sultan, and Shipra Narang-Suri. "War, Cities and Planning: Making a Case for Urban Planning in Conflict-Affected Cities." *Cities and Crises*, edited by Dennis Day, Annette Grindsted, Brigitte Piquard, and David Zammit, 105–29. Bilbao: University of Deusto, 2009,

Bayat, Asef. "Politics in the City Inside-Out." *City & Society* 24, no. 2 (2012), 110–28.

———. *Street Politics: Poor People's Movements in Iran*. New York: Columbia University Press, 1997.

Beauregard, Robert A. "The Multiplicities of Planning." *Journal of Planning Education and Research* 20, no. 4 (2001): 437–39.

"Beirut Apartments Second Most Pricey in MENA." *Daily Star*, February 21, 2012.

Bello, Walden. "Globalization and Social Change." Keynote speech at *Globalization and Social Change*, the 7th Annual Berkeley Journal of Sociology Conference, University of California, Berkeley, March 9, 2007.

Bergman, Ronen. "The Hezbollah Connection." *New York Times*, February 10, 2015.

Berman, Marshall. *All That Is Solid Melts into Air: The Experience of Modernity*. New York: Verso, 1983.

Beshara, Adel. *Lebanon: The Politics of Frustration—the Failed Coup of 1961*. London: Routledge, 2011.

Beyhum, Nabil. "Espaces Éclatés, Espaces Dominés: Étude de la Recomposition des Espaces Publics Centraux de Beyrouth de 1975 à 1990." Dissertation, Université de Lyon, 1991.

Boal, Frederick W. *Ethnicity and Housing: Accommodating Differences*. Farnham: Ashgate, 2000.

Bou Akar, Hiba. "Contesting Beirut's Frontiers." *City & Society* 24, no. 2 (2012): 150–72.

———. "Displacement, Politics, and Governance: Access to Low-Income Housing in a Beirut Suburb." Unpublished master's thesis, MIT, 2005.

———. "From Poor Peripheries to Sectarian Frontiers: Planning, Development, and the Spatial Production of Sectarianism in Beirut." In *Territories of Poverty: Rethinking North and South*, edited by Ananya Roy and Emma Shaw Crane, 264–88. Athens: University of Georgia Press, 2015.

Bou Akar, Hiba, and Mohamad Hafeda, eds. *Narrating Beirut from Its Borderlines*. Berlin: Heinrich Böll Foundation, 2011.

Brenner, Neil. "Theses on Urbanization." *Public Culture* 25, no. 1 69 (2013): 85–114.

Brooks, Michael P. *Planning Theory for Practitioners.* Chicago: APA Planners Press, 2002.

Brundiers, Katja, and André Odermatt. "Analyzing Socio-Spatial Processes of Integration and Disintegration by Examining the Local Housing Market: A Case Study of Beirut, Lebanon." *Arab World Geographer* 5, no. 4 (2002).

Buck-Morss, Susan. *The Dialectics of Seeing: Walter Benjamin and the Arcades Project.* Cambridge, MA: MIT Press, 1991.

Caldeira, Teresa P. R. *City of Walls: Crime, Segregation, and Citizenship in São Paulo.* Berkeley: University of California Press, 2000.

Cammett, Melani. *Compassionate Communalism: Welfare and Sectarianism in Lebanon.* Ithaca, NY: Cornell University Press, 2014.

Cammett, Melani, and Sukriti Issar. "Bricks and Mortar Clientelism: Sectarianism and the Logics of Welfare Allocation in Lebanon." *World Politics* 62, no. 03 (2010): 381–421.

Castells, Manuel. *The City and the Grassroots.* London: Edward Arnold, 1983.

———. *The Rise of the Network Society.* Malden, MA: Blackwell, 1996.

Castells, Manuel, and Alan Sheridan. *The Urban Question: A Marxist Approach.* London: Edward Arnold, 1977.

Central Administration of Statistics. *Household Living Conditions in Lebanon 1997.* Beirut, February 1998.

Chance, Kerry Ryan. "Transitory Citizens: Contentious Housing Practices in Contemporary South Africa." *Social Analysis* 59, no. 3 (2015): 62–84.

Charafeddine, Wafa. "L'Habitat Illégal de la Banlieue-Sud de Beyrouth." In *Reconstruire Beyrouth—Les Paris sur le Possible*, edited by Beyhum Nabil, 227–38. Lyon: Maison de L'Orient et de la Méditerranée, 1991.

———. "The Lebanese National Master Plan: Concerned Institutions and Beneficiaries." In *Conference City Debates, The Lebanese National Master Plan, City Debates 2003 Proceedings*, edited by Mona Harb, 40–45. Beirut, American University of Beirut, 2004.

Clerc, Valerie. *Les Quartiers Irréguliers de Beyrouth: Une Histoire des Enjeux Fonciers et Urbanistiques de la Banlieue Sud.* Beirut: IFPO, 2008.

Cobban, Helena. "The Growth of Shi'i Power in Lebanon and its Implications for the Future." In *Shi'ism and Social Protest*, edited by Juan Ricardo Cole and Nikki R. Keddie, 137–55. Yale University Press, 1986.

The Consultative Center for Studies and Documentation (CCSD). *Al-Khuṭṭa al-Shāmila li-Tartīb al-Arāḍī al-Lubnāniyya: Niqāsh fī al-Mabādi' wa-l-Khiyārāt: Awrāq Warshat al-ʿAmal allati Naẓẓamahā al-Markaz al-Istishārī lil-Dirāsāt wa-l-Tawthīq bi-l-Taʿāwun maʿ al-Tajammuʿ al-Islāmī lil-Muhandisīn, Bayrūt fī 29–30 Ḥazīrān 2006.* Beirut: Al-Markaz al-Istishari lil-Dirasat wa-l-Tawthiq, 2008.

———. *Alīssār: Al-Wāqiʿ wa-l-Taḥawwulāt: Madīnīyyan, Iqtiṣādiyyan, Ijtimāʿiyyan.* Beirut: Markaz al-Istishari lil-Dirasat wa-l-Tawthiq, 1998.

Council for Development and Reconstruction. *National Physical Master Plan for the Lebanese Territory.* Beirut, 2005.

———. *Roads, Highways and Public Transport.* Beirut, July 2008.

Coward, Martin. "Urbicide in Bosnia." In *Cities, War, and Terrorism: Towards an Urban Geopolitics*, edited by Stephen Graham, 154–71. London: Wiley-Blackwell, 2004.

Dar al-Aytam al-Islamiya. *Mujamma' Inmā' al-Qudurāt al-Insāniyya*. Beirut: Dar al-Aytam al-Islamiya, May 21, 2017.

Davie, Michael F. "Demarcation Lines in Contemporary Lebanon." In *World Boundaries Series: The Middle East and North Africa*, vol. 2, edited by Clive Schofield and Richard Schofield, 35–58. New York: Routledge, 1994.

Davis, Diane E. "Non-State Armed Actors, New Imagined Communities, and Shifting Patterns of Sovereignty and Insecurity in the Modern World." *Contemporary Security Policy* 30, no. 2 (2011): 221–45.

Davis, Mike. "Planet of Slums." *New Left Review* 2, no. 26 (2004): 5–34.

Deboulet, Agnès, and Mona Fawaz. "Contesting the Legitimacy of Urban Restructuring and Highways in Beirut's Irregular Settlements." In *Cities & Sovereignty: Identity Politics in Urban Spaces*, edited by Diane E. Davis and Nora Libertun de Duren, 117–51. Bloomington: Indiana University Press, 2011.

De Certeau, Michel. *The Practice of Everyday Life*. Berkeley: University of California Press, 1984.

Deeb, Lara. *An Enchanted Modern: Gender and Public Piety in Shi'i Lebanon*. Princeton, NJ: Princeton University Press, 2006.

Deeb, Lara, and Mona Harb. *Leisurely Islam: Negotiating Geography and Morality in Shi'ite South Beirut*. Princeton, NJ: Princeton University Press, 2013.

Dikeç, Mustafa. "Revolting Geographies: Urban Unrest in France." *Geography Compass* 1, no. 5 (2007): 1190–1206.

Drake, St. C., and Horace R. Cayton. *Black Metropolis: A Study of Negro Life in a Northern City*. Chicago: University of Chicago Press, 1970.

Elyachar, Julia. *Markets of Dispossession: NGOs, Economic Development, and the State in Cairo*. Durham, NC: Duke University Press, 2005.

Fainstein, Susan S. "Planning Theory and the City." *Journal of Planning Education and Research* 25, no. 2 (2005): 121–30.

Faour, Ghaleb, and Mario Mhawej. "Mapping Urban Transitions in the Greater Beirut Area Using Different Space Platforms." *Land* 3, no. 3 (2014): 941–56.

Farah, Jihad. "Différenciations Sociospatiales et Gouvernance Municipale dans les Banlieues de Beyrouth: À Travers l'Exemple de Sahel al-Matn al-Janoubi et des Municipalités de Chiyah, Ghobeiri et Furn al-Chebbak." Unpublished PhD dissertation, University of Liège, 2011.

Fawaz, Mohamad. *Inmā' Lubnān*. Beirut: Dar Sadir, 2002.

———. "The Role of DGU in Providing Low-Cost Housing in Lebanon." In *Proceedings of the Symposium on Low Cost Housing in the Arab Region*, 438–59. Beirut: United Nations Economic and Social Commission for Western Asia, 1992.

———. *Al-Tanzīm al-Mudunī fī Lubnān*. Beirut: ALBA, 2004.

Fawaz, Mona. "Agency and Ideology in the Service Provision of Islamic Organizations in the Southern Suburb of Beirut, Lebanon." Paper presented at the UNESCO conference *NGOS and Governance in the Arab Countries*, Cairo, March 2000.

———. "Exceptions and the Actually Existing Practice of Planning: Beirut (Lebanon) as Case Study." *Urban Studies* 54, no. 8 (2017): 1938–55.

———. "Hezbollah as Urban Planner? Questions to and from Planning Theory." *Planning Theory* 8, no. 4 (2009): 323.

———. "Neoliberal Urbanity and the Right to the City: A View from Beirut's Periphery." *Development and Change* 40, no. 5 (2009): 827–52.

———. "Notes on Beirut's Historiography: Towards a People's History of the City." In *Des Banlieues à la Ville*. Beirut: IFPO, 2013.

———. "The Politics of Property in Planning: Hezbollah's Reconstruction of Haret Hreik (Beirut, Lebanon) as Case Study." *International Journal of Urban and Regional Research* 38, no. 3 (2014): 922–34.

———. "Strategizing for Housing: An Investigation of the Production and Regulation of Low-Income Housing in the Suburbs of Beirut." Doctoral dissertation, Massachusetts Institute of Technology, 2004.

Fawaz, Mona, and Marwan Ghandour. *The Reconstruction of Haret Hreik: Design Options for Improving the Livability of the Neighborhood*. Beirut: Reconstruction Unit, Department of Architecture and Design, American University of Beirut, 2007.

Fawaz, Mona, Mona Harb, and Ahmad Gharbieh. "Living Beirut's Security Zones: An Investigation of the Modalities and Practice of Urban Security." *City & Society* 24, no. 2 (2012): 173–95

Fawaz, Mona, and Isabelle Peillen. "The Case of Beirut, Lebanon." In *Understanding Slums: Case Studies for the Global Report on Human Settlements*, by University College, London, Development Planning Unit and United Nations Human Settlements Programme. London: University College, London, Development Planning Unit, 2003.

Fawaz, Mustafa. *Mabādi' Tanẓīm al-Mudun*. Beirut: Arab Development Institute, 1980.

Fawz, Nader. "Al-Ḥadath: Timthāl al-Masīḥ Rāji'." *Al-Akhbar*, May 3, 2010, 1107 edition.

Feldman, Allen. "Ethnographic States of Emergency." In *Fieldwork under Fire: Contemporary Studies of Violence and Survival*, edited by Carolyn Nordstrom and Antonius C.G.M. Robben, 224–52. Berkeley: University of California Press, 1996.

———. *Formations of Violence: The Narrative of the Body and Political Terror in Northern Ireland*. Chicago: University of Chicago Press, 1991.

Flyvbjerg, Bent. "Phronetic Planning Research: Theoretical and Methodological Reflections." *Planning Theory & Practice* 5, no. 3 (2004): 283–306.

Flyvbjerg, Bent, and Tim Richardson. "Planning and Foucault: In Search of the Dark Side of Planning Theory." In *Planning Futures: New Directions for Planning Theory*, 44–62. London: Psychology Press, 2002.

Forester, John. *Planning in the Face of Power*. Berkeley: University of California Press, 1989.

Foucault, Michel. *The Birth of Biopolitics: Lectures at the Collège de France, 1978–79*. New York: Palgrave Macmillan, 2008.

Fregonese, Sara. "Beyond the 'Weak State': Hybrid Sovereignties in Beirut." *Environment and Planning D: Society and Space* 30, no. 4 (2012): 655–74.

———. "The Urbicide of Beirut? Geopolitics and the Built Environment in the Lebanese Civil War (1975–1976)." *Political Geography* 28, no. 5 (2009): 309–18.

Friedmann, John. 1987. *Planning in the Public Domain: From Knowledge to Action*. Princeton, NJ: Princeton University Press, 1987.

Friedmann, John, and William Alonso, eds. *Regional Development and Planning: A Reader*. Cambridge, MA: MIT Press, 1964.

Gendzier, Irene L. *Notes from the Minefield: United States Intervention in Lebanon and the Middle East, 1945–1958*. New York: Columbia University Press, 2006.

Ghannam, Farha. *Remaking the Modern: Space, Relocation, and the Politics of Identity in a Global Cairo*. Berkeley: University of California Press, 2002.

Ghorayeb, Marlène. "The Work and Influence of Michel Ecochard in Lebanon." In *Projecting Beirut: Episodes in the Construction and Reconstruction of a Modern City*, edited by Peter G. Rowe and Hashim Sarkis, 106–21. New York: Prestel, 1998.

Global IDP. *Profile of Internal Displacement: Lebanon*. Geneva: Norwegian Refugee Council/Global IDP Project, 2004. http://www.refworld.org/pdfid/3bd98d5e0.pdf.

Goldman, Michael. "Development and the City." In *Cities of the Global South Reader*, edited by Faranak Miraftab and Neema Kudva, 54–65. New York: Routledge, 2015.

Graham, Stephen. *Cities under Siege: The New Military Urbanism*. New York: Verso, 2011.

———. *Cities, War, and Terrorism: Towards an Urban Geopolitics*. London: Wiley-Blackwell, 2004.

———. "The Urban 'Battlespace.'" *Theory, Culture & Society* 26, no. 7–8 (2009): 278–88.

———. "When Life Itself Is War: On the Urbanization of Military and Security Doctrine." *International Journal of Urban and Regional Research* 36, no. 1:136–55.

Gregory, Derek. *The Colonial Present: Afghanistan, Palestine, Iraq*. Oxford: Blackwell, 2004.

———. "'In Another Time-Zone, the Bombs Fall Unsafely. . . .' Targets, Civilians and Late Modern War." *Arab World Geographer* 9, no. 2 (2006): 88–111.

Gupta, Akhil, and James Ferguson. "Space, Identity, and the Politics of Difference." *Cultural Anthropology* 7, no. 1 (1992): 6–23.

Guy, Simon. "Shadow Architectures: War, Memories, and Berlin's Futures." In *Cities, War, and Terrorism*, edited by Stephen Graham, 75–92. London: Wiley-Blackwell, 2004.

Hackworth, Jason. *Faith Based: Religious Neoliberalism and the Politics of Welfare in the United States*. Athens: University of Georgia Press, 2012.

Hadifa, Saleh. "Durūz Sāhil Jabal Lubnān 'Hunūd Ḥumr' Yantaẓirūn . . . al-Inqirāḍ." *Now Lebanon*, September 26, 2012.

Hafeda, Mohamad. "Bordering Practices: Negotiating and Narrating Political-Sectarian Conflict in Contemporary Beirut." Doctoral thesis, University College London, 2015.

Haidar, Jad. "Bayn Mārātūn Bayrūt wa Mārātūn al-Sariqāt." *Lebanon Files*, November 8, 2010.

Hall, Peter. *Cities of Tomorrow: An Intellectual History of Urban Planning and Design in the Twentieth Century*. 3rd ed. Malden, MA: Wiley-Blackwell, 2002.

Hamadeh, Shirine. "A Housing Proposal against All Odds: The Case of Squatter Settlements in Beirut." Unpublished master's thesis, Rice University, 1987.

Harb, Mona. *City Debates 2003: The Lebanese National Master Plan*. Beirut: American University of Beirut, 2004.

———. "Deconstructing Hizballah and Its Suburb." *Middle East Report* 37, no. 242 (2007): 12.

———. "Faith-Based Organizations as Effective Development Partners? Hezbollah and Post-War Reconstruction in Lebanon." In *Development, Civil Society and Faith-Based*

Organizations: Bridging the Sacred and the Secular, edited by Gerard Clarke and Michael Jennings, 214–39. New York: Palgrave Macmillan, 2008.

———. "On Religiosity and Spatiality: Lessons from Hezbollah in Beirut." In *The Fundamentalist City? Religiosity and the Remaking of Urban Space*, edited by Nezar AlSayyad and Mejgan Massoumi, 125–154. New York: Routledge, 2011.

———. "Urban Governance in Post-War Beirut: Resources, Negotiations, and Contestations in the Elyssar Project." In *Capital Cities: Ethnographies of Urban Governance in the Middle East*, edited by Seteney Khalid Shami, 111–33. Toronto: University of Toronto Press, 2001.

Harb, Mona, and Reinoud Leenders. "Know Thy Enemy: Hizbullah, 'Terrorism' and the Politics of Perception." *Third World Quarterly* 26, no. 1 (2005): 173–97.

Harb el-Kak, Mona. *Politiques Urbaines dans la Banlieue Sud de Beyrouth*. Beirut: Presses de l'Ifpo, 1996.

Hart, Gillian. "D/developments after the Meltdown." *Antipode* 41, no. S1 (2010): 117–41.

———. "Development Critiques in the 1990s: Culs de Sac and Promising Paths." *Progress in Human Geography* 25, no. 4 (2001): 649–58.

Harvey, David. *The Condition of Postmodernity: An Enquiry into the Origins of Cultural Change*. Oxford: Blackwell, 1989.

———. *The Limits to Capital*. Updated ed. New York: Verso, 2007.

———. "On Planning the Ideology of Planning." In *Reading in Planning Theory*, edited by Scott Campbell and Susan Fainstein, 176–97. Malden, MA: Wiley-Blackwell, 1996.

———. "The Political Economy of Public Space." In *The Politics of Public Space*, edited by Setha Low and Neil Smith, 17–34. New York: Routledge, 2013.

———. "The Right to the City." *International Journal of Urban and Regional Research* 27, no. 4 (2003): 939–41.

———. *Social Justice and the City*. Baltimore: Johns Hopkins University Press, 1973.

Haskins, Ekaterina V., and Justin P. DeRose. "Memory, Visibility, and Public Space: Reflections on Commemoration(s) of 9/11." *Space and Culture* 6, no. 4 (2003): 377–93.

Hayek, Ghenwa. *Beirut, Imagining the City: Space and Place in Lebanese Literature*. London: I. B. Tauris, 2014.

"Highlights of Speech by Nasrallah on 11th Anniversary of 2006 War." *Daily Star*, August 13, 2017.

Holston, James. "Insurgent Citizenship in an Era of Global Urban Peripheries." *City & Society* 21, no. 2 (2009): 245–67.

———. *The Modernist City: An Anthropological Critique of Brasília*. Chicago: University of Chicago Press, 1989.

Hourani, Najib. "Capitalists in Conflict: The Lebanese Civil War Reconsidered." *Middle East Critique* 24, no. 2 (2015): 137–60.

———. "Lebanon: Hybrid Sovereignties and U.S. Foreign Policy." *Middle East Policy* 20, no. 1 (2013): 39–55.

Huyssen, Andreas. "Nostalgia for Ruins." *Grey Room*, no. 23 (2006): 6–21.

Ide, Kanako. "A Symbol of Peace and Peace Education: The Genbaku Dome in Hiroshima." *Journal of Aesthetic Education* 41, no. 4 (2007): 12–23.

InfoPro. *Business Opportunities in Lebanon*. Beirut: Infopro, 2014.

"Intihāʾ al-Ishkāl bayn Lubnāniyyīn wa Sūriyyīn fī Dawḥat ʿĀramūn wa-l-Jaysh Yūqif ʿĀdadan min Muṭliqī al-Nār." *An-Nahar*, September 20, 2016.

International Monetary Fund. *World Economic Outlook Database for April 2006*. Washington, DC: International Monetary Fund, 2006.

Ismail, Salwa. *Political Life in Cairo's New Quarters: Encountering the Everyday State*. Minneapolis: University of Minnesota Press, 2006.

Johnson, Michael. *All Honourable Men: The Social Origins of War in Lebanon*. London: I. B. Tauris, 2001.

———. *Class & Client in Beirut: The Sunni Muslim Community and the Lebanese State, 1840–1985*. London: Ithaca Press, 1986.

Joseph, Suad. "The Politicization of Religious Sects in Borj Hammoud, Lebanon." Doctoral dissertation, Columbia University, 1975.

"Junblāṭ fī al-Khalwa al-Durziyya: Maḥkūmūn bi-l-Taʿāyush maʿ al-Shīʿa . . . aw Qulūlī Mā al-ʿAmal?" *Al-Akhbar*, May 28, 2009, 829 edition.

"Junblāṭ: Naḥnu wa-l-Mawārina Hunūd Ḥumr." *Beirut Observer*, November 10, 2009.

Kanafani, Samar. "South Now Has 'High-Speed' Link to Downtown Beirut: Development Council Inaugurates New Overpass." *Daily Star*, March 15, 2002.

Kassir, Samir. *Ḥarb Lubnān: Min NizāʿAhlī ilā Ṣirāʿ fī al-Manṭiqa*. Beirut: An-Nahar, 2007.

Kassir, Samir, and Robert Fisk. *Beirut*. Translated by M. B. DeBevoise. Berkeley: University of California Press, 2010.

Kazzaz, Tarek, Jamal Abed, Deema Husseini, Ralph Gakenheimer, Adel Mardelli, Omar Razzaz, Hashim Sarkis, and Maha Yahya. "Rebuilding the Residential Sector of Beirut." Joint research project between MIT, School of Architecture and Planning and the American University of Beirut, 1993.

"Khafāyā Ishtibākāt 'Dawḥat ʿĀramūn' . . . wa Qiṣṣat 'al-Qulūb al-Malyāna.'" *Only Lebanon News*, September 21, 2016.

Khalaf, Samir. "Some Sociological Reflections on the Urban Reconstruction of Beirut." In *Beirut of Tomorrow*, edited by Friedrich Ragette, 18–24. Beirut: American University of Beirut, 1983.

Khalaf, Samir, and Philip S. Khoury. *Recovering Beirut: Urban Design and Post-War Reconstruction*. Leiden: Brill, 1993.

Khalaf, Samir, and Per Kongstad. *Hamra of Beirut: A Case of Rapid Urbanization*. Leiden: Brill, 1973.

Khaled, Hassan. *Al-Muslimūn fī-Lubnān wa Ḥarb al-Sanatayn: Dār al-Fatwā fī al-Aḥdāth, Maḥāḍir Ijtimāʿāt Qimmat ʿĀramūn athnāʾ al-Ḥarb al-Ahliyya*. Beirut: Dar al-Kanadi, 1978.

Khouri, Rami G. "Beirut Madinati: Is This the Way Out of Our Awful Situation?" *The Washington Report on Middle East Affairs* 35, no. 4 (2016): 38–39.

Khuri, Fuad I. "The Changing Class Structure in Lebanon." *Middle East Journal* 23, no. 1 (1969): 29–44.

———. *From Village to Suburb: Order and Change in Greater Beirut*. Chicago: University of Chicago Press, 1975.

———. "Sectarian Loyalty among Rural Migrants in Two Lebanese Suburbs: A Stage between Family and National Allegiance." In *Rural Politics and Social Change in the*

Middle East, edited by Richard T. Antoun and Iliya F. Harik, 198–213. Bloomington: Indiana University Press, 1972.

Krayem, Hasan. "The Lebanese Civil War and the Taif Agreement." In *Conflict Resolution in the Arab World*, edited by Paul Salem, 411–35. Beirut: American University of Beirut, 1997.

Krijnen, Marieke, and Mona Fawaz. "Exception as the Rule: High-End Developments in Neoliberal Beirut." *Built Environment* 36, no. 2 (2010): 245–59.

Lang, Frederick W. *Housing Activities 1956–1958: A Summary of Operations*. Beirut: USOM Housing Division, 1959.

Larkin, Craig. *Memory and Conflict in Lebanon: Remembering and Forgetting the Past*. New York: Routledge, 2012.

Lebanese National News Agency. "Al-Maʻlūf Qaddam Iqtirāḥ Qānūn Yarmī ilā Taʻdīl Qānūn al-Istimlāk." May 26, 2015. http://nna-leb.gov.lb/ar/show-news/160411/.

Lebanese Parliament. "Taʻdīl al-Qānūn Raqm 58 Tarīkh 29/5/1991 Qānūn al-Istimlāk." *Al-Jarida al-Rasmiyya*, December 8, 2006.

"Lebanese Soldier Killed in Gunfight in Dohet Aramoun." *Daily Star*, May 28, 2008.

Lefebvre, Henri. *The Production of Space*. Oxford: Blackwell, 1991.

———. *Writings on Cities*. Oxford: Blackwell, 1996.

Leitner, Helga, Eric Sheppard, and Kristin M. Sziarto. "The Spatialities of Contentious Politics." *Transactions of the Institute of British Geographers* 33, no. 2 (2008): 157–72.

LeVine, Mark. *Overthrowing Geography: Jaffa, Tel Aviv, and the Struggle for Palestine, 1880–1948*. Berkeley: University of California Press, 2005.

Lewis, Oscar. *Five Families: Mexican Case Studies in the Culture of Poverty*. New York: Basic Books, 1975.

Li, Tania M. *The Will to Improve: Governmentality, Development, and the Practice of Politics*. Durham, NC: Duke University Press, 2007.

Luca, Anna Maria. "The Alley Flag War." *NOW Lebanon*, June 16, 2010.

MacKinnon, Colin. "Trade and Finance—Lebanon: Poised for a Massive Reconstruction Undertaking." *Washington Report on Middle East Affairs*, January 1994.

Makdisi, Samar. *The Lessons of Lebanon: The Economics of War and Development*. London: I. B. Tauris, 2004.

Makdisi, Saree. "Laying Claim to Beirut: Urban Narrative and Spatial Identity in the Age of Solidere." *Critical Inquiry* 23, no. 3 (1997): 661–705.

Makdisi, Ussama S. *The Culture of Sectarianism: Community, History, and Violence in Nineteenth-Century Ottoman Lebanon*. Berkeley: University of California Press, 2000.

"Maʻlūmāt Daqīqa li-Maṣādir Amniyya: Takhrīb wa Qannāṣūn wa Tawzīʻ al-Silāh ʻind al-Sāʻa Ṣifr." May 21, 2017. www.saidaonline.com.

Martin, Deborah G., and Byron Miller. "Space and Contentious Politics." *Mobilization* 8, no. 2 (2003): 143–56.

Massey, Douglas S., and Nancy A. Denton. *American Apartheid: Segregation and the Making of the Underclass*. Cambridge, MA: Harvard University Press, 1993.

Mbembe, Achille. "Chinua Achebe and the African Century." Address presented at *Forty Years After: Chinua Achebe and Africa in the Global Imagination*, the Chinua Achebe Symposium, 2015, University of Massachusetts, Amherst, October 15, 2015.

McAdam, Doug, Sidney G. Tarrow, and Charles Tilly. *Dynamics of Contention*. New York: Cambridge University Press, 2001.

Merriam-Webster Dictionary, s.v. "price-fixing (noun)." Accessed May 29, 2017. https://www.merriam-webster.com/dictionary/price-fixing.

Mitchell, Timothy. *Colonising Egypt*. Berkeley: University of California Press, 1988.

Mohsen, Ahmad. "Dawḥat ʿAramūn: Adghāl Ismantiyya fawq Baqāyā al-Nahr." *Al-Akhbar*, February 2, 2012, 1625 edition.

MTV. *Bi Mawdouiyeh—Land Sales in Ḥadath*, 2011.

———. *Interview with Boutrous Harb*, 2010.

Munby, Denys Lawrence, Vatican Commission on Peace and Freedom, and World Council of Churches. *World Development: Challenge to the Churches; The Official Report and the Papers*. Washington, DC: Corpus Books, 1969.

Muschamp, Herbert. "Architecture View; 'Things Generally Wrong in the Universe.'" *New York Times*, May 30, 1993, sec. Arts.

Nagel, Caroline. "Reconstructing Space, Re-Creating Memory: Sectarian Politics and Urban Development in Post-War Beirut." *Political Geography* 21, no. 5 (2002): 717–25.

Naharnet Newsdesk. "Lebanon Eyes Future for Famed Hotel Turned Civil War Relic." *Naharnet*, May 4, 2014.

———. "Security Forces Complete Deployment in Dahieh and Charbel Hopes Step Would Extend to Tripoli." *Naharnet*, September 23, 2013.

Nasr, Joe, and Eric Verdeil. "The Reconstructions of Beirut." In *The City in the Islamic World*, edited by Salma Jayyusi, Renata Holod, Attilio Petruccioli, and André Raymond, 1121–48, 2008.

Nasr, Salim. "Backdrop to Civil War: The Crisis of Lebanese Capitalism." *MERIP Reports*, no. 73 (1978): 3–13.

———. "Lebanon's War: Is the End in Sight?" *Middle East Report*, no. 162 (1990): 4–30.

———. "New Social Realities and Post-War Lebanon: Issues for Reconstruction." In *Recovering Beirut: Urban Design and Post-War Reconstruction*, edited by Samir Khalaf and Philip S. Khoury, 63–80. Leiden: Brill, 1993.

Nasr, Salim, and Diane James. "Roots of the Shiʿi Movement." *MERIP Reports*, no. 133 (1985): 10–16.

Nasr, Samir. *Investor's Guide: A Portrait of the Lebanese Market*. Beirut: Etudes et Consultations Economiques (SARL), 1997.

Nsouli, Mustafa. "Design and Development." Keynote address at the Pillars of the Lebanese House lecture series, 1962.

Nucho, Joanne Randa. *Everyday Sectarianism in Urban Lebanon: Infrastructures, Public Services, and Power*. Princeton, NJ: Princeton University Press, 2016.

Odeh, B. J. *Lebanon, Dynamics of Conflict: A Modern Political History*. London: Zed Books, 1985.

Olsen, Donald. *The City as a Work of Art: London, Paris, Vienna*. New Haven, CT: Yale University Press, 1986.

Ong, Aihwa. *Neoliberalism as Exception: Mutations in Citizenship and Sovereignty*. Durham, NC: Duke University Press, 2006.

Oxford Dictionaries, s.v. "capital project (noun)." Accessed October 16, 2016. https://en.oxforddictionaries.com/definition/capital_project.

Pant, Mohan. "The Impulse to Remember: Thoughts on the Conservation of World War II Ruins in Germany." In *Authenticity in Architectural Heritage Conservation*, edited by Katharina Weiler and Niels Gutschow, 73–83. New York: Springer, 2017.

Parnell, Susan, and Jennifer Robinson. "(Re)theorizing Cities from the Global South: Looking beyond Neoliberalism." *Urban Geography* 33, no. 4 (2012): 593–617.

Peet, Richard. "The Social Origins of Environmental Determinism." *Annals of the Association of American Geographers* 75, no. 3 (1985): 309–33.

Pew Research Center. *Mapping the Global Muslim Population*. Washington, DC: Pew Research Center, October 7, 2009.

Picard, Elizabeth. "The Lebanese Shi'a and Political Violence in Lebanon." In *The Legitimization of Violence*, edited by David E. Apter, 189–233. New York: Palgrave Macmillan, 1997.

———. *Lebanon, a Shattered Country: Myths and Realities of the Wars in Lebanon*. Teaneck, NJ: Holmes & Meier, 2002.

Rabinow, Paul. *French Modern: Norms and Forms of the Social Environment*. Cambridge, MA: MIT Press, 1989.

Robinson, Jennifer. "Global and World Cities: A View from off the Map." *International Journal of Urban and Regional Research* 26, no. 3 (2002): 531–54.

———. *The Power of Apartheid: State, Power, and Space in South African Cities*. Oxford: Butterworth-Heinemann, 1996.

———. *Ordinary Cities: Between Modernity and Development*. London: Routledge, 2004.

Robson, James. "Bid'a." In *The Encyclopaedia of Islam*, New ed. Leiden: Brill.

Rostow, Walt Whitman. *The Stages of Economic Growth: A Non-Communist Manifesto*. Cambridge: Cambridge University Press, 1990.

Rowe, Peter G., and Hashim Sarkis. *Projecting Beirut: Episodes in the Construction and Reconstruction of a Modern City*. New York: Prestel, 1998.

Roy, Ananya. "The Blockade of the World-Class City: Dialectical Images of Indian Urbanism." In *Worlding Cities: Asian Experiments and the Art of Being Global*, edited by Ananya Roy and Aihwa Ong, 259–78. Malden, MA: Wiley-Blackwell, 2011.

———. *City Requiem, Calcutta: Gender and the Politics of Poverty*. Minneapolis: University of Minnesota Press, 2002.

———. "Civic Governmentality: The Politics of Inclusion in Beirut and Mumbai." *Antipode* 41, no. 1 (2009): 159–79.

———. "Praxis in the Time of Empire." *Planning Theory* 5, no. 1 (2006): 7–29.

———. "Why India Cannot Plan Its Cities: Informality, Insurgence and the Idiom of Urbanization." *Planning Theory* 8, no. 1 (2009): 76–87.

Roy, Ananya, and Nezar AlSayyad. *Urban Informality: Transnational Perspectives from the Middle East, Latin America, and South Asia*. Lanham, MD: Lexington Books, 2004.

Sachs, Wolfgang. *The Development Dictionary: A Guide to Knowledge as Power*. London: Zed Books, 1992.

Said, Edward W. *Orientalism*. New York: Pantheon Books, 1978.

Saint-Amour, Paul K. *Tense Future: Modernism, Total War, Encyclopedic Form*. New York: Oxford University Press, 2015.

Salibi, Kamal S. "Lebanon under Fuad Chehab 1958–1964." *Middle Eastern Studies* 2, no. 3 (1966): 211–26.

Salloukh, Bassel. "Syria and Lebanon: A Brotherhood Transformed." *Middle East Report*, no. 236 (2005):14–21.

Sandler, Daniela. "Counterpreservation: Decrepitude and Memory in Post-Unification Berlin." *Third Text* 25, no. 6 (2011): 687–97.

Sarkis, Hashim. *Circa 1958: Lebanon in the Pictures and Plans of Constantinos Doxiadis*. Beirut: Editions Dar An-Nahar, 2003.

———. "Dances with Margaret Mead: Planning Beirut since 1958." In *Recovering Beirut: Urban Design and Post-War Reconstruction*, edited by Samir Khalaf and Philip S. Khoury, 187–201. Leiden: Brill, 1993.

Sassen, Saskia. *The Global City: New York, London, Tokyo*. Princeton, NJ: Princeton University Press, 1991.

Sawalha, Aseel. *Reconstructing Beirut: Memory and Space in a Postwar Arab City*. Austin: University of Texas Press, 2010.

Schrecker, Ellen. "McCarthyism: Political Repression and the Fear of Communism." *Social Research* 71, no. 4 (2004):1041–86.

Scott, James C. *Seeing like a State: How Certain Schemes to Improve the Human Condition Have Failed*. New Haven, CT: Yale University Press, 1998.

Seligman, Amanda. *Block by Block: Neighborhoods and Public Policy on Chicago's West Side*. Chicago: University of Chicago Press, 2005.

Sfeir, Rita. "Ijtimāʿ Bkirkī 'Yuthmir' Iqtirāḥāt li-Taʿdīl Qānūn al-Milkiyya al-ʿAqāriyya. Hal Yashfaʿ 'Ḥaqq al-Shufʿa' bi-ʿAmaliyyāt al-Bayʿ al-Mashbūha?" *An-Nahar*. June 2011.

Shaery-Eisenlohr, Roschanack. *Shiʿite Lebanon: Transnational Religion and the Making of National Identities*. New York: Columbia University Press, 2008.

Shahin, George. "Abʿad bi-Kathīr min Intiqād Taʿyīn al-Sayyid Husayn." *Al Joumhouria*, October 8, 2011.

Sharara, Waddah. *Al-Silm al-Ahlī al-Bārid: Lubnān al-Mujtamaʿ wa-l-Dawla, 1964–1967*. Vol. 2. Beirut: Maʿhad al-Inmaa al-ʿArabi, 1980.

Shirlow, Peter. "Ethno-Sectarianism and the Reproduction of Fear in Belfast." *Capital & Class* 27, no. 2 (2003): 77–93.

Simone, AbdouMaliq. "At the Frontier of the Urban Periphery." In *Sarai Reader 07: Frontiers*, 462–70. Delhi: Center for the Study of Developing Societies, 2007.

———. *City Life from Jakarta to Dakar: Movements at the Crossroads*. New York: Routledge, 2010.

———. *For the City Yet to Come: Changing African Life in Four Cities*. Durham, NC: Duke University Press, 2004.

Smith, Neil. *The New Urban Frontier: Gentrification and the Revanchist City*. New York: Routledge, 1996.

Stoler, Ann Laura. *Imperial Debris: On Ruins and Ruination*. Durham, NC: Duke University Press, 2013.

Sturken, Marita. "The Aesthetics of Absence: Rebuilding Ground Zero." *American Ethnologist* 31, no. 3 (2004): 311–25.

Tabet, Jad. "From Colonial Style to Regional Revivalism: Modern Architecture in Lebanon and the Cultural Problem of Identity." In *Recovering Beirut: Urban Design and Post-War Reconstruction*, edited by Samir Khalaf and Philip S. Khoury, 83–105. Leiden: Brill, 1993.

Taleb, Ahmad, and Hasan Saab. *Al-Mushāraka al-'Arabiyya wa-l-Duwaliyya fī Inmā' Lubnān mā ba'd al-Ḥarb: Abḥāth wa Tawṣiyāt Mu'tamar al-Mushāraka al-'Arabiyya wa-l-Duwaliyya fī Inmā' Lubnān*. Development Studies Association Symposium, vol. 34. Beirut: Development Studies Association, 1978.

Taussig, Michael. "Culture of Terror—Space of Death. Roger Casement's Putumayo Report and the Explanation of Torture." *Comparative Studies in Society and History* 26, no. 3 (1984): 467–97.

Taylor, John Laverack. "Planning for Urban Growth: British Perspectives on the Planning Process." Westport, CT: Praeger, 1972.

Taylor, Nigel. *Urban Planning Theory since 1945*. Thousand Oaks, CA: Sage, 1998.

Tayyar. "Utimm bi-Tishrīn al-Thānī Injāz Binā' al-Quwā al-'Askariyya. Ma'lūmāt Daqīqa li-Maṣādir Amniyya: Takhrīb wa Qannāṣūn wa Tawzī' al-Silāḥ 'ind al-Sā'a Ṣifr." January 13, 2011. Tayyar.org Facebook page.

Theodosis, Lefteris. "'Containing' Baghdad: Constantinos Doxiadis' Program for a Developing Nation." *DC Papers: Revista de Crítica i Teoria de l'Arquitectura*, special issue (2008): 167–172.

Townsend, Janet G., Gina Porter, and Emma Mawdsley. "Creating Spaces of Resistance: Development NGOs and their Clients in Ghana, India and Mexico." *Antipode* 36, no. 5 (2004): 871–89.

Traboulsi, Fawwaz. *A History of Modern Lebanon*. London: Pluto, 2007.

———. "Social Classes and Political Power in Lebanon." Beirut: Heinrich Böll Foundation, 2014.

Tsing, Anna Lowenhaupt. *Friction: An Ethnography of Global Connection*. Princeton, NJ: Princeton University Press, 2005.

Tuathail, Gearóid Ó, and Carl Dahlman. "The 'West Bank of the Drina': Land Allocation and Ethnic Engineering in Republika Srpska." *Transactions, Institute of British Geographers*, n.s. 31, no. 3 (2006): 304–22.

Tuğal, Cihan Ziya. *Passive Revolution: Absorbing the Islamic Challenge to Capitalism*. Palo Alto: Stanford University Press, 2009.

United Nations. *The United Nations Development Decade, Proposals for Action: Report of the Secretary-General*. New York: United Nations, 1962.

United Nations, Department of Economic and Social Affairs, Population Division. *World Population Prospects: The 2017 Revision*. DVD Edition, File POP/1-1: Total population (both sexes combined) by region, subregion and country, annually for 1950-2100 (thousands): Estimates, 1950-2015.

United Nations High Commissioner for Refugees. *UNHCR Syria Regional Refugee Response*. New York, United Nations, 2016.

United Nations Relief and Works Agency for Palestine Refugees. *Where We Work; Lebanon.* 2014. https://www.unrwa.org/where-we-work/lebanon.

United States Operations Mission to Lebanon. *Lebanon: USOM Report.* Beirut, 1955.

USAID. *Lebanon: History.* 2016. https://www.usaid.gov/lebanon/history.

Verdeil, Eric. *Beyrouth et Ses Urbanistes: Une Ville en Plans (1946–1975).* Beyrouth: IFPO, 2010.

———. "Methodological and Political Issues in the Lebanese Planning Experiences." In *Conference City Debates, The Lebanese National Master Plan, City Debates 2003 Proceedings,* edited by Mona Harb, 16–22. Beirut, American University of Beirut, 2004.

———. "Michel Ecochard in Lebanon and Syria (1956–1968): The Spread of Modernism, the Building of the Independent States and the Rise of Local Professionals of Planning." *Planning Perspectives* 27, no. 2 (2012): 249–266.

———. "State Development Policy and Specialised Engineers: The Case of Urban Planners in Post-War Lebanon." *Knowledge Work Society* 5, no. 1 (2008): 29–51.

Verdeil, Eric, Ghaleb Faour, and Sébastien Velut. *Atlas du Liban: Territoires et Société.* Beirut: IFPO Press, 2008.

Watson, Vanessa. "Seeing from the South: Refocusing Urban Planning on the Globe's Central Urban Issues." *Urban Studies* 46, no. 11 (2009): 2259–75.

Watts, Michael. "Development and Governmentality." *Singapore Journal of Tropical Geography* 24, no. 1 (2003): 6–34.

———. "Revolutionary Islam." In *Violent Geographies: Fear, Terror, and Political Violence,* edited by Derek Gregory and Allan Pred, 175–203. New York: Routledge, 2007.

Wedeen, Lisa. *Ambiguities of Domination: Politics, Rhetoric, and Symbols in Contemporary Syria.* Chicago: University of Chicago Press, 1999.

Wehbe, Mouhamad. "Living Sectarianism: Lebanon's Demographic Cold War." *Al-Akhbar English,* September 5, 2011.

Weiss, Max. *In the Shadow of Sectarianism: Law, Shi'ism, and the Making of Modern Lebanon.* Cambridge, MA: Harvard University Press, 2010.

Weizman, Eyal. *Hollow Land: Israel's Architecture of Occupation.* New York: Verso, 2007.

Whitmarsh, Andrew. " 'We Will Remember Them': Memory and Commemoration in War Museums." *Journal of Conservation and Museum Studies* 7 (2001): 11–15. DOI: http://doi.org/10.5334/jcms.7013.

Wilson, Elizabeth. "Architecture and Consciousness in Central Europe." In *The Sphinx in the City: Urban Life, the Control of Disorder, and Women,* 84–99 Berkeley: University of California Press, 1991.

World Bank. *World Bank's Response to the Syrian Conflict.* Washington, DC: World Bank, 2016.

World Bank Group. "Registering Property in Lebanon—Doing Business." 2017. http://www.doingbusiness.org/data/exploreeconomies/lebanon/registering-property.

Wright, Robin. "Beirut's Museums of War and Memories." *The New Yorker,* October 12, 2016.

Yassin, Nasser. "Violent Urbanization and Homogenization of Space and Place: Reconstructing the Story of Sectarian Violence in Beirut." In *Urbanization and Development:*

Multidisciplinary Perspectives, edited by Jo Beall, Basudeb Guha-Khasnobis, and S. M. Ravi Kanbur, 205–18. New York: Oxford University Press, 2010.

Yiftachel, Oren. *Ethnocracy: Land and Identity Politics in Israel/Palestine*. Philadelphia: University of Pennsylvania Press, 2006.

———. "Planning and Social Control: Exploring the Dark Side." *Journal of Planning Literature* 12, no. 4 (1998): 395–406.

———. *The Power of Planning: Spaces of Control and Transformation*. Boston: Kluwer Academic, 2001.

———. "Social Control, Urban Planning and Ethno-class Relations: Mizrahi Jews in Israel's 'Development Towns.'" *International Journal of Urban and Regional Research* 24, no. 2 (2000): 418–38.

———. "Towards a New Typology of Urban Planning Theories." *Environment and Planning B: Planning and Design* 16, no. 1 (1989): 23–39.

Zakhem Group. "Business Activities." 2014. http://zakhem.com/projects.

Zarakit, Ali. "Dhikrā 13 Nīsān Ḥarb Kādat Tustaʿād. Al-Ḥarb . . . khalf Kanīsat Mār Mikhāyil." *Al-Mustaqbal*, April 13, 2007.

INDEX

Lightning Source UK Ltd.
Milton Keynes UK
UKHW030338251121
394567UK00008B/467

9 781503 605602